Integrated Chinese

CHENG & TSUI PUBLICATIONS OF RELATED INTEREST

Making Connections: Enhance Your Listening Comprehension in Chinese
(Text & Audio CD Set)
Madeline K. Spring

| Simplified Characters | 0-88727-366-1 |
| Traditional Characters | 0-88727-365-3 |

Chinese BuilderCards: The Lightning Path to Mastering Vocabulary
Song Jiang

| Simplified Characters | 0-88727-434-X |
| Traditional Characters | 0-88727-426-9 |

Cheng & Tsui Chinese-Pinyin-English Dictionary for Learners
Wang Huan, Editor-in-Chief

| Paperback | 0-88727-316-5 |

Cheng & Tsui Chinese Character Dictionary
Wang Huidi, Editor-in-Chief

| Paperback | 0-88727-314-9 |

Crossing Paths: Living and Learning in China,
An Intermediate Chinese Course
Hong Gang Jin and De Bao Xu, with Der-lin Chao, Yea-fen Chen, and Min Chen

| Paperback & Audio CD Set | 0-88727-370-X |

Shifting Tides: Culture in Contemporary China,
An Intermediate Chinese Course
Hong Gang Jin and De Bao Xu, with Songren Cui, Yea-fen Chen, and Yin Zhang

| Paperback & Audio CD Set | 0-88727-3726 |

Pop Chinese: A Cheng & Tsui Handbook of Contemporary Colloquial
Expressions
Yu Feng, Yaohua Shi, Zhijie Jia, Judith M. Amory, and Jie Cai

| Paperback | 0-88727-424-2 |

Please visit www.cheng-tsui.com for more information on these and many other language-learning resources, or visit www.webtech.cheng-tsui.com for information on web-based and downloadable products.

Integrated Chinese

中文聽說讀寫／中文听说读写

Traditional and Simplified Character Edition

WORKBOOK

2nd Edition

Yuehua Liu and Tao-chung Yao

Nyan-Ping Bi and Yaohua Shi

CHENG & TSUI COMPANY ▲ Boston

Second Edition

10 09 08 07 06   1 2 3 4 5 6 7 8 9 10

Published by
Cheng & Tsui Company
25 West Street
Boston, MA 02111-1213 USA
Fax (617) 426-3669
www.cheng-tsui.com
"Bringing Asia to the World"™

Integrated Chinese Level 2 Workbook
ISBN-13 978-0-88727-481-7
ISBN 0-88727-481-1

The *Integrated Chinese* series includes textbooks, workbooks, character workbooks, audio products, multimedia products, teacher's resources, and more. Visit www.cheng-tsui.com for more information on the other components of *Integrated Chinese*.

Printed in the United States of America

THE INTEGRATED CHINESE SERIES

The *Integrated Chinese* series is a two-year course that includes textbooks, workbooks, character workbooks, audio CDs, CD-ROMs, DVDs, and teacher's resources.

Textbooks introduce Chinese language and culture through a series of dialogues and narratives, with culture notes, language use and grammar explanations, and exercises.

Workbooks follow the format of the textbooks and contain a wide range of integrated activities that teach the four language skills of listening, speaking, reading, and writing.

Character Workbooks help students learn Chinese characters in their correct stroke order. Special emphasis is placed on the radicals that are frequently used to compose Chinese characters.

Audio CDs include the narratives, dialogues and vocabulary presented in the textbooks, as well as pronunciation and listening exercises that correspond to the workbooks.

Teacher's Resources contain answer keys, transcripts of listening exercises, grammar notes, and helpful guidance on using the series in the classroom. Visit www.webtech.cheng-tsui.com to obtain the latest teacher resources.

Multimedia CD-ROMs are divided into sections of listening, speaking, reading, and writing, and feature a variety of supplemental interactive games and activities for students to test their skills and get instant feedback.

Workbook DVD dialogues from the Level 1 Part 1 Workbook are presented in contemporary settings in color video format.

PUBLISHER'S NOTE

When *Integrated Chinese* was first published in 1997, it set a new standard with its focus on the development and integration of the four language skills (listening, speaking, reading, and writing). Today, to further enrich the learning experience of the many users of *Integrated Chinese* worldwide, the Cheng & Tsui Company is pleased to offer the revised, updated and expanded second edition of *Integrated Chinese*. We would like to thank the many teachers and students who, by offering their valuable insights and suggestions, have helped *Integrated Chinese* evolve and keep pace with the many positive changes in the field of Chinese language instruction. *Integrated Chinese* continues to offer comprehensive language instruction, with many new features.

The Cheng & Tsui Asian Language Series is designed to publish and widely distribute quality language learning materials created by leading instructors from around the world. We welcome readers' comments and suggestions concerning the publications in this series. Please feel free to send feedback to our Editorial Department (e-mail: editor@cheng-tsui.com), or to contact the following members of our Editorial Board.

Professor Shou-hsin Teng, Chief Editor
3 Coach Lane, Amherst, MA 01002

Dana Scott Bourgerie
Asian and Near Eastern Languages
Brigham Young University, Provo, UT 84602

Professor Samuel Cheung
Dept. of Chinese, Chinese University of Hong Kong
Shatin, Hong Kong

Professor Ying-che Li
Dept. of East Asian Languages, University of Hawaii
Honolulu, HI 96822

Professor Timothy Light
Dept. of Comparative Religion, Western Michigan University
Kalamazoo, MI 49008

CONTENTS

Lesson 5: 選專業 ／ 选专业   67

Lesson 6: 租房子   83

Lesson 7: 男朋友   99

Lesson 8: 電影和電視的影響 ／ 电影和电视的影响 115

▼▼▼▼▼▼▼▼▼▼▼▼▼▼▼▼▼▼▼▼▼▼▼▼▼▼▼▼▼▼▼▼▼▼▼▼▼▼▼

Lesson 13: 談體育／谈体育   207

Lesson 14: 家庭   223

Lesson 15: 男女平等   241

Lesson 16: 健康與保險／健康与保险   257

Indices   333

PREFACE

In designing the Level Two Workbook exercises for *Integrated Chinese*, we strove to give equal emphasis to students' listening, speaking, reading, and writing skills. There are different difficulty levels in order to provide variety and flexibility to suit different curriculum needs. Teachers can assign the exercises at their discretion; they need not feel pressure to use all of them. If appropriate, teachers can use them out of sequence. Moreover, teachers can supplement this workbook with their own exercises.

What's New in the Second Edition

Thanks to all those who have used *Integrated Chinese* and given us the benefit of their suggestions and comments, we have been able to produce a second edition that includes the following improvements.

▲ **Level 2 Workbook offers full text in simplified and traditional characters.** The original Workbook, although geared toward both traditional- and simplified-character learners, contained sections in which only the traditional characters were given. This was of course problematic for students who were principally interested in learning simplified characters. This difficulty has been resolved in the new edition, as we now provide both traditional and simplified characters for every Chinese sentence. The only exception is the authentic materials. All authentic materials used in the Workbook are presented in their original characters to preserve their authenticity. An appendix containing alternate character versions is provided as a learning tool for those interested in reading both forms.

▲ The Workbook's **exercises have been revised extensively** to recycle vocabulary learned and to provide a contextualized language environment. New and different varieties of exercises have been added, and more authentic materials are included. Teachers can choose exercises that best suit their needs. When words that have not been taught are used in the exercises, glosses have been provided.

▲ A **Chinese-English vocabulary index** and an **English-Chinese vocabulary index** have been added to the Workbook. The indices contain new vocabulary words that are glossed in the exercises. (See the Textbook indices for vocabulary words appearing in the lessons.)

▲ In addition to written instructions, **new illustrations and photos** provide the reader with visual interest, linguistic clues, and relevant cultural information.

▲ Typographical errors present in the first edition have been corrected, and the content has been carefully edited to ensure accuracy and minimize errors.

How to Use This Workbook

Listening Comprehension

All too often listening comprehension is sacrificed in a formal classroom setting because of time constraints. Students tend to focus their time and energy on the mastery of a few grammar points, rather than on developing strong listening skills. This workbook tries to remedy this imbalance by including a substantial number of listening comprehension exercises. There are two categories of listening exercises;

both can be done on the students' own time or in the classroom. In either case, it is important to have the instructor review the students' answers for accuracy.

The first category of listening exercises, which is at the beginning of each listening section, is based on the text of each lesson. For the exercises to be meaningful, students should *first* study the vocabulary list, and *then* listen to the recordings of the texts. The questions are provided to help students' aural understanding of the texts.

The second category of listening exercises consists of an audio CD recording of two or more mini-dialogues or narratives. These exercises are designed to give students extra practice on the vocabulary and grammar points introduced in the lesson. Some of the exercises, especially ones that ask students to choose among several possible answers, are significantly more difficult than others. These exercises should be assigned toward the end of the lesson, when the students have become familiar with the content of the lesson.

Speaking Exercises

Here, too, there are two types of exercises. They are designed for different levels of proficiency within each lesson and should be assigned at the appropriate time.

To help students apply their newly acquired vocabulary and grammatical understanding to meaningful communication, we first ask them questions related to the dialogues and narratives, and then ask them questions related to their own lives. These questions require one- or two-sentence answers. By stringing together short questions and answers, students can construct their own mini-dialogues, practice in pairs, or take turns asking or answering questions.

Once they have gained some confidence, students can progress to the more difficult questions, where they are invited to express opinions on a number of topics. Typically, these questions are abstract, so they gradually teach students to express their opinions in longer conversations. As the school year progresses, these types of questions should take up more class discussion time. Because this second type of speaking exercise is quite challenging, it should be attempted only **after** students are well grounded in the grammar and vocabulary of a particular lesson. Usually, this occurs not *immediately* after students have completed the first part of the speaking exercises.

Reading Comprehension

There are three types of reading exercises in the Workbook: 1) short passages incorporating new vocabulary and grammatical structures from the lesson; 2) authentic materials such as advertisements, personal ads, and short news articles (some slightly modified); and 3) ancient Chinese parables. The sequence generally reflects the degree of difficulty of the materials, with the short passages being the most straightforward. The authentic materials are included not only because of their pedagogical value but also for their sociological interest. The various parables, on the other hand, originate from classical "wisdom texts" and have long been familiar set phrases. The variety of the readings is a way to bring culture—contemporary and ancient—into language learning while also allowing flexibility to the instructor. Occasionally, words that may be unfamiliar to some students appear in the reading passages, and these words are not glossed. But they will not prevent students from completing the tasks assigned successfully. Students are encouraged to guess the meaning of these words from the context of the reading passage.

▼▼

Writing and Grammar Exercises

Grammar and Usage

These drills and exercises are designed to solidify students' grasp of important grammar points. Through brief exchanges, students answer questions using specific grammatical forms, or are given sentences to complete. These exercises are not simple mechanical drills since their completion depends on students correctly understanding the contextual clues.

In the second half of the Level 2 Textbook, students are introduced to increasingly sophisticated and abstract vocabulary. Corresponding exercises in this Workbook help them to grasp the nuances of new words. For example, synonyms are a source of great difficulty; so exercises are provided to help students distinguish them.

Translation

Translation has been a tool for language teaching throughout the ages, and positive student feedback confirms our belief that it continues to play an important role. The exercises we have devised serve to reinforce two primary areas: one, to help students use specific grammatical structures in their speech; and two, to allow students to build their ever-increasing vocabulary. Ultimately, our hope is that this dual-pronged approach will enable students to understand that it takes more than just literal translation to convey an idea in a foreign language.

Writing Practice

This is the culmination of the written exercises, and it is where students learn to express themselves in writing. Many of the topics overlap with those used in oral practice. We expect that students will find it easier to put in writing what they have already learned to express orally.

Acknowledgments

Since publication of the first edition of *Integrated Chinese*, in 1997, many teachers and students have given us helpful comments and suggestions. We cannot list all of these individuals here, but we would like to reiterate our genuine appreciation for their help. We do wish to recognize the following individuals who have made recent contributions to the *Integrated Chinese* revision. We are indebted to Tim Richardson, Jeffrey Hayden, Ying Wang, and Xianmin Liu for field-testing the new edition and sending us their comments and corrections. We would also like to thank Chengzhi Chu for letting us try out his "Chinese TA," a computer program designed for Chinese teachers to create and edit teaching materials. This software saved us many hours of work during the revision. Last, but not least, we want to thank James Dew for his superb, professional editorial job, which enhanced both the content and the style of the new edition. We are also grateful to our editors at Cheng & Tsui, Sandra Korinchak and Kristen Wanner, for their painstaking work throughout the editing and production process. Naturally, the authors assume full responsibility for the content.

As much as we would like to eradicate all errors in the new edition, some will undoubtedly remain, so please continue to send your comments and corrections to editor@cheng-tsui.com, and accept our sincere thanks for your help.

第一课 ▲ 開學
第一课 ▲ 开学

 I. LISTENING COMPREHENSION

A. Listen to the audio for the Textbook and answer the questions.

1. What year in school is Zhang Tianming?

2. How did Zhang Tianming get to the campus?

3. Who is Ke Lin?

4. Where does Ke Lin live?

5. What does Ke Lin offer to do for Zhang Tianming?

6. What did Zhang's mother tell him right before he left for college?

B. Listen to the audio for the Workbook.

1. Listen to the recording and answer the following questions.
   a. What does "zhù xiào" mean?

   b. What is a "shìyǒu"? What is a "tóngwū"?

2. Listen to the recording and answer the following questions.
   a. Why does Little Wang want to move out of his dorm?

   b. What is good about Little Wang's new place?

   c. Do you think Little Wang will live at his new place alone? Why or why not?

3. After listening to the recording, fill out Zhang's daily schedule in Chinese and answer the questions below in English.

Zhang's Daily Schedule

起床	起床
———	———
———	———
吃早飯	吃早饭
———	———
———	———
———	———
———	———
吃午飯	吃午饭
———	———
———	———
———	———
吃晚飯	吃晚饭

Questions:

a. How long does Little Zhang listen to the tape every day?

b. How many classes does Little Zhang have?

c. Where does Little Zhang have dinner every night?

4. Write the friend's name in Chinese characters after you listen to the recording.

5. Write the name in characters on the basis of the recording.

▼▼

II. SPEAKING EXERCISES

A. In order to know your Chinese language partner/classmate better, find out and report the following information in Chinese.

1. What's his or her name?
2. Where is he or she from?
3. Where was he or she born?
4. Where did he or she grow up?
5. Is he or she a college freshman?
6. Has he or she ever lived on campus or off campus? Which does he or she prefer? Why?
7. How long has he or she been studying Chinese?
8. Has he or she gotten used to the Chinese instructor's teaching style?
9. What kinds of activities have helped him or her to learn Chinese?
10. How long has it been since your classmate last saw his or her parents?

B. Practice asking and answering the following questions with a partner before class.

1. 你是在什麼地方出生的？
   你是在什么地方出生的？

2. 你是在什麼地方長大的？
   你是在什么地方长大的？

3. 你的暑假過得怎麼樣？是怎麼過的？
   你的暑假过得怎么样？是怎么过的？

4. 你今天是幾點到教室的？
   你今天是几点到教室的？

5. 你今天是怎麼來的？走路, 開車, 還是坐公共汽車？
   你今天是怎么来的？走路, 开车, 还是坐公共汽车？

6. 學校是幾號開的學？
   学校是几号开的学？

7. 你住校內還是住校外？
   你住校内还是住校外？

8. 要是你有錢, 你想搬到什麼地方去住？為什麼？
   要是你有钱, 你想搬到什么地方去住？为什么？

開學搬進宿舍 / 开学搬进宿舍

C. Practice speaking on the following topics.

1. 請你做一個簡單的自我介紹。
   请你做一个简单的自我介绍。

2. 請你談一談你上大學的第一天是怎麼過的。
   请你谈一谈你上大学的第一天是怎么过的。

3. 你認為住在學校宿舍好, 還是住在校外好? 為什麼?
   你认为住在学校宿舍好, 还是住在校外好? 为什么?

III. READING COMPREHENSION

A. Read the passage and answer the questions. (True/False)

(Traditional Characters)

柯林: 嘿, 王強! 你怎麼又搬家了? 你上個學期剛剛從校內搬到校外, 現在
      又要搬回學校宿舍了?

▼▼▼▼▼▼▼▼▼▼▼▼▼▼▼▼▼▼▼▼▼▼▼▼▼▼▼▼▼▼▼▼▼▼▼▼▼▼▼

王强: 住在宿舍的時候覺得房租太貴, 而且不自由。可是住在校外很不方便。上個星期三早上我考試又去晚了。想來想去, 還是搬回宿舍吧。

柯林: 哈, 你這個人真有意思。在學校宿舍住上兩個月, 你可能又想搬出去了!

王强: 説真的, 平時住在宿舍覺得又方便又安全, 可是一到週末我還會想起住在校外的好處: 房租便宜得多, 而且沒人管你。

柯林: 我有個好辦法。你可以租兩套房子, 一套在校內, 另一套在校外。你星期一到星期五住在校內, 一到週末就住到校外去。這樣你會覺得又方便又安全, 而且又自由又省錢。

王强: 省錢? 哈哈, 想不到你還有點經濟頭腦 (smarts for finance), 過幾年你一定要去學 MBA.

(Simplified Characters)

柯林: 嘿, 王强! 你怎么又搬家了? 你上个学期刚刚从校内搬到校外, 现在又要搬回学校宿舍了?

王强: 住在宿舍的时候觉得房租太贵, 而且不自由。可是住在校外很不方便。上个星期三早上我考试又去晚了。想来想去, 还是搬回宿舍吧。

柯林: 哈, 你这个人真有意思。在学校宿舍住上两个月, 你可能又想搬出去了!

王强: 说真的, 平时住在宿舍觉得又方便又安全, 可是一到周末我还会想起住在校外的好处: 房租便宜得多, 而且没人管你。

柯林: 我有个好办法。你可以租两套房子, 一套在校内, 另一套在校外。你星期一到星期五住在校内, 一到周末就住到校外去。这样你会觉得又方便又安全, 而且又自由又省钱。

王强： 省钱？哈哈，想不到你还有点经济头脑 (smarts for finance)，过几年你一定要去学MBA.

Questions (True/False):

( ) 1. Wang Qiang has been living in the student dorm for a semester.

( ) 2. Ke Lin thinks Wang Qiang has moved too many times.

( ) 3. One of the reasons that Wang Qiang moved out of the dorm was it was too expensive.

( ) 4. Wang Qiang had never been late for his examinations until last Wednesday.

( ) 5. It was not easy for Wang Qiang to make the decision to move one more time.

( ) 6. Wang Qiang has made the decision to move again in two months.

( ) 7. Ke Lin thinks Wang Qiang is never sure about where he should live.

( ) 8. According to Wang Qiang, it is much less expensive to live off campus.

( ) 9. If Wang Qiang follows Ke Lin's suggestion, he will be able to save money.

( ) 10. Wang Qiang truly thinks Ke Lin will make an excellent MBA student.

B. Read the passage and answer the questions.

(Traditional Characters)

　　張天明的家在波士頓，他們在那兒已經住了十多年了。張天明的父母都工作，每天早出晚歸 (1)，只有晚上下班以後，一家人才能在一起，一邊吃飯，一邊聊天。張天明排行老三，上邊有一個哥哥，一個姐姐，下邊還有一個妹妹。張天明上大學以前從來沒離開過家，到學校才一天，他已經非常想家了。

(1) 歸 guī: return; 回來

(Simplified Characters)

　　张天明的家在波士顿，他们在那儿已经住了十多年了。张天明的父母都工作，每天早出晚归 (1)，只有晚上下班以后，一家人才能在一起，一边吃饭，一边聊天。张天明排行老三，上边有一个哥哥，一个姐姐，下边还有一个妹妹。张天明上大学以前从来没离开过家，到学校才一天，他已经非常想家了。

(1) 归 guī: return; 回来

Questions:

1. 張天明的父母為什麼只有晚上才有時間？
   张天明的父母为什么只有晚上才有时间？

2. 張天明一共有幾個兄弟姐妹?

　　張天明一共有几个兄弟姐妹?

3. 張天明為什麼很想家?

　　张天明为什么很想家?

C. *Take a look at the business card and answer the questions.*

(Traditional Characters)

北京文化學院中國文學系

張百華　教授

地址: 北京文化學院19樓門502

100083

電話: 82017531-480(辦公室)

(Simplified Characters)

北京文化学院中国文学系

张百华　教授

地址: 北京文化学院19楼5门502

100083

电话: 82017531-480(办公室)

Questions:

1. 這個人在什麼地方工作?

　　这个人在什么地方工作?

▼▼▼▼▼▼▼▼▼▼▼▼▼▼▼▼▼▼▼▼▼▼▼▼▼▼▼▼▼▼▼▼▼▼

2. 他是做什麼的?

    他是做什么的?

3. 他家在哪兒?

    他家在哪儿?

4. 這上邊有沒有他家的電話?

    这上边有没有他家的电话?

D. *Read the story and answer the questions.*

(Traditional Characters)

    從前, 有一個人, 姓張, 叫張文, 他很有錢。可是他的兒子很笨 (1), 已經十幾歲了, 連一個字都不認識。張文想, 他已經六十多歲了, 兒子不認識字, 他死了以後, 不會寫信, 不會記賬 (2), 怎麼辦?所以就請了一位老師來教他兒子念書, 識字。老師先教他"一"字, 他覺得很容易, 又教他"二"字, 他也覺得很容易, 等老師教完"三"字, 他就說"寫字太容易了!"老師走了以後, 他對爸爸說:"爸爸, 明天不用請老師了, 我把中國字都學會了。"爸爸聽了很高興地

▼▼▼

説："過幾天是我的生日，我要請很多客人，你趕快寫一些請柬(3)吧。我的好朋友叫萬千，你先給他寫吧。"兒子説："沒問題。"張文給兒子準備了很多紙，兒子寫了十幾張紙，還沒寫完。爸爸走過來問他："快寫完了嗎？"兒子説："沒有，才寫了三百多筆，還有很多很多呢。"

(1) 笨(bèn): stupid

(2) 記賬(jì zhàng): keep accounts; do bookkeeping

(3) 請柬(qǐngjiǎn): invitation letter

(Simplified Characters)

从前，有一个人，姓张，叫张文，他很有钱。可是他的儿子很笨 (1)，已经十几岁了，连一个字都不认识。张文想，他已经六十多岁了，儿子不认识字，他死了以后，不会写信，不会记账 (2)，怎么办？所以就请了一位老师来教他儿子念书，识字。老师先教他"一"字，他觉得很容易，又教他"二"字，他也觉得很容易，等老师教完"三"字，他就说："写字太容易了！"老师走了以后，他对爸爸说："爸爸，明天不用请老师了，我把中国字都学会了。"爸爸听了很高兴地说："过几天是我的生日，我要请很多客人，你赶快写一些请柬 (3) 吧。我的好朋友叫万千，你先给他写吧。"儿子说："没问题。"张文给儿子准备了很多纸，儿子写了十几张纸，还没写完。爸爸走过来问他："快写完了吗？"儿子说："没有，才写了三百多笔，还有很多很多呢。"

(1) 笨(bèn): stupid

(2) 记账(jì zhàng): keep accounts; do bookkeeping

(3) 请柬(qǐngjiǎn): invitation letter

Questions:

1. Why is Zhang Wen worried about his son?

2. What does Zhang Wen do to help his son?

3. Why does the son say that he does not need help any more?

4. Does the son learn to write in Chinese? How do you know?

IV. GRAMMAR & USAGE

A. *Answer the following questions on the basis of your personal experience.*

1. a: 學校開學幾天了?

   学校开学几天了?

   b: _____。

2. a: 你學中文學了幾個學期了?

   你学中文学了几个学期了?

   b: _____。

3. a: 每天吃了晚飯以後, 你做什麼?

   每天吃了晚饭以后, 你做什么?

   b: _____。

B. *Review Zhang Tianming's schedule and complete the passage.*

早上	起床	起床
	吃早飯	吃早饭
	上漢語課	上汉语课
	上化學課	上化学课
	聽錄音	听录音
下午	吃午飯	吃午饭
	上歷史課	上历史课
	打球	打球
	回宿舍	回宿舍
晚上	吃晚飯	吃晚饭
	做功課	做功课
	看電視	看电视
	睡覺	睡觉

去語言實驗室聽錄音？　／　去语言实验室听录音？

(Traditional Characters)

　　張天明今天早上＿＿＿＿＿以後, 很快地吃了點早飯, 就去上課。＿＿＿＿＿, 沒能休息, 就去上化學課。＿＿＿＿＿, 他到語言實驗室去＿＿＿＿＿。吃午飯的時候, 柯林坐在他的旁邊。柯林説:"我今天有四節課, 已經上了三節了, 你呢?"小張回答説:"我＿＿＿＿＿, 還有一節歷史課"。下午回宿舍前, 張天明跟朋友去＿＿＿＿＿。＿＿＿＿＿, 才回宿舍吃晚飯。張天明今天的功課不多, ＿＿＿＿＿一個鐘頭就＿＿＿＿＿。然後, ＿＿＿＿＿半個鐘頭的電視, 就上床睡覺了。

(Simplified Characters)

　　张天明今天早上＿＿＿＿＿以后, 很快地吃了点早饭, 就去上课。＿＿＿＿＿, 没能休息, 就去上化学课。＿＿＿＿＿, 他到语言实验室去＿＿＿＿＿。吃午饭的时候, 柯林坐在他的旁边。柯林说:"我今天有四节课, 已经上了三节了, 你呢?"小张回答说:"我＿＿＿＿＿, 还有一节历史课。"下午回宿舍前, 张天明跟朋友去＿＿＿＿＿。＿＿＿＿＿, 才回宿舍吃晚饭。张天明今天的功课不多,＿＿＿＿＿一个钟头就＿＿＿＿＿。然后,＿＿＿＿＿半个钟头的电视, 就上床睡觉了。

C. Use 是…的 *to complete the dialogues.*

1. a: 你今天是幾點起的床?
   你今天是几点起的床?

   b: _____。

2. a: _____?

   b: 我今天是走路回家的。

3. a: 你身上穿的衣服真漂亮, 是在哪兒買的?
   你身上穿的衣服真漂亮, 是在哪儿买的?

   b: _____。

4. a: 我是從上海來的。你呢?你是從哪兒來的?
   我是从上海来的。你呢?你是从哪儿来的?

   b: _____。

5. a: 你漢語說得很好, 是什麼時候開始學的?
   你汉语说得很好, 是什么时候开始学的?

   b: _____。

6. a: 你會開車嗎?
   你会开车吗?

   b: 會呀。
   会呀。

   a: _____?

   b: 我是去年學的。
   我是去年学的。

D. Rewrite the sentences using 除了...以外, 還/还...

1. 這個學校開的語言課很多, 有中文, 日文, 法文和德文。
   这个学校开的语言课很多, 有中文, 日文, 法文和德文。

   → 這個學校開的語言課很多,
   　　这个学校开的语言课很多,

   _____。

2. 我們這兒飯館很多, 有三家中國飯館, 一家法國飯館和一家日本飯館。
   我们这儿饭馆很多, 有三家中国饭馆, 一家法国饭馆和一家日本饭馆。

   → 我們這兒
   　　我们这儿_____。

3. 學校剛開學, 校園裏人很多, 有老生, 有新生, 還有新生的父母。
   学校刚开学, 校园里人很多, 有老生, 有新生, 还有新生的父母。

   → 學校剛開學,
   　　学校刚开学, _____。

4. 他昨天去紐約看了父母, 和朋友吃了一頓飯。
   他昨天去纽约看了父母, 和朋友吃了一顿饭。

   → 他昨天_____。

E. Rewrite the sentences using 除了...以外, 都...

1. 我這個星期只有星期四晚上有空。
   我这个星期只有星期四晚上有空。

   → _____。

2. 大學二、三、四年級的學生都不用住校, 只有一年級的新生得住校。
   大学二、三、四年级的学生都不用住校, 只有一年级的新生得住校。

   → _____。

3. 每到週末，學校裏只有圖書館沒人，別的地方人都很多。
   每到周末，学校里只有图书馆没人，别的地方人都很多。

→ _____。

4. 新生只有小張還沒辦註冊手續，別的人都辦好了。
   新生只有小张还没办注册手续，别的人都办好了。

→ _____。

圖書館沒人 / 图书馆没人

F. Use 再說 / 再说 *to answer the following questions.*

EXAMPLE: a: 你為什麼今天沒去註冊？
          你为什么今天没去注册？

        b: <u>因為我去機場送我的父母了</u>, <u>再說今天註冊的人也太多</u>。
           <u>因为我去机场送我的父母了</u>, <u>再说今天注册的人也太多</u>。

1. a: 你為什麼學中文？
      你为什么学中文？

  b: _____, _____。

2. a: 你為什麼上這個學校?

   你为什么上这个学校?

   b: _____, _____。

3. a: 柯林説他為什麼住在校外?

   柯林说他为什么住在校外?

   b: 他説:

   他说: "_____, _____。"

4. a: 你為什麼喜歡買美國車?

   你为什么喜欢买美国车?

   b: _____, _____。

G. Complete the following exchanges using 不見得 ／ 不见得.

EXAMPLE:　a: 他父母是中國人, 雖然他生在美國, 但是學中文應該很容易吧?

　　　　　　　他父母是中国人, 虽然他生在美国, 但是学中文应该很容易吧?

　　　　b: 在美國長大的中國孩子, <u>學中文也不見得容易</u>。

　　　　　在美国长大的中国孩子, <u>学中文也不见得容易</u>。

1. a: 這個宿舍又小又貴, 我真想搬出去住, 省一點錢。

   这个宿舍又小又贵, 我真想搬出去住, 省一点钱。

   b: 很多校外的房子也很小很貴,

   很多校外的房子也很小很贵, _____。

2. a: 你們這個宿舍很安靜, 下個學期我打算搬進來。

   你们这个宿舍很安静, 下个学期我打算搬进来。

   b: 這個宿舍房間不多, 好像都有人住,

   这个宿舍房间不多, 好像都有人住, _____。

3. a: 他是老生, 我們有什麼事都可以去問他。

   他是老生, 我们有什么事都可以去问他。

b: 他只比我們早來一年,

他只比我们早来一年, _____。

4. a: 我想找一家又好吃又便宜的飯館, 學校旁邊那家去吃飯的人很多, 我們去那兒怎麼樣?

我想找一家又好吃又便宜的饭馆, 学校旁边那家去吃饭的人很多, 我们去那儿怎么样?

b: 那家飯館的菜可能很好吃, 可是

那家饭馆的菜可能很好吃, 可是

_____。

V. TRANSLATION

A. Translate the following into Chinese.

1. a: When will the school year start?
   b: Next Wednesday.

2. a: What time did you get to school today?
   b: I came at 10:15 AM.

3. a: Did you go to Boston by plane or by car?
   b: I went by car.

4. Living in the dormitory is very convenient. However, it does not save you any money.

B. Translate the following passages into Chinese.

1. That first-year student was born in China, but she was raised in America. Yesterday I helped her to register. Her parents wanted her to live in the dorm to get used to college life. She felt that living in the dorm was too restrictive. She said that she wanted to live off campus next semester.

▼ ▼

2. Zhang Tianming made a new friend this morning. His name was Ke Lin. Zhang Tianming met Ke Lin in the dorm. There were many people in the dorm. Except for Ke Lin, Zhang Tianming didn't know anyone else. Ke Lin helped Zhang Tianming move. He also helped other new students move. After finishing moving, Ke Lin said to Zhang Tianming, "If you need any help, call me."

3. Little Zhang is from China. He just moved to the States last year. He has been living in Boston for more than a year, and hasn't adapted to life in America. He thinks that it is really inconvenient to live in the United States without a car. He had to depend on other people to drive him around. Next semester he would like to buy a car. He'd like to help other new students from China.

VI. COMPOSITION

《開學的第一天》

《开学的第一天》

Describe your first day in college. Include information such as when and how you got to the campus, whether you liked your living quarters and why, and classmates or roommates you met that day.

第二課 ▲ 宿舍

A. Listen to the audio for the Textbook and answer the questions.

1. Who moved in first—Zhang Tianming or John?

2. What furniture do Zhang Tianming and John both have?

3. Is their dorm close to the main street?

4. What are the advantages of living in the dorm?

5. What are the disadvantages of living in the dorm?

B. Listen to the audio for the Workbook.

1. Write the character you hear on the recording.

2. Write the character you hear on the recording.

3. Listen to the recording and answer the following questions.

Questions:

    a. What year in school is Ke Lin?

    b. When did Ke Lin study French?

    c. With whom did Ke Lin practice his Chinese?

4. Listen to the recording and answer the following questions.
    a. How many pieces of furniture are there in the room?

    b. What is the room's only shortcoming?

5. Draw a picture of Little Li's room based on the recording. Then answer the question you hear at the end of the recording.

II. SPEAKING EXERCISES

A. *Practice asking and answering the following questions with a partner before class.*

1. 你的房間有什麼傢俱?

   你的房间有什么家具?

2. 你的書桌上擺著一些什麼東西?

   你的书桌上摆着一些什么东西?

3. 你住的地方離學校哪一棟樓最近?

   你住的地方离学校哪一栋楼最近?

4. 你去過的中國餐館, 哪一家的菜最地道?

   你去过的中国餐馆, 哪一家的菜最地道?

B. *Practice speaking on the following topics.*

1. 自己的房間(我現在住在...)

   自己的房间(我现在住在...)

2. 你喜歡什麼樣的房間?

   你喜欢什么样的房间?

▼ ▼

C. *Choose one of the six rooms and describe it in detail.*

III. READING COMPREHENSION

A. *Read the passage and answer the questions.*

(Traditional Characters)

　　在中國, 學生高中畢業以後都需要考試才能上大學。考試考得好, 就上好一點的大學, 考得不太好, 就上差一點的大學。如果考試考得很不好, 就不能上大學。很多大學新生一進學校, 就已經知道自己的專業 (1) 是什麼了, 要是不喜歡, 也可以轉系或者轉學。但是轉系, 轉學還是得考試。

(1)　專業(zhuānyè): major

(Simplified Characters)

　　在中国, 学生高中毕业以后都需要考试才能上大学。考试考得好, 就上好一点的大学, 考得不太好, 就上差一点的大学。如果考试考得很不好, 就不能上大学。很多大学新生一进学校, 就已经知道自己的专业 (1) 是什么了, 要是不喜欢, 也可以转系或者转学。但是转系, 转学还是得考试。

(1)　专业(zhuānyè): major

Questions:

1. How does the college admissions process in China differ from the process in America?

2. What are 轉系 / 转系 and 轉學 / 转学 in English?

B. *Draw a picture and answer the questions after reading the following passage.*

(Traditional Characters)

　　小高的新家有兩層樓。樓上有三個房間。左邊的房間是小高的書房。書房中間是一張很大的書桌，書桌後邊是兩個又高又大的書架。中間的房間是廁所。廁所的右邊是小高的臥房，臥房中間放著一張床，床旁邊擺著一個衣櫃。樓下有客廳，餐廳和洗衣房。洗衣房在右邊，裏邊有烘乾機和洗衣機。洗衣房的隔壁是餐廳，再過去才是客廳。客廳的外邊是車庫，裏邊停著兩輛車，一輛大的，一輛小的。小高非常喜歡他的新家。

(Simplified Characters)

　　小高的新家有两层楼。楼上有三个房间。左边的房间是小高的书房。书房中间是一张很大的书桌，书桌后边是两个又高又大的书架。中间的房间是厕所。厕所的右边是小高的卧房，卧房中间放着一张床，床旁边摆着一个衣柜。楼下有客厅，餐厅和洗衣房。洗衣房在右边，里边有烘乾机和洗衣机。洗衣房的隔壁是餐厅，再过去才是客厅。客厅的外边是车库，里边停着两辆车，一辆大的，一辆小的。小高非常喜欢他的新家。

▼▼▼▼▼▼▼▼▼▼▼▼▼▼▼▼▼▼▼▼▼▼▼▼▼▼▼▼▼▼▼▼▼▼▼▼▼▼▼

Questions (True/False):

(   ) 1.   這個房子有五個房間。

             这个房子有五个房间。

(   ) 2.   小高不用到外邊洗衣服了。

             小高不用到外边洗衣服了。

(   ) 3.   要是小高的朋友來家裏聊天、吃飯, 他們應該到樓上去。

             要是小高的朋友来家里聊天、吃饭, 他们应该到楼上去。

C. Read the passage and answer the questions.

(Traditional Characters)

    有一天, 張文去參加李朋的生日晚會, 看到李朋畫的畫兒很好, 就说:"李朋, 你可以給我畫一張嗎?"李朋說:"可以, 你下個星期六來拿吧。"到了星期六, 張文又來到李朋家。他進門以後就問:"你給我的畫兒畫好了嗎?"李朋说:"畫好了。"張文問:"在哪兒呢?"李朋說:"在這兒。"張文一看, 是一張白紙, 就说:"你還沒畫呀?"李朋說:"畫了, 我畫的是牛吃草 (1)。"張文問:"這兒沒有草啊!"李朋説:"草都被牛吃了。"張文說:"那牛呢?"李朋說:"沒有草了, 牛還在這裏做什麼!"

(1) 草(cǎo): grass

(Simplified Characters)

    有一天, 张文去参加李朋的生日晚会, 看到李朋画的画儿很好, 就说:"李朋, 你可以给我画一张吗?"李朋说:"可以, 你下个星期六来拿吧。"到了星期六, 张文又来到李朋家。他进门以后就问:"你给我的画儿画好了吗?"李朋说:"画好了。"张文问:"在哪儿呢?"李朋说:"在这儿。"张文一看, 是一张白纸, 就说:"你还没画呀?"李朋说:"画了, 我画的是牛吃草 (1)。"张文问:"这儿没有草啊!"李朋说:"草都被牛吃了。"张文说:"那牛呢?"李朋说:"没有草了, 牛还在这里做什么!"

(1) 草(cǎo): grass

Questions:

1. Why did Zhang ask Li to paint for him?

2. When did Li ask Zhang to pick up the painting?

3. What did Li call his painting?

4. What did Zhang see on the painting?

5. How did Li explain his painting?

IV. GRAMMAR & USAGE

A. *Complete the dialogues using* 比較／比较.

1. a: 學校附近有很多飯館, 你比較喜歡哪一家的菜?

   學校附近有很多饭馆, 你比较喜欢哪一家的菜?

   b: _____。

2. a: 你覺得住校內比較省錢, 還是住校外比較省錢?

   你觉得住校內比较省钱, 还是住校外比较省钱?

   b: _____。

3. a: 你家誰的胃口好?

   你家谁的胃口好?

   b: _____。

B. Complete the dialogues using 比較 / 比较.

EXAMPLE:　a: 我不想住校, 房間太小了。

　　　　　　　我不想住校, 房间太小了。

　　　　　　b: 宿舍房間雖然比較小, 但是離教室近, 上課很方便。

　　　　　　　宿舍房间虽然比较小, 但是离教室近, 上课很方便。

1. a: 這個店的傢俱很貴, 我想看一看別的店怎麼樣。

　　　这个店的家具很贵, 我想看一看别的店怎么样。

　　b: ＿＿＿＿＿＿＿＿＿＿＿＿＿＿＿＿＿＿＿＿, 但是比別的店都好得多。

2. a: 這個洗衣機和烘乾機太吵了, 應該買新的。

　　　这个洗衣机和烘乾机太吵了, 应该买新的。

　　b: ＿＿＿＿＿＿＿＿＿＿＿＿＿＿＿＿＿＿＿＿＿＿＿,

　　　但是還可以用。 / 但是还可以用。

3. a: 你怎麼帶我來這家餐館? 你看他們的設備那麼舊。

　　　你怎么带我来这家餐馆? 你看他们的设备那么旧。

　　b: ＿＿＿＿＿＿＿＿＿＿＿＿＿＿＿＿＿＿＿＿＿＿＿,

　　　但是菜又好吃又便宜。

C. Rewrite the sentences using 得很.

EXAMPLE:　　那家飯館的菜非常地道。→ <u>那家飯館的菜地道得很</u>。

　　　　　　那家饭馆的菜非常地道。→ <u>那家饭馆的菜地道得很</u>。

1. 他住的那棟宿舍非常安靜。

　　他住的那栋宿舍非常安静。

　　→ ＿＿＿＿＿＿＿＿＿＿＿＿＿＿＿＿＿＿＿＿＿＿。

2. 這個學校非常安全。

　　这个学校非常安全。

　　→ ＿＿＿＿＿＿＿＿＿＿＿＿＿＿＿＿＿＿＿＿＿＿。

3. 那家商店非常遠。

   那家商店非常远。

   → _____。

D. Complete the dialogues using 恐怕.

EXAMPLE: a: 哎, 你的房間怎麼這麼熱?

                哎, 你的房间怎么这么热?

           b: 我也不知道, <u>恐怕空調壞了</u>。

                我也不知道, <u>恐怕空调坏了</u>。

1. a: 他明天能來嗎?

   他明天能来吗?

   b: 他這兩天忙得很,

   他这两天忙得很,

   _____。

2. a: 我剛下課, 肚子餓得很。今天宿舍餐廳的晚飯怎麼樣?

   我刚下课, 肚子饿得很。今天宿舍餐厅的晚饭怎么样?

   b: 還不錯。可是現在已經快九點了。這麼晚了,

   还不错。可是现在已经快九点了。这么晚了,

   _____。

3. a: 已經十二點半了, 他怎麼還沒來?

   已经十二点半了, 他怎么还没来?

   b: 波士頓的路不好找,

   波士顿的路不好找,

   _____。

4. a: 你覺得我應該買多少傢俱?

   你觉得我应该买多少家具?

▼▼▼

b: 你的新家不大, 如果傢俱太多, _____, 最好少买一些。

你的新家不大, 如果家具太多, _____, 最好少买一些。

E. Rearrange the words into complete sentences. Pay attention to the word order.

1. 書　　一本　　買了　　我妹妹　　很有意思

   书　　一本　　买了　　我妹妹　　很有意思

2. 從華盛頓　　前天　　我　　是　　來的　　坐飛機

   从华盛顿　　前天　　我　　是　　来的　　坐飞机

3. 六個月　　兩年前　　工作了　　他　　在中國

   六个月　　两年前　　工作了　　他　　在中国

4. 一頓　　在那家中國飯館　　我們　　昨天　　吃了　　很好吃的　　飯

   一顿　　在那家中国饭馆　　我们　　昨天　　吃了　　很好吃的　　饭

5. 寫　　中國字　　小王　　很快　　寫得

   写　　中国字　　小王　　很快　　写得

F. Describe the picture. What are the two people wearing? What is on the table? Include the background and the restaurant decor. Remember to use 著/着 *in your description.*

Some helpful vocabulary words:

抽煙 ／ 抽烟(chōu yān): to smoke a cigarette

手提箱(shǒutíxiāng): briefcase

抽煙斗 ／ 抽烟斗(chōu yāndǒu): to smoke a pipe

戴眼鏡 ／ 戴眼镜(dài yǎnjìng): to wear glasses

火柴(huǒchái): matches

手錶 ／ 手表(shǒubiǎo): wristwatch

掛/挂(guà): to hang

畫/画(huà): picture; painting

▼ ▼

V. TRANSLATION

A. *Translate the dialogues into Chinese.*

1. a: Where is your roommate from?

    b: He's from Washington.

2. a: I am starving.

    b: Then let's go eat.

3. a: Does the store on campus sell furniture?

    b: No, the campus stores generally don't sell furniture. They only sell daily necessities and stationery.

B. *Translate the following sentences into Chinese. Pay attention to the word order.*

1. I read a new book in the library yesterday afternoon.

2. My brother drove from Boston to Washington, D.C., last weekend to visit a friend.

3 . He was doing laundry on the second floor when his father called.

4. Little Zhang is going to play basketball with his friends after the class.

5. This is the restaurant that my roommate mentioned.

6. The dorm where I used to live was very small and very old.

7. The food that your mom made last night was extremely tasty.

8. The bookstore we went to this morning also sells sportswear.

C. *Translate the passages into Chinese using the grammar and vocabulary from this lesson.*

1. Near the campus there is a Chinese restaurant and a Japanese restaurant. The Japanese restaurant is relatively more expensive. The Chinese restaurant is much cheaper than the Japanese restaurant. The restaurants are very close to the campus. It's really convenient.

2. This is Zhang Tianming's room. There is a bed in the middle of the room. There is a blanket and a comforter on the bed. On the right side of the room is a wardrobe. However, the wardrobe is empty. There is a picture hanging on the door, and there's a bookshelf below the picture. There are some books on the shelf.

3. I am moving into the dorm in a few days. The facilities of the dorm are relatively new. My room is close to the bathroom. There are washers and dryers on my floor. It's really convenient to live there. However, I'm afraid it will be a bit noisy.

VI. COMPOSITION

Describe your living quarters. Be sure to mention the location, the layout, whether it is quiet for study and convenient for shopping, and finally whether you like living there and why.

房間裏有什麽？／房间里有什么？

第三課 ▲ 在飯館
第三课 ▲ 在饭馆

 **I. LISTENING COMPREHENSION**

A. Listen to the audio for the Textbook and answer the following questions.

1. Why did Zhang Tianming want to go to Chinatown?

2. Who went to Chinatown with Zhang Tianming?

3. Who was a frequent patron of the restaurant?

4. What did they order?

5. Did they agree with the reporter?

B. Listen to the audio for the Workbook.

1. Listen to the passage and answer the multiple-choice question.
   ( ) Why did Little Chen decide to quit?
      a. He was not allowed to smoke in the restaurant.
      b. The boss didn't like him.
      c. His customers didn't tip him well.
      d. He became a vegetarian.

   New Vocabulary:

   飯碗／饭碗 (fànwǎn): rice bowl
   盤子／盘子 (pánzi): plate

2. According to the passage, in what four ways do Chinese and American people differ when it comes to eating and drinking?
   a.

   b.

   c.

   d.

   Are these four things perhaps changing among the Chinese? Why?

▼ ▼

3. Listen to the passage and answer the following questions.

   a.   What was Little Zhang's adventure about?

   b.   Was his adventure a successful one?

   c.   What did Little Zhang finally do?

II. SPEAKING EXERCISES

A. Practice asking and answering the questions with a partner before class.

1. 開學已經多長時間了？
    开学已经多长时间了？

2. 你多久沒吃中國飯了？
    你多久没吃中国饭了？

3. 你媽媽的拿手菜是什麼？
    你妈妈的拿手菜是什么？

一家中國餐館 / 一家中国餐馆

(See the Alternate Character Appendix for simplified characters.)

▼ ▼

B. *Practice speaking on the following topics.*

1. 你一般都到什麼樣的餐館吃飯？為什麼？

   你一般都到什么样的餐馆吃饭？为什么？

2. 你覺得吃什麼東西對身體健康有好處？

   你觉得吃什么东西对身体健康有好处？

3. Find a partner and make up a dialogue about eating out. One could invite the other to eat at a Chinese restaurant. Ask about each other's favorite restaurants and dishes. Arrange how and when the two of you will meet. Discuss how to order or cook healthy Chinese food.

III. READING COMPREHENSION

A. *Look at the dishes below. Which ones do you think are meatless? Consult with your instructor or your Chinese friends if you have never had any of the dishes listed. You can also ask them if any of the dishes can be made either with or without meat. Fill out the chart with your answers.*

Traditional	Simplified	Meatless	Not meatless	Either
1. 酸辣湯	酸辣汤			
2. 涼拌黃瓜	凉拌黄瓜			
3. 紅燒牛肉	红烧牛肉			
4. 清蒸魚	清蒸鱼			
5. 菠菜豆腐湯	菠菜豆腐汤			
6. 糖醋魚	糖醋鱼			
7. 芥蘭牛肉	芥兰牛肉			
8. 家常豆腐	家常豆腐			

B. *Read the passage and answer the questions.*

(Traditional Characters)

　　吸煙的人覺得在美國越來越不自由。對他們來說，到飯館吃飯，到商店買東西什麼的，都很不方便。他們覺得跟別的客人付的錢一樣多，但是不能做自己想做的事, 這沒有什麼道理。有些飯館的老闆也覺得, 不讓客人吸煙, 客人會越來越少, 對飯館沒有好處。可是不吸煙的人認為, 身體健康最重要, 不能讓吸煙的人跟他們一起吃飯, 要不然, 他們就到別的飯館去吃飯。他們還說, 要是有人想吸煙, 可以到沒有人的地方去吸。所以現在很多人只好站在門外, 一邊吸煙, 一邊吹風。

(Simplified Characters)

吸烟的人觉得在美国越来越不自由。对他们来说, 到饭馆吃饭, 到商店买东西什么的, 都很不方便。他们觉得跟别的客人付的钱一样多, 但是不能做自己想做的事, 这没有什么道理。有些饭馆的老板也觉得, 不让客人吸烟, 客人会越来越少, 对饭馆没有好处。可是不吸烟的人认为, 身体健康最重要, 不能让吸烟的人跟他们一起吃饭, 要不然, 他们就到别的饭馆去吃饭。 他们还说, 要是有人想吸烟, 可以到没有人的地方去吸。所以现在很多人只好站在门外, 一边吸烟, 一边吹风。

Questions:

1. In which two situations do smokers feel shortchanged?

2. Who else is worried about this national trend?

3. What is the non-smokers' argument?

4. What are smokers forced to do?

C. *Answer the questions after reading the passage.*

(Traditional Characters)

小柯常到學校附近的一家中國餐館吃飯。那家飯館的菜又便宜又地道。小柯是那兒的常客, 老闆, 服務員都認識他。小柯今天又去那兒吃午飯。但是他一進門, 就覺得跟以前不一樣了。飯館原來是不讓人吸煙的, 可是今天怎麼

▼▼▼▼▼▼▼▼▼▼▼▼▼▼▼▼▼▼▼▼▼▼▼▼▼▼▼▼▼▼▼▼

那麼多人吸煙? 還有, 那裏的服務員小柯一個也沒見過。菜單上的菜也比以前貴多了。除了這些以外, 小柯點的菜裏還放了很多味精。小柯想下次再也不到這家餐館來吃飯了。

(Simplified Characters)

　　小柯常到学校附近的一家中国餐馆吃饭。那家饭馆的菜又便宜又地道。小柯是那儿的常客, 老板, 服务员都认识他。小柯今天又去那儿吃午饭。但是他一进门, 就觉得跟以前不一样了。饭馆原来是不让人吸烟的, 可是今天怎么那么多人吸烟? 还有, 那里的服务员小柯一个也没见过。菜单上的菜也比以前贵多了。除了这些以外, 小柯点的菜里还放了很多味精。小柯想下次再也不到这家餐馆来吃饭了。

Questions:

1. What attracted Little Ke to the restaurant?

2. What four changes did Little Ke notice on this visit?

3. Did he eat? How do you know?

4. Will he eat there again?

D. Read the passage and answer the following questions. (True/False)

(Traditional Characters)

　　今天是太太的生日, 李先生很早就下班回家, 給太太做一個他最拿手的紅燒魚。魚做好了, 李先生覺得味道太淡。他加了一點鹽, 還是太淡, 又加了一點鹽, 还是太淡。李先生覺得不對, 原來自己把糖當成鹽了。他就在菜裏放了一些醋, 把紅燒魚做成了糖醋魚。太太笑著說: "我不是愛吃醋的女人。" 李先生說 "嘿, 多吃醋對身體有好處!"

(Simplified Characters)

　　今天是太太的生日, 李先生很早就下班回家, 给太太做一个他最拿手的红烧鱼。鱼做好了, 李先生觉得味道太淡。他加了一点盐, 还是太淡, 又加了一点盐, 还是太淡。李先生觉得不对, 原来自己把糖当成盐了。他就在菜里放了一些醋, 把红烧鱼做成了糖醋鱼。太太笑着说: "我不是爱吃醋的女人。" 李先生说 : "嘿, 多吃醋对身体有好处!"

Questions (True/False):

(   ) 1.   Mr. Li didn't go to work today.

(   ) 2.   Ordinarily, fish braised in soy sauce is one of Mr. Li's best dishes.

(   ) 3.   Vinegar is one of the essential ingredients of Mr. Li's fish recipe.

(   ) 4.   Mr. Li put a lot of salt in the fish.

(   ) 5.   Mr. Li put a lot of vinegar in the fish because Mrs. Li likes vinegar.

(   ) 6.   Mrs. Li says she is not a jealous woman.

E.   *Answer the questions after reading the passage.*

(Traditional Characters)

        法國人跟美國人對吃的看法好像很不同。法國人認為想吃什麼就應該吃什麼, 不要怕油多, 卡路里高, 而且最重要的是每天一定要喝些紅酒。他們認為喝紅酒對身體有好處。美國人認為菜越清淡越好, 應該多吃青菜, 少吃肉, 尤其是牛肉。做菜的時候, 要少放油, 少放鹽。如果你問我這兩種看法哪一種對? 我想, 這就要看每個人的情況 (1) 了。一個人應該根據 (2) 自己的身體情況, 生活習慣來決定 (3) 自己應該吃什麼, 不應該吃什麼。

(1)   情況 (qíngkuàng): situation

(2)   根據 (gēnjù): on the basis of

(3)   決定 (juédìng): to decide

(Simplified Characters)

        法国人跟美国人对吃的看法好像很不同。法国人认为想吃什么就应该吃什么, 不要怕油多, 卡路里高, 而且最重要的是每天一定要喝些红酒。他们认为喝红酒对身体有好处。美国人认为菜越清淡越好, 应该多吃青菜, 少吃肉, 尤其是牛肉。做菜的时候, 要少放油, 少放盐。如果你问我这两种看法哪一种对? 我想, 这就要看每个人的情况了 (1)。一个人应该根据 (2) 自己的身体情况, 生活习惯来决定 (3) 自己应该吃什么, 不应该吃什么。

▼▼▼▼▼▼▼▼▼▼▼▼▼▼▼▼▼▼▼▼▼▼▼▼▼▼▼▼▼▼▼▼▼▼

(1) 情况(qíngkuàng): situation

(2) 根据(gēnjù): on the basis of

(3) 决定(juédìng): to decide

Questions:

1. Does the author prefer the American or the French diet? How do you know?

2. Why do the French drink red wine every day?

3. How does the French diet differ from the American diet, according to this passage?

4. Is one diet better than the other, according to the author?

F. Read the passage and answer the question.

(Traditional Characters)

這是我的中文老師學中文的時候聽過的一個故事：

今天是小明的生日, 爸爸媽媽帶他到外邊飯館吃飯。爸爸説他們要去的飯館是小朋友最喜歡的。但是到了飯館門前, 小明看見飯館的名字, 就哭起來説: "我不進去!" 媽媽説: "你為什麼不進去呀?" 小明説: "我怕!"

後來爸爸看到飯館的名字是 "友朋小吃", 就笑了起來。你們知道小明為什麼怕, 爸爸為什麼笑嗎?

(Simplified Characters)

这是我的中文老师学中文的时候听过的一个故事:

今天是小明的生日, 爸爸妈妈带他到外边饭馆吃饭。爸爸说他们要去的饭馆是小朋友最喜欢的。但是到了饭馆门前, 小明看见饭馆的名字, 就哭起来说: "我不进去!" 妈妈说: "你为什么不进去呀?" 小明说: "我怕!"

后来爸爸看到饭馆的名字是 "友朋小吃", 就笑了起来。你们知道小明为什么怕, 爸爸为什么笑吗?

What is the cause of Little Ming's alarm? What does 小吃 mean and why is 友朋小吃 a plausible although unlikely name for a restaurant? Hint: The sign can be read as an anagram. Ask your teacher to explain how shop signs and placards were inscribed traditionally.

IV. GRAMMAR & USAGE

A. Topics

Answer the questions using the words in parentheses.

EXAMPLE: a: 學校附近有很多飯館, 還有一家中國餐館, 不知道那兒的菜怎麼樣? (那家餐館)

學校附近有很多饭馆, 还有一家中国餐馆, 不知道那儿的菜怎么样? (那家餐馆)

▼▼▼▼▼▼▼▼▼▼▼▼▼▼▼▼▼▼▼▼▼▼▼▼▼▼▼▼▼▼▼▼▼▼▼▼

　　　　b: 那家餐館我去過。菜做得很地道。
　　　　　　那家餐館我去过。菜做得很地道。

1. a: 我聽説小柯剛交了一個女朋友。你認識嗎?(那個女孩)
　　　我听说小柯刚交了一个女朋友。你认识吗?(那个女孩)

　　b: ＿＿＿＿＿＿＿＿＿＿＿＿＿＿＿＿＿＿＿＿＿＿＿＿＿。

2. a: 這個餐館我第一次來, 想吃他們的清蒸魚。你説怎麽樣?(他們的清蒸魚)
　　　这个餐馆我第一次来, 想吃他们的清蒸鱼。你说怎么样?(他们的清蒸鱼)

　　b: ＿＿＿＿＿＿＿＿＿＿＿＿＿＿＿＿＿＿＿＿＿＿＿＿＿。

3. a: 你昨天買什麽了?
　　　你昨天买什么了?

　　b: 我昨天買了一本書。(那本書)
　　　我昨天买了一本书。(那本书)

　　a: ＿＿＿＿＿＿＿＿＿＿＿＿＿＿＿＿＿＿＿＿＿＿＿＿＿。

4. a: 你喜歡不喜歡你新買的家俱?(床, 衣櫃)
　　　你喜欢不喜欢你新买的家具?(床, 衣柜)

　　b: ＿＿＿＿＿＿＿＿＿＿＿＿＿＿＿＿＿＿＿＿＿＿＿＿＿。

B. Complete the sentences using 一…就…

EXAMPLE:　　小明病了, 吃什麽東西都不行, <u>一吃就跑廁所</u>。
　　　　　　　小明病了, 吃什么东西都不行, <u>一吃就跑厕所</u>。

1. 書店離這兒很近／书店离这儿很近, ＿＿＿＿＿＿＿＿＿＿＿＿＿＿＿。
　　(only have to walk a bit…)

2. 我的錢不多／我的钱不多, ＿＿＿＿＿＿＿＿＿＿＿＿＿＿＿＿。
　　(only have to spend a little…)

3. 他很聰明, 你教他什麼, 很快就會了。

他很聪明, 你教他什么, 很快就会了。

→ _____。

4. 那個地方很近, 很快就能走到。

那个地方很近, 很快就能走到。

→ _____。

C. *Summarize the sentences using* 原來 / 原来 *(originally).*

EXAMPLE:　　三年前我認識他的時候, 他在學日文。過了幾個月就不學了。

　　　　　　三年前我认识他的时候, 他在学日文。过了几个月就不学了。

　　→ <u>他原來學日文, 後來不學了</u>。

　　　　<u>他原来学日文, 后来不学了</u>。

1. 他上高中的時候, 常常喝酒, 上大學, 有了女朋友以後, 就不喝了。

他上高中的时候, 常常喝酒, 上大学, 有了女朋友以后, 就不喝了。

→ _____

2. 他小時候常常吃肉, 現在只吃素菜, 不吃肉了。

他小时候常常吃肉, 现在只吃素菜, 不吃肉了。

→ _____

3. 約翰想買一台空調, 但是太貴, 就買了一台電扇 (diànshàn: electric fan)。

约翰想买一台空调, 但是太贵, 就买了一台电扇 (diànshàn: electric fan)。

→ _____

4. 我想叫清蒸魚, 但是服務員说賣完了, 只好叫了一盤炒青菜。

我想叫清蒸鱼, 但是服务员说卖完了, 只好叫了一盘炒青菜。

→ _____

▼▼▼▼▼▼▼▼▼▼▼▼▼▼▼▼▼▼▼▼▼▼▼▼▼▼▼▼▼▼▼▼▼▼▼▼▼▼

湯　類	
海鮮酸辣湯（2-4 人）……… 7.95	大腸豬血湯（2-4 人）……… 6.95
海鮮豆腐羹（2-4 人）……… 7.95	沙茶豬血湯（2-4 人）……… 6.95
西湖牛肉羹（2-4 人）……… 7.95	薑絲腰花湯（2-4 人）……… 7.25
香菇肉羹（2-4 人）……… 7.95	薑絲魚乾空心菜湯(2-4 人) 6.95
花枝羹（2-4 人）……… 7.95	薑絲蛤蜊湯（2-4 人）……… 7.95
魷魚羹（2-4 人）……… 7.95	蚵仔湯（2-4 人）……… 7.95
酸菜魷魚湯（2-4 人）……… 7.95	酸菜豆腐湯(2-4 人) ……… 6.25
酸菜肚絲湯（2-4 人）……… 6.95	菠菜豆腐湯(2-4 人) ……… 6.25
麻辣肚絲湯（2-4 人）……… 6.95	榨菜肉絲湯(2-4 人) ……… 6.25
	雞茸玉米湯(2-4 人) ……… 6.50

菜單上有豆腐湯、酸辣湯嗎？ ／菜单上有豆腐汤、酸辣汤吗？

(See the Alternate Character Appendix for simplified characters.)

D. Complete the sentences using 原來 ／ 原来 *(as it turns out)*.

1. 屋子裏怎麼這麼熱, 噢,
   屋子里怎么这么热, 噢,

   _____。

2. 小張晚飯沒吃什麼, 我以為他不喜歡吃我做的牛肉, 後來才知道
   小张晚饭没吃什么, 我以为他不喜欢吃我做的牛肉, 后来才知道

   _____。

3. 我找了你半天, 找不到你,
   我找了你半天, 找不到你,

   _____。

4. 小柯三個星期沒來上課了,
   小柯三个星期没来上课了,

   _____。

E. Rewrite the sentences using 又…又…

EXAMPLE:　　那棟宿舍很新, 也很漂亮。→ 那棟宿舍又新又漂亮。

　　　　　　那栋宿舍很新, 也很漂亮。→ 那栋宿舍又新又漂亮。

1. 我媽媽做的牛肉很嫩, 而且很好吃。

   我妈妈做的牛肉很嫩, 而且很好吃。

   → _____ 。

2. 有些記者寫文章寫得很長, 而且沒有意思。

   有些记者写文章写得很长, 而且没有意思。

   → _____ 。

3. 聽說那家商店的青菜水果非常新鮮, 而且很便宜。

   听说那家商店的青菜水果非常新鲜, 而且很便宜。

   → _____ 。

F. Answer the questions using 這就要看...了 / 这就要看...了.

EXAMPLE: a: 你今天想點什麼菜呢?

   你今天想点什么菜呢?

   b: <u>這就要看這家餐館什麼菜最好吃了。</u>
   <u>这就要看这家餐馆什么菜最好吃了。</u>

1. a: 你下個學期還要學中文嗎?

   你下个学期还要学中文吗?

   b: _____ 。

2. a: 你這個週末打算做什麼?

   你这个周末打算做什么?

   b: _____ 。

3. a: 你覺得大學新生應該住校內還是住校外?

   你觉得大学新生应该住校内还是住校外?

   b: _____ 。

G. *Complete the sentences using* 其實／其实.

EXAMPLE:　　　我的同學都認為這次考試有一點兒難, <u>其實這次考試不太難</u>。

　　　　　　　　我的同学都认为这次考试有一点儿难, <u>其实这次考试不太难</u>。

1. 大家都覺得那個女孩長得很漂亮,

   大家都觉得那个女孩长得很漂亮,

   _____。

2. 很多人都覺得住在校外比較好,

   很多人都觉得住在校外比较好,

   _____。

3. 最近有一些文章說中國菜太油,

   最近有一些文章说中国菜太油,

   _____。

H. *Complete the sentences using* 特別是.

EXAMPLE:　　　開學大家都很忙, <u>特別是新生</u>。

　　　　　　　　开学大家都很忙, <u>特别是新生</u>。

1. 小林非常喜歡吃中國菜,

   小林非常喜欢吃中国菜,

   _____。

2. 我的同屋喜歡去外邊活動,

   我的同屋喜欢去外边活动,

   _____。

3. 小張這學期每門課的功課都很多,

   小张这学期每门课的功课都很多,

   _____。

I. Complete the sentences using 要不然.

EXAMPLE: 租房子最好租帶傢俱的, <u>要不然得花很多錢買傢俱</u>。

                      租房子最好租带家具的, <u>要不然得花很多钱买家具</u>。

1. 學中文最好天天聽錄音,

    学中文最好天天听录音,

    _____。

2. 在中國飯館吃飯, 常常得告訴老闆少放點兒鹽和味精,

    在中国饭馆吃饭, 常常得告诉老板少放点儿盐和味精,

    _____。

3. 找房子最好不要找在大馬路旁邊的,

    找房子最好不要找在大马路旁边的,

    _____。

J. Fill in the blanks with 的, 地, *or* 得.

(Traditional Characters)

    前些日子, 校園報紙做了一個調查, 看看附近哪一家餐館____菜做____最好吃。結果, 是城裏一家中國飯館____菜最受歡迎。聽說, 那家餐館上菜上____快, 菜也做____很地道。地方又大又安靜, 客人雖多, 但是一定有地方坐。大家都喜歡在那兒慢慢兒____吃, 邊吃飯, 邊聊天。

(Simplified Characters)

    前些日子, 校园报纸做了一个调查, 看看附近哪一家餐馆____菜做____最好吃。结果, 是城里一家中国饭馆____菜最受欢迎。听说, 那家餐馆上菜上____快, 菜也做____很地道。地方又大又安静, 客人虽多, 但是一定有地方坐。大家都喜欢在那儿慢慢儿____吃, 边吃饭, 边聊天。

▼▼

K. Fill in the blanks with the words and phrases provided.

(Traditional Characters)

　　要不然, 又…又…, 這就要看你, 非常, 比較, 特別是

　　這家餐館的菜做得_____好, _____他們的炒青菜, _____新鮮_____好吃。但是有的人覺得他們的菜太清淡。其實_____你喜歡吃什麼樣的菜。我自己吃的_____清淡, _____, 我就不會說這家餐館的菜好吃了。

(Simplified Characters)

　　要不然, 又…又…, 这就要看你, 非常, 比较, 特别是

　　这家餐馆的菜做得_____好, _____他们的炒青菜, _____新鲜_____好吃。但是有的人觉得他们的菜太清淡。其实_____你喜欢吃什么样的菜。我自己吃的_____清淡, _____, 我就不会说这家餐馆的菜好吃了。

又好吃又地道的中國芥蘭
又好吃又地道的中国芥兰

V. TRANSLATION

A. Translate the sentences into Chinese.

1. I finished reading the book I bought yesterday. (topic-comment)

2. Your younger sister is very pretty. (長得 / 长得)

3. The steamed fish tastes delicious.

4. The beef with broccoli at this restaurant is superb. The beef is tender and smells wonderful.
   (又...又...)

5. The waiter said that the fish was fresh. But it wasn't. (並/并 + Neg.)

6. Could I trouble you to tell the boss not to put MSG in the dishes?

B. *Translate the sentences using* 原來 / 原来 *(as it turns out).*

1. I thought he didn't like the sweet-and-sour fish I made. As it turns/turned out, he is allergic to fish.

2. We all thought that Little Gao had left. As it turns/turned out, he went outside to smoke.

3. The landlord couldn't find a tenant for the apartment downstairs. As it turns/turned out, the apartment didn't have air-conditioning.

C. *Translate the sentences using* 其實 / 其实.

1. Everyone thought she was Chinese. She's actually Japanese.

2. I thought the food in the dorm must be terrible. Actually, it is not as bad as I thought.

3. I don't listen to my parents too much. But as a matter of fact, what they say does make sense.

4. Many college freshmen thought it would be more economical to rent an apartment. In fact, it is not necessarily so.

D. *Translate the passages into Chinese.*

1. Ke Lin and Zhang Tianming went out to eat last night. Ke Lin drove very fast. They got to Chinatown very quickly. Originally they wanted to order four dishes. In the end they only ordered three. The dishes that they ordered were all delicious. As soon as they finished eating, they went back to school. On their way home (在回家的路上), they talked and laughed. They were very happy.

2. I haven't had Chinese food for three weeks and was thinking about having some authentic Chinese food in Chinatown. As it happened, my friend Little Lin also wanted to have some Chinese food. But neither of us had a car. There was no other way but to walk. It took us an hour to get there. We ordered three dishes, and they smelled good and tasted great. We both felt that we should have ordered more.

VI. COMPOSITION

《我最喜歡的飯館》

《我最喜欢的饭馆》

Write a restaurant review. In your review, describe the decor of the restaurant, the service, the prices, and your favorite dishes.

第四课 ▲ 買東西
第四课 ▲ 买东西

I. LISTENING COMPREHENSION

A. *Listen to the audio for the Textbook and answer the questions.*

1. Why doesn't Zhang Tianming like the clothes that his mother bought for him?

2. What is Zhang Tianming's philosophy when it comes to shopping for clothes?

3. What are Ke Lin's criteria for buying clothes?

4. Who does Lin Xuemei agree with?

B. *Listen to the audio for the Workbook.*

1. Listen to the passage and answer the questions.
   a. Will you write a check to pay for your purchases in China? Why or why not?

   b. In which two ways do Chinese and American people differ when it comes to shopping?

2. Listen to the passage and answer the questions.
   a. What does Little Lin look for when buying clothes?

   b. What does Little Wang think about Little Lin's criteria for choosing what to wear?

   c. Would you go shopping with Lin and Wang together? Why or why not?

3. Listen to the passage and answer the questions.
   a. What is the name of the shopping center?

   b. How many floors are there?

   c. If you want to buy children's clothes, which floor should you go to?

d. Why is there a sale at the shopping center? How big is the discount?

e. What extra incentive is the shopping center offering to lure customers to spend more money?

4. Listen to the passage and answer the question by circling the correct item.

If you have to buy a T-shirt for Little Zhang, which of the three shown above will you choose?

5. Listen to the passage and answer the questions.
    a. What do the hotels prepare for their guests?

    b. How can the guests pay their bills?

    c. What is the disadvantage of staying at any of the hotels in the area?

    d. How high could the hotel tax be?

II. SPEAKING EXERCISES

A. Practice asking and answering the questions with a partner before class.

1. 你差不多多久買一次衣服？
    你差不多多久买一次衣服？

2. 你現在身上穿的衣服／襯衫／褲子是什麼顏色的？
    你现在身上穿的衣服／衬衫／裤子是什么颜色的？

3. 你買衣服的標準是什麼?

　　你买衣服的标准是什么?

4. 一般來說, 買完東西以後, 你付現金, 寫支票還是用信用卡?

　　一般来说, 买完东西以后, 你付现金, 写支票还是用信用卡?

5. 這一州買衣服需要付稅嗎?

　　这一州买衣服需要付税吗?

B. Practice speaking on the following topics.

1. 你跟你的朋友一起去買東西, 他看到什麼東西都想買, 你怎麼讓他少買一些?

　　你跟你的朋友一起去买东西, 他看到什么东西都想买, 你怎么让他少买一些?

2. 請你說說你對名牌衣服的看法。你買衣服一定要買名牌的嗎? 為什麼?

　　请你说说你对名牌衣服的看法。你买衣服一定要买名牌的吗? 为什么?

3. You are a salesperson and have to sell this T-shirt. Talk to a potential customer about the T-shirt based on the information on the sales tag, and try to convince the customer that the T-shirt is wonderful in style, color, material, and price and is ideal for him or her.

DKNY
ORIGINAL: $40
NOW: $20

MADE IN CHINA

100% COTTON

MACHINE WASH

TUMBLE DRY

▼ ▼

III. READING COMPREHENSION

A. Read the passage and answer the question.

(Traditional Characters)

在美國, 上餐館吃飯跟在中國有很多地方不一樣。比方説, 幾個朋友在一起吃飯, 中國人吃完飯以後, 常常每個人都爭 (zhēng) 著付錢。美國人一般不會這樣。付錢的時候, 在美國可以用現金, 支票, 或者信用卡, 但是在中國, 一般來説都付現金。在美國, 吃完飯以後得給服務員小費, 但是在中國不用付小費。還有一點就是, 中國人一般不要收據。

(Simplified Characters)

在美国, 上餐馆吃饭跟在中国有很多地方不一样。比方说, 几个朋友在一起吃饭, 中国人吃完饭以后, 常常每个人都争 (zhēng) 着付钱。美国人一般不会这样。付钱的时候, 在美国可以用现金, 支票, 或者信用卡, 但是在中国, 一般来说都付现金。在美国, 吃完饭以后得给服务员小费, 但是在中国不用付小费。还有一点就是, 中国人一般不要收据。

Question:
What are the four major differences between eating out in America and in China?

B. Read the passage and answer the questions.

(Traditional Characters)

報紙上有一篇文章説, 城裏有一家新的購物中心, 他們的東西質量雖然不錯, 可是價錢太貴。購物中心的老闆看了文章以後打電話給記者説:"你説得不對。我們的東西物美價廉。"他一定要記者再寫一篇文章。記者説:"你們的購物中心買東西只能付現金, 不能用信用卡, 而且也不給收據。如果你叫我再寫一篇文章, 我就寫這個。"老闆聽了以後著急 (jí) 得不得了。

(Simplified Characters)

　　报纸上有一篇文章说, 城里有一家新的购物中心, 他们的东西质量虽然不错, 可是价钱太贵。购物中心的老板看了文章以后打电话给记者说："你说得不对。我们的东西物美价廉。"他一定要记者再写一篇文章。记者说："你们的购物中心买东西只能付现金, 不能用信用卡, 而且也不给收据。如果你叫我再写一篇文章, 我就写这个。"老板听了以后着急 (jí) 得不得了。

Questions:

1. What was reported in the first article?

2. What was the owner's reaction?

3. What other things did the reporter say he would reveal in his second article about the restaurant?

4. What do you think the owner should do after all this?

C. Read the passage and answer the questions. (True/False)

(Traditional Characters)

　　柯林買衣服從來不挑剔, 只要樣子和顏色合適就行, 不在乎是不是名牌。他的女朋友林雪梅卻認為名牌衣服質量好得多, 穿起來也更舒服。雖然雪梅經常為買衣服的事和柯林爭論, 可是柯林還是不同意雪梅的看法。上個週末柯林買了一件襯衫, 是雪梅最不喜歡的黃色, 然後穿著去見她。雪梅一看見就叫起來："你怎麼買了一件這麼難看的衣服？"柯林笑著說："這是阿迪達斯的！難道你不喜歡嗎？"

(Simplified Characters)

　　柯林买衣服从来不挑剔，只要样子和颜色合适就行，不在乎是不是名牌。他的女朋友林雪梅却认为名牌衣服质量好得多，穿起来也更舒服。虽然雪梅经常为买衣服的事和柯林争论，可是柯林还是不同意雪梅的看法。上个周末柯林买了一件衬衫，是雪梅最不喜欢的黄色，然后穿着去见她。雪梅一看见就叫起来："你怎么买了一件这么难看的衣服？"柯林笑着说："这是阿迪达斯的！难道你不喜欢吗？"

Questions (True/False):

( ) 1. Ke Lin is not picky when shopping for clothes.

( ) 2. To Lin Xuemei, a good brand means good quality.

( ) 3. Finally, Lin Xuemei succeeded in convincing Ke Lin that he should buy brand-name clothing.

( ) 4. Last weekend Ke Lin and Lin Xuemei went shopping together.

( ) 5. Ke Lin thought that Lin Xuemei would like his new shirt.

( ) 6. Ke Lin maintained that brand name clothes are not necessarily good.

D. *Since the mid-1990s retailers from overseas have been setting up camp in coastal cities in mainland China. Upscale boutiques and department stores are becoming commonplace in big cities. The following advertisement appeared in a Shanghai evening paper. Skim through it and complete the following tasks.*

(See the Alternate Character Appendix for traditional characters.)

1. Circle the Chinese name of the store.

2. Circle the address of the store.

▼▼▼▼▼▼▼▼▼▼▼▼▼▼▼▼▼▼▼▼▼▼▼▼▼▼▼▼▼▼▼▼▼▼▼▼

3. Circle the description that is used to try to persuade the customer of the prestige of the store.

4. What will the first 60 customers receive?

E. Read the advertisement for a department store's sale and answer the questions.

(See the Alternate Character Appendix for simplified characters.)

Questions:

1. Which department will offer a 40 percent discount?

2. Will each item in that department be 40 percent off? How do you know?

3. Will customers get a discount if they go shopping on a Friday?

IV. GRAMMAR & USAGE

A. Practice using time phrases by answering the following questions.

1. a: 今天是幾月幾號, 星期幾？

   今天是几月几号, 星期几？

   b: _____。

2. a: 這個學期開學多久了？

   这个学期开学多久了？

   b: _____。

3. a: 你一個星期上幾次中文課? 什麼時候上？

   你一个星期上几次中文课? 什么时候上？

b: _____。

4. a: 你昨天做功課做了多長時間?

   你昨天做功课做了多长时间?

   b: _____。

5. a: 你多長時間沒聽錄音了?

   你多长时间没听录音了?

   b: _____。

6. a: 你一天吃幾頓飯?

   你一天吃几顿饭?

   b: _____。

7. a: 你多久洗一次衣服?

   b: _____。

8. a: 從你住的地方開車到購物中心要開多長時間?

   从你住的地方开车到购物中心要开多长时间?

   b: _____。

B. *Complete the sentences using* 什麼的 / 什么的.

EXAMPLE:　　這個購物中心真大, <u>衣服、日用品什麼的</u>, 你都買得到。

　　　　　　这个购物中心真大, <u>衣服、日用品什么的</u>, 你都买得到。

1. 這家飯館的菜很好, _____, 都很好吃。

   这家饭馆的菜很好, _____, 都很好吃。

2. 他買衣服非常挑剔, _____, 他都很在乎。

   他买衣服非常挑剔, _____, 他都很在乎。

3. 跟他一起租房子真不容易, _____, 他都要問清楚。

   跟他一起租房子真不容易, _____, 他都要问清楚。

▼▼▼▼▼▼▼▼▼▼▼▼▼▼▼▼▼▼▼▼▼▼▼▼▼▼▼▼▼▼▼▼▼▼▼▼

C. Rewrite the sentences using 無論...都／无论...都.

EXAMPLE: 這兩天他沒什麼胃口, 清蒸魚、芥蘭牛肉、菠菜豆腐什麼的, 他都
不想吃。

這兩天他沒什么胃口, 清蒸鱼、芥兰牛肉、菠菜豆腐什么的, 他都
不想吃。

→ 這兩天他沒什麼胃口, <u>無論什麼菜, 他都不想吃</u>。

這兩天他沒什么胃口, <u>无论什么菜, 他都不想吃</u>。

1. 他吸煙吸得真多, 上班也吸, 上課也吸, 在家也吸。
他吸烟吸得真多, 上班也吸, 上课也吸, 在家也吸。

→ _____。

2. 美國的稅很重。買吃的要稅, 買穿的要稅, 買用的也要稅。
美国的税很重。买吃的要税, 买穿的要税, 买用的也要税。

→ _____。

3. 附近新開的購物中心非常大。吃的, 穿的, 用的, 都能買到。
附近新开的购物中心非常大。吃的, 穿的, 用的, 都能买到。

→ _____。

人民幣一百元／人民币一百元

▼▼▼

人民幣五十元／人民币五十元

D. You disagree with your friend on many issues, but you are always tactful. You always acknowledge the partial validity of your friend's view before stating your own opinion. Complete the sentences using Adj./V + 是 *+ Adj./V,* 可是...

EXAMPLE: a: 你為什麼不喜歡去那家餐館吃飯？他們的菜做得很地道。

你为什么不喜欢去那家餐馆吃饭？他们的菜做得很地道。

b: <u>他們的菜地道是地道, 可是有點油</u>。

<u>他们的菜地道是地道, 可是有点油</u>。

1. a: 中文太難了。

中文太难了。

b: ＿＿＿＿＿＿＿＿＿＿＿＿＿＿＿＿＿, ＿＿＿＿＿＿＿＿＿＿＿＿＿＿＿＿＿。

2. a: 住在校內很好, 你為什麼要搬出去？

住在校内很好, 你为什么要搬出去？

b: ＿＿＿＿＿＿＿＿＿＿＿＿＿＿＿＿＿, ＿＿＿＿＿＿＿＿＿＿＿＿＿＿＿＿＿。

3. a: 這棟樓的設備那麼舊, 你為什麼不搬到別的地方去？

这栋楼的设备那么旧, 你为什么不搬到别的地方去？

b: ＿＿＿＿＿＿＿＿＿＿＿＿＿＿＿＿＿, ＿＿＿＿＿＿＿＿＿＿＿＿＿＿＿＿＿。

▼▼▼▼▼▼▼▼▼▼▼▼▼▼▼▼▼▼▼▼▼▼▼▼▼▼▼▼▼▼▼▼▼▼▼▼▼

4. a: 這條褲子你穿起很好看, 為什麼不買?

     这条裤子你穿起很好看, 为什么不买?

    b: _____, _____。

E. Complete the sentences using 非...不可...

EXAMPLE: 天氣又悶又熱, <u>非下雨不可</u>, 你別去打球了。

             天气又闷又热, <u>非下雨不可</u>, 你别去打球了。

1. 今天是我母親的生日, 晚上的生日晚會我_____。

    今天是我母亲的生日, 晚上的生日晚会我_____。

2. 他每次出去吃飯, _____, 別的菜他都不喜歡吃。

    他每次出去吃饭, _____, 别的菜他都不喜欢吃。

3. 你天天吃那麼多肉, 又那麼喜歡吃糖, _____。

    你天天吃那么多肉, 又那么喜欢吃糖, _____。

V. TRANSLATION

A. Translate the passages into English.

1.

(Traditional Characters)

　　小張買東西的標準是: 只要是名牌的, 無論樣子好不好, 價錢貴不貴, 他都要買。小林買東西跟小張不一樣, 很在乎質量, 而且要價錢便宜。他們兩個一起出去買東西的時候, 常會有爭論: 小張認為小林只圖便宜, 不在乎牌子; 小林覺得小張只圖牌子, 不在乎衣服穿著合適不合適。所以他們常常出去的時候很高興, 回來的時候很不高興。

(Simplified Characters)

　　小张买东西的标准是: 只要是名牌的, 无论样子好不好, 价钱贵不贵,他都要买。小林买东西跟小张不一样, 很在乎质量, 而且要价钱便宜。他们两个一起出去买东西的时候, 常会有争论: 小张认为小林只图便宜, 不在乎牌子; 小林觉得小张只图牌子, 不在乎衣服穿着合适不合适。所以他们常常出去的时候很高兴, 回来的时候很不高兴。

2.

(Traditional Characters)

小李只有在打折的時候才買衣服, 一聽说哪家商店打折, 就去買。我说: "打折的東西便宜是便宜, 但是質量也差一些。"小李说: "衣服便宜可以多買幾件, 質量差一點也沒關係, 穿壞了可以再買新的呀。"

(Simplified Characters)

小李只有在打折的时候才买衣服, 一听说哪家商店打折, 就去买。我说: "打折的东西便宜是便宜, 但是质量也差一些。"小李说: "衣服便宜可以多买几件, 质量差一点也没关系, 穿坏了可以再买新的呀。"

▼▼▼▼▼▼▼▼▼▼▼▼▼▼▼▼▼▼▼▼▼▼▼▼▼▼▼▼▼▼▼▼▼▼▼▼▼▼

B. Translate the sentences into Chinese.

1. Zhang Tianming doesn't have a car. He has to depend on Ke Lin wherever he wants to go.
   (無論／无论)

2. They had dinner at a restaurant in Chinatown. The dishes that they ordered, such as Chinese broccoli, steamed fish, etc., were all very delicious. (什麼的／什么的)

3. a: I feel living on campus is better. It's very convenient.

   b: Living on campus is convenient, but it's too expensive. (A是A)

4. Would you please sign your name on the receipt? (簽字／签字)

5. Will you accompany me to the shopping center to buy a pair of athletic shoes? (陪)

6. Teacher, could you tell us how to study Chinese? (reduplication of verb)

C. Translate the sentences into Chinese. Pay special attention to the position of the time phrases.

1. a: How long has your teacher been teaching Chinese?
   b: My teacher has been teaching Chinese for five years.

2. a: How long have you gone without Chinese food?
   b: I haven't had any Chinese food for two weeks.

▼ ▼

3. a: How often does your sister shop?

    b: My sister goes shopping once a week.

4. a: How many hours did your roommate sleep last night?

    b: My roommate slept for three hours last night.

5. a: How long do you work every day?

    b: I have to work two hours a day.

6. The doctor said that you have to drink water ten times a day.

7. Little Zhang writes to his parents every other month.

8. He moved three times last year.

9. My brother hasn't talked to me for four days.

10. He lived in the dorm for six months and moved off campus last week.

D. Translate the passage into Chinese.

Little Zhang came to the States from China in 2005. He has been living in Boston for more than a year, and hasn't had authentic Chinese food for six months. Before he came to the States, he heard that it was very convenient to live there. But now that he is in America he doesn't think so, since he doesn't have a car and has to depend on others to take him grocery shopping, etc. He misses his parents very much and plans to return to China right after the semester ends in December.

VI. COMPOSITION

《我買衣服的標準》

《我买衣服的标准》

Describe what you look for when shopping for clothes.

人民幣二十元／人民币二十元

人民幣十元／人民币十元

第五課　▲　選專業
第五课　▲　选专业

A. Listen to the audio for the Textbook and answer the questions.

1. What courses is Zhang Tianming taking this semester?

2. What do Zhang's parents want him to do after he graduates from college?

3. What does Li Zhe plan to do after he graduates from college?

4. What does Zhang think that Li should do after he graduates from college?

B. Listen to the audio for the Workbook.

1. Listen to the passage and answer the questions.
   a. How many schools does the university have?

   b. What are they?

   c. Which school is the most expensive?

   d. Which school has the most students?

   e. Which school has the best library?

   f. Which school has the best professors?

   g. What was the controversy about?

   h. What were the two opposing positions?

2. Listen to the passage and answer the questions.
   a. Why are more and more students interested in having double majors?

b. What two examples of double majors are mentioned in the passage?

3. Listen to the passage and answer the questions.
    a. What are the two things that many college students complain about?

    b. What is the school's reaction?

II. SPEAKING EXERCISES

A. Practice asking and answering the questions with a partner before class.

1. 你這學期選了幾門課?
    你这学期选了几门课?

2. 你最喜歡哪一門課? 為什麼?
    你最喜欢哪一门课? 为什么?

3. 哪門課最讓你受不了? 為什麼?
    哪门课最让你受不了? 为什么?

4. 中文聽、説、讀、寫, 什麼最難? 為什麼?
    中文听、说、读、写, 什么最难? 为什么?

5. 你下個學期有什麼打算?
    你下个学期有什么打算?

B. Practice speaking on the following topics.

1. 請談一談你的專業以及畢業以後的打算。
    请谈一谈你的专业以及毕业以后的打算。

2. 請談一談你父母對你選專業有什麼影響。
    请谈一谈你父母对你选专业有什么影响。

3. 請談一談你跟指導教授之間(zhījiān)的關係(guānxi)怎麼樣。
    请谈一谈你跟指导教授之间(zhījiān)的关系(guānxi)怎么样。

▼▼▼▼▼▼▼▼▼▼▼▼▼▼▼▼▼▼▼▼▼▼▼▼▼▼▼▼▼▼▼▼▼▼▼▼▼▼▼

III. READING COMPREHENSION

A. Answer the questions after reading the passage.

(Traditional Characters)

　　小李是大學三年級的學生，因為他打算明年五月就畢業，所以每個學期都選六門課，每個暑假都實習。要是學分夠，他還打算拿雙學位。他的指導教授覺得他課選得太多了，建議他少選一點，要不然對身體健康沒有好處。小李說他希望早一點畢業，這樣他可以把大學第四年的錢省下來。至於身體健康不健康，他並不在乎。

(Simplified Characters)

　　小李是大学三年级的学生，因为他打算明年五月就毕业，所以每个学期都选六门课，每个暑假都实习。要是学分够，他还打算拿双学位。他的指导教授觉得他课选得太多了，建议他少选一点，要不然对身体健康没有好处。小李说他希望早一点毕业，这样他可以把大学第四年的钱省下来。至于身体健康不健康，他并不在乎。

Questions:

1. Why does Little Li want to graduate before the rest of his class?

2. What did Little Li's adviser say to him?

3. Do you think it is possible for Little Li to achieve his goal? Why or why not?

4. Would you do the same thing if you were Little Li? Why or why not?

B. Answer the questions after reading the passage.

(Traditional Characters)

　　大學生每個學期都得註冊。在註冊前，每個學生都會和指導教授討論選哪些課。新生常常不知道應該選什麼課，指導教授就會給他們一些建議。可是因為有些課一定得上，很多學生都得選，所以這些課有時可能選不上，這對新生來說是個大問題。

(Simplified Characters)

　　大学生每个学期都得注册。在注册前，每个学生都会和指导教授讨论选哪些课。新生常常不知道应该选什么课，指导教授就会给他们一些建议。可是因为有些课一定得上，很多学生都得选，所以这些课有时可能选不上，这对新生来说是个大问题。

Questions:

1. According to the passage, why do freshmen have to talk to their advisers?

2. What kinds of problems do freshmen face when signing up for courses?

C. Read the passage and answer the questions. (True/False)

(Traditional)

　　有一天張天明跟他的幾個朋友談選專業的事：張天明的父母一直想讓他畢業以後念醫學院。林雪梅很想上工學院，可是她父母認為還是學醫最好。柯林的爸爸媽媽認為他學什麼專業都可以。柯林原來選了歷史專業，可是為了跟林雪梅在一起，也打算上醫學院。王強聽了以後就說："你們大家都學醫，那我只好學'生病專業'了。要不然，將來你們這麼多醫生到哪兒去找病人啊？"

(Simplified)

　　有一天张天明跟他的几个朋友谈选专业的事：张天明的父母一直想让他毕业以后念医学院。林雪梅很想上工学院，可是她父母认为还是学医最好。柯林的爸爸妈妈认为他学什么专业都可以。柯林原来选了历史专业，可是为了跟林雪梅在一起, 也打算上医学院。王强听了以后就说 : "你们大家都学医, 那我只好学'生病专业'了。要不然, 将来你们这么多医生到哪儿去找病人啊?"

Questions (True/False):

(　) 1. 張天明的父母不在乎他選什麼專業。

張天明的父母不在乎他选什么专业。

(　) 2. 林雪梅覺得學工比學醫有意思。

林雪梅觉得学工比学医有意思。

(　) 3. 林雪梅的父母認為她上醫學院比較合適。

林雪梅的父母认为她上医学院比较合适。

(　) 4. 柯林的父母希望他學歷史。

柯林的父母希望他学历史。

(　) 5. 王强身體不好, 常常生病。

王强身体不好, 常常生病。

(　) 6. 王强認為學醫的人太多了。

王强认为学医的人太多了。

D. Look at the degree certificate issued by a mainland Chinese college and answer the questions.

(See the Alternate Character Appendix for traditional characters.)

Note: This is an authentic certificate. Only the name and dates have been changed.

Questions:

1. What is the degree recipient's name?_____

2. What is his date of birth? _____

3. What is the name of the college? _____

4. What is the degree recipient's major? _____

5. How long is the degree program? _____

6. What degree was awarded? _____

7. Circle the college president's name.

8. When was the degree awarded? _____

E. *Read the story and answer the questions.*

(Traditional Characters)

名落孫山(1)

　　中國宋朝 (960–1279) 的時候, 有一個人叫孫山, 他很會說笑話。有一年, 他離開家到外地參加考試, 結果考上了, 可是發榜 (2) 時, 他的名字在最後。孫山回到家裏以後, 很多人來看他。孫山的一個朋友的兒子也參加了考試, 就來問孫山, 他兒子考上沒有, 孫山沒有直接回答。他說: "我的名字在榜上是最後一個, 你兒子的名字在我的後面。"

(1) 孫山(Sūn Shān): a person's name

(2) 發榜(fā bǎng): to publish a list of successful candidates or applicants

(Simplified Characters)

名落孙山(1)

　　中国宋朝 (960-1279) 的时候, 有一个人叫孙山, 他很会说笑话。有一年, 他离开家到外地参加考试, 结果考上了, 可是发榜(2)时, 他的名字在最后。孙山回到家里以后, 很多人来看他。孙山的一个朋友的儿子也参加了考试, 就来问孙山, 他儿子考上没有, 孙山没有直接回答。他说: "我的名字在榜上是最后一个, 你儿子的名字在我的后面。"

(1) 孙山(Sūn Shān): a person's name

(2) 发榜(fā bǎng): to publish a list of successful candidates or applicants

Questions:

1. What was Sun Shan good at?

2. Why did he leave home?

3. Did he succeed with what he headed out to do?

4. What did his friend want to know?

5. Why didn't Sun Shan answer his friend directly?

6. What did Sun Shan tell his friend? What was he really saying?

7. What do you think the final sentence means?

IV. GRAMMAR & USAGE

A. As the saying goes, you can't have your cake and eat it, too. Complete the sentences using 就是 or 只是 to show what prevents each situation from being perfect.

EXAMPLE:　　這條運動褲質量好, 價錢便宜, <u>就是樣子不太好看</u>。

　　　　　　　這条运动裤质量好, 价钱便宜, <u>就是样子不太好看</u>。

1. 中國歷史課很有意思, 老師也很好,

　　中国历史课很有意思, 老师也很好,

　　_____。

2. 夏天去上海學中文, 時間沒問題, 那裏我也有很多朋友,

　　夏天去上海学中文, 时间没问题, 那里我也有很多朋友,

　　_____。

3. 當醫生很好, 能幫很多人, 賺很多錢,

　　当医生很好, 能帮很多人, 赚很多钱,

　　_____。

B. Answer the questions using 至於／至于.

EXAMPLE:　a: 聽説暑假你打算實習。去哪兒實習? 什麼時候開始實習?

　　　　　　　听说暑假你打算实习。去哪儿实习? 什么时候开始实习?

　　　　　b: 我去一家電腦公司實習, <u>至於什麼時候開始, 他們還沒告訴我</u>。

　　　　　　　我去一家电脑公司实习, <u>至于什么时候开始, 他们还没告诉我</u>。

1. a: 你們去旅行, 幾個人去? 什麼時候去?

　　你们去旅行, 几个人去? 什么时候去?

　b: 我們五個人去,

　　我们五个人去, _____。

2. a: 你的老師是從哪兒來的？大學的專業是什麼？

   你的老师是从哪儿来的？大学的专业是什么？

   b: 他是從波士頓來的，

   他是从波士顿来的，＿＿＿＿＿＿＿＿＿＿＿＿＿＿＿＿＿＿＿。

3. a: 你買衣服的標準是什麼？

   你买衣服的标准是什么？

   b: 我買衣服的標準第一是顏色好，

   我买衣服的标准第一是颜色好，＿＿＿＿＿＿＿＿＿＿＿＿＿＿＿＿。

C. Use 至於／至于 *to complete the tasks.*

1. Your younger brother is trying to choose a major. Help him decide by comparing the following two possibilities.

   談一談電腦和醫學這兩個專業。

   谈一谈电脑和医学这两个专业。

2. Your roommate is thinking about whether to stay in the dorm or move off campus next year. She is asking you for advice.

   談一談住在校內和住在校外的好處和壞處。

   谈一谈住在校内和住在校外的好处和坏处。

3. You are a salesperson. A customer is examining a sports outfit. You try to be helpful by talking about different aspects of the outfit, including its brand, color, material, price, etc.

D. Fill in the blanks with the correct resultative complements and answer the questions.

1. a: 第四課的漢字你都記＿＿＿＿＿＿了嗎？

   第四课的汉字你都记＿＿＿＿＿了吗？

   b: ＿＿＿＿＿＿＿＿＿＿＿＿＿＿＿＿＿＿＿＿＿＿＿＿＿＿＿＿＿＿＿＿＿。

2. a: 昨天老師給你的功課你都做＿＿＿＿＿＿了嗎？

   昨天老师给你的功课你都做＿＿＿＿＿＿了吗？

   b: ＿＿＿＿＿＿＿＿＿＿＿＿＿＿＿＿＿＿＿＿＿＿＿＿＿＿＿＿＿＿＿＿＿。

3. a: 張天明買＿＿＿＿＿＿他要的運動服了嗎？

   张天明买＿＿＿＿＿＿他要的运动服了吗？

   b: ＿＿＿＿＿＿＿＿＿＿＿＿＿＿＿＿＿＿＿＿＿＿＿＿＿＿＿＿＿＿＿＿＿。

4. a: 李哲下學期的課選＿＿＿＿＿＿了嗎？

   李哲下学期的课选＿＿＿＿＿＿了吗？

   b: ＿＿＿＿＿＿＿＿＿＿＿＿＿＿＿＿＿＿＿＿＿＿＿＿＿＿＿＿＿＿＿＿。

E. Complete the dialogues using 另外 (another).

EXAMPLE: a: 你的同屋都是美國人嗎？

           你的同屋都是美国人吗？

       b: 我有三個同屋，兩個美國人，<u>另外一個是日本人</u>。

           我有三个同屋，两个美国人，<u>另外一个是日本人</u>。

1. a: 這附近有幾家購物中心？離這兒遠嗎？

   这附近有几家购物中心？离这儿远吗？

▼▼

b: 有兩家。一家很近,

　有兩家。一家很近, _____。

2. a: 我們放三天假, 你打算做什麼?

　我们放三天假, 你打算做什么?

b: 我打算一天洗衣服, _____。

3. a: 你的三個弟弟都大學畢業了吧?

　你的三个弟弟都大学毕业了吧?

b: 我大弟弟已經畢業了,

　我大弟弟已经毕业了, _____。

F. Complete the dialogues using 另外 (besides).

EXAMPLE:　a: 學校宿舍裏有什麼設備?

　　　　　学校宿舍里有什么设备?

　　　　b: 每層都有洗衣機和烘乾機, <u>另外每層樓也都有電腦</u>。

　　　　　每层都有洗衣机和烘乾机, <u>另外每层楼也都有电脑</u>。

1. a: 你這學期上什麼課?

　你这学期上什么课?

b: 中文, _____。

2. a: 張天明, 柯林和林雪梅三個人去中國飯館吃飯, 點了些什麼菜?

　张天明, 柯林和林雪梅三个人去中国饭馆吃饭, 点了些什么菜?

b: 他們點了芥蘭牛肉,

　他们点了芥兰牛肉, _____。

3. a: 張天明去購物中心買了些什麼東西?

　张天明去购物中心买了些什么东西?

▼ ▼

b: 他買了一套運動服，

他买了一套运动服，＿＿＿＿＿＿＿＿＿＿＿＿＿＿＿＿＿＿＿＿。

G. Use 要麼…要麼… ／ 要么…要么… *and the illustrations to complete the dialogues.*

1. a: 這個週末你打算做什麼？

   这个周末你打算做什么？

   b: ＿＿＿＿＿＿＿＿＿＿＿＿＿＿＿＿＿＿＿＿＿＿＿＿＿＿＿＿＿＿。

2. a: 你今天晚飯想吃什麼？

   你今天晚饭想吃什么？

   b: ＿＿＿＿＿＿＿＿＿＿＿＿＿＿＿＿＿＿＿＿＿＿＿＿＿＿＿＿＿＿。

3. a: 你下午去購物中心想買些什麼日用品？

   你下午去购物中心想买些什么日用品？

   b: ＿＿＿＿＿＿＿＿＿＿＿＿＿＿＿＿＿＿＿＿＿＿＿＿＿＿＿＿＿＿。

H. Complete the dialogues using 跟…打交道.

EXAMPLE:　a: 你為什麼不念醫學院？ (patients)

　　　　　　　你为什么不念医学院？

　　　　　b: 因爲我不願意跟病人打交道。
　　　　　　因为我不愿意跟病人打交道。

1. a: 你為什麼不當售貨員了？ (money, customers, etc.)

   你为什么不当售货员了？

   b: ＿＿＿＿＿＿＿＿＿＿＿＿＿＿＿＿＿＿＿＿＿＿＿＿＿＿＿＿＿＿。

2. a: 你的房子這麼大, 房間這麼多, 為什麼不出租? (tenants)

     你的房子这么大, 房间这么多, 为什么不出租?

   b: _____。

3. a: 快開學了, 學校需要一些老生幫新生辦註冊手續, 你願意幫忙嗎? (freshmen)

     快开学了, 学校需要一些老生帮新生办注册手续, 你愿意帮忙吗?

   b: _____。

I. Complete the dialogues using 肯定.

EXAMPLE: a: 已經這麼晚了, 他還會來嗎?

           已经这么晚了, 他还会来吗?

       b: <u>他肯定不會來了</u>, 我們別等了。

         <u>他肯定不会来了</u>, 我们别等了。

1. a: 他下個學期會搬到校外去嗎?

     他下个学期会搬到校外去吗?

   b: _____,

     他已經找好房子了。／ 他已经找好房子了。

2. a: 小張大學畢業以後, 打算工作還是念研究所?

     小张大学毕业以后, 打算工作还是念研究所?

   b: _____,

     他早就找到工作了。

3. a: 他五月畢得了業嗎?

     他五月毕得了业吗?

b: 他還少三個學分, 今年五月

他还少三个学分, 今年五月

_____。

J. The following is a dialogue between two friends. Complete their conversation using the information provided.

a: 這個週末你打算做什麼?

這个周末你打算做什么?

b: _____, 你呢?

(要麼...要麼... / 要么...要么...)

a: 星期六我打算在家洗衣服,

星期六我打算在家洗衣服,

_____。

(至於 / 至于)

V. TRANSLATION

A. Translate the dialogue into Chinese.

Zhang Tianming: This sports jacket is really nice.

Ke Lin: Adidas sportswear is very nice, but it's just too expensive.

Zhang Tianming: It's not that I don't want to save money. It's just that other sportswear is too

                  poorly made. (質量 / 质量)

Ke Lin: As long as quality is good, no matter how expensive it is, you'll get it?

                  (無論 ...都 / 无论 ...都)

Zhang Tianming: To me the most important thing is quality, not price.

Ke Lin: I agree. Either you buy good quality or you don't buy.

                  (要麼...要麼... / 要么...要么...)

B. *Translate the following passages into Chinese.*

1. My younger brother plans to go to graduate school after he graduates next semester. He says he will study either engineering or medicine. My parents hope that he will study computer science and make a lot of money in the future. They know that my brother might make even more money by going to medical school. However, they don't want him to deal with patients all day long.

2. Little Lin wants to take Chinese next year. She thinks learning Chinese will be helpful for her future studies and career. But she's afraid that Chinese is too hard for her to master. She went to talk to her adviser and hoped to get some advice. Her adviser told her that as long as she did her homework, listened to the tapes, and practiced writing characters repeatedly every day, Little Lin would definitely learn it well.

▼▼▼▼▼▼▼▼▼▼▼▼▼▼▼▼▼▼▼▼▼▼▼▼▼▼▼▼▼▼▼▼▼▼▼▼▼▼

VI. COMPOSITION

1. 請你介紹一下你的專業。

   请你介绍一下你的专业。

What is your major? Why did you choose it? If you do not have a major yet, what do you hope to major in? Why?

2. 你父母對你選專業有什麼影響?

   你父母对你选专业有什么影响?

Do your parents have any influence on you when it comes to choosing a major?

第六課 ▲ 租房子

I. LISTENING COMPREHENSION

A. *Listen to the audio for the Textbook and answer the questions.*

1. Why does Zhang Tianming want to move out?

2. Why doesn't Zhang Tianming check out the first place he called?

3. Why isn't Zhang Tianming interested in the second place?

4. What is great about the third place?

B. *Listen to the audio for the Workbook.*

1. Listen to the passage and answer the questions.
    a. According to the passage, what are the things that you need to consider when you plan to buy a house?

    b. According to the passage, what are the advantages of renting a place versus buying a house?

2. Listen to the passage and answer the questions.
    a. According to the passage, what four things should be taken into consideration when looking for a place to rent?

    b. Based on the passage, how difficult is it to find a good roommate?

    c. Why did John move off campus?

    d. How did John get sick?

    e. What incidents made John decide to move back to campus? List two.

II. SPEAKING EXERCISES

A. Practice asking and answering the following questions with a partner.

1. 你每個月的房租多少錢? 包不包水電?
   你每个月的房租多少钱? 包不包水电?

2. 如果你有一個房子想出租, 廣告上會寫些什麼?
   如果你有一个房子想出租, 广告上会写些什么?

3. 如果你的同屋或者你隔壁的同學吵得你不能學習, 你怎麼辦?
   如果你的同屋或者你隔壁的同学吵得你不能学习, 你怎么办?

B. Practice speaking on the following topics.

1. 請你談一談找什麼樣的人做同屋最理想。
   请你谈一谈找什么样的人做同屋最理想。

2. 請你談一談租什麼樣的房子最理想。
   请你谈一谈租什么样的房子最理想。

3. 報紙廣告欄一般有些什麼樣的廣告?
   报纸广告栏一般有些什么样的广告?

4. With a partner, make up a dialogue about renting an apartment. One person could be the landlord and the other could be the tenant.

▼▼

III. READING COMPREHENSION

A. *Read the passage and answer the questions. (True/False)*

(Traditional)

　　安德森是個球迷，差不多每天晚上都要看電視裏的球賽，一看球賽就激動得大喊大叫。張天明就住在安德森的隔壁。安德森知道自己影響張天明的學習，很不好意思，打算搬家。安德森想，他搬走了以後，張天明就能安靜地學習了。

　　安德森找到了一套兩室一廳的公寓，覺得很合適，就租了一間臥室，打算下個星期就搬。他先付了一個月的房租給房東，房東告訴他那套公寓裏的另一個房間也租出去了，新房客也是下個星期搬進來。房東還說，新房客也是學生，叫張天明。

(Simplified)

　　安德森是个球迷，差不多每天晚上都要看电视里的球赛，一看球赛就激动得大喊大叫。张天明就住在安德森的隔壁。安德森知道自己影响张天明的学习，很不好意思，打算搬家。安德森想，他搬走了以后，张天明就能安静地学习了。

　　安德森找到了一套两室一厅的公寓，觉得很合适，就租了一间卧室，打算下个星期就搬。他先付了一个月的房租给房东，房东告诉他那套公寓里的另一个房间也租出去了，新房客也是下个星期搬进来。房东还说，新房客也是学生，叫张天明。

Questions (True/False):

(　　) 1.　安德森不是一個很安靜的人。
　　　　安德森不是一个很安静的人。

(　　) 2.　安德森不在乎張天明能不能學習。
　　　　安德森不在乎张天明能不能学习。

(　　) 3.　張天明常常在自己的房間裏學習。
　　　　张天明常常在自己的房间里学习。

( ) 4. 張天明跟安德森都覺得自己現在住的環境不太理想。

張天明跟安德森都觉得自己现在住的环境不太理想。

( ) 5. 安德森沒告訴張天明他正在找房子。

安德森没告诉张天明他正在找房子。

( ) 6. 安德森找到的那套公寓有兩個臥室。

安德森找到的那套公寓有两个卧室。

( ) 7. 房東不知道安德森認識張天明。

房东不知道安德森认识张天明。

( ) 8. 下個星期沒有人會影響張天明學習了。

下个星期没有人会影响张天明学习了。

B. Read the passage and answer the questions.

(Traditional Characters)

小張剛剛大學畢業, 正在找工作。他翻開報紙廣告欄一看: 人家要麼要醫學院的, 要麼要管理學院的, 跟文科有關係的工作, 一定要有工作經驗。小張拿的是文科雙學位, 不過履歷上並沒有什麼實習經驗。沒有辦法, 最後他考慮上研究所, 但是怕申請不到錢。還好, 他父親昨天打電話告訴他, 給他買了一棟樓房, 可以出租, 每個月收的租金夠付學費的了。

(Simplified Characters)

小张刚刚大学毕业, 正在找工作。他翻开报纸广告栏一看: 人家要么要医学院的, 要么要管理学院的, 跟文科有关系的工作, 一定要有工作经验。小张拿的是文科双学位, 不过履历上并没有什么实习经验。没有办法, 最后他考虑上研究所, 但是怕申请不到钱。还好, 他父亲昨天打电话告诉他, 给他买了一栋楼房, 可以出租, 每个月收的租金够付学费的了。

Questions:

1. How is the job market for Little Zhang?

2. What is Little Zhang's field?

3. What is his plan for the near future?

4. How is his money problem solved?

C. ***Read the advertisement and answer the questions.***

(Traditional Characters)

> 有公寓一套, 三房一廳, 不帶傢俱,
>
> 有地毯, 洗碗機和有綫電視。
>
> 月租: $1500。房客不可以吸煙或養狗,
>
> 最好是學生, 研究生更好。
>
> 請電: 555-2456(日); 555-3654(夜)。

(Simplified Characters)

> 有公寓一套, 三房一厅, 不带家具,
>
> 有地毯, 洗碗机和有线电视。
>
> 月租$1500。房客不可以吸烟或养狗,
>
> 最好是学生, 研究生更好。
>
> 请电: 555-2456(日); 555-3654(夜)。

Questions:

1. How many bedrooms are there in the apartment?

2. What is the daytime phone number?

3. Who will be the ideal tenant?

4. What is provided in the apartment?

D. If you were looking for an apartment in the Boston area, which of the two ads below would you be interested in? Why?

Ad 1 (Traditional Characters)

公寓出租
東波士頓一房一廳
交通購物方便
安全安靜。月組:$800
請電:(617) 555-7548
晚11時前

Ad 1 (Simplified Characters)

公寓出租
东波士顿一房一厅
交通购物方便
安全安静。月租: $800
请电:(617) 555-7548
晚11时前

Ad 2 (Traditional Characters)

房室出租
房間大而明亮
近BU及Harvard, 近公共汽車沾
包水電、暖氣,帶傢俱
供晚餐。兩人合住一房
月組$390。請電:(617) 555-9736

Ad 2 (Simplified Characters)

房屋出租
房间大而明亮
近BU及Harvard, 近公共汽车站
包水电、暖气,带家具
供晚餐。两人合住一房
月租$390。请电:(617) 555-9736

E. Read the story and answer the questions.

(Traditional Characters)

孟母三遷(1)

　　孟子(2)是中國歷史上影響最大的思想家(3)之一。他很小的時候，父親就去世了，孟子是他的母親帶大的。孟子的家附近是一塊墓地(4)，他經常去那兒玩，跟著別人學挖墓(5)。孟子的母親看見了就說：“這地方對小孩不好。”所以她就把家搬到別的地方去了。新家在一個市場旁邊，孟子常常去市場玩。孟子的母親又說：“這地方對小孩也不好。”就把家搬到了一個學校旁邊。孟子看到學校裏的學生都念書，也跟著念書。孟子的母親高興地說：“這才是小孩子應該住的地方。”所以孟子的母親跟孟子就在那兒住下來了。孟子後來成了一個很有學問的人。

(1)　遷(qiān): to move (to another place); 搬
(2)　孟子(Mèngzǐ): Mencius
(3)　思想家(sīxiǎngjiā): philosopher; 哲學家
(4)　墓地(mùdì): graveyard; cemetery
(5)　挖墓(wā mù): to dig graves

(Simplified Characters)

孟母三迁(1)

　　孟子(2)是中国历史上影响最大的思想家(3)之一。他很小的时候，父亲就去世了，孟子是他的母亲带大的。孟子的家附近是一块墓地(4)，他经常去那儿玩，跟着别人学挖墓(5)。孟子的母亲看见了就说：“这地方对小孩不好。”所以她就把家搬到别的地方去了。新家在一个市场旁边，孟子常常去市场玩。孟子的母亲又说：“这地方对小孩也不好。”就把家搬到了一个学校旁边。孟子看到学校里的学生都念书，也跟着念书。孟子的母亲高兴地说：“这才是小孩子应该住的地方。”所以孟子的母亲跟孟子就在那儿住下来了。孟子后来成了一个很有学问的人。

(1)　迁(qiān): to move (to another place); 搬
(2)　孟子(Mèngzǐ): Mencius
(3)　思想家(sīxiǎngjiā): philosopher; 哲学家

(4) 墓地(mùdì): graveyard; cemetery

(5) 挖墓(wā mù): to dig graves

Questions:

1. When did Mencius lose his father?

2. Why did Mencius' mother decide to move?

3. Where did they first move?

4. What did Mencius take up playing?

5. Where did they end up living?

6. Why did Mencius' mother decide to stay there?

IV. GRAMMAR & USAGE

A. *Rewrite the sentences using* 一直.

EXAMPLE: 他上次吃過那家素菜館的菜以後, 就一直想再去吃一頓。
他上次吃过那家素菜馆的菜以后, 就一直想再去吃一顿。

1. 小李的父母從他上大學以來,
   小李的父母从他上大学以来,

   _____。

2. 安德森上了中學以後,
   安德森上了中学以后,

   _____。

▼▼▼▼▼▼▼▼▼▼▼▼▼▼▼▼▼▼▼▼▼▼▼▼▼▼▼▼▼▼▼▼▼▼▼▼

3. 房東的一套公寓又舊, 房租又貴,
   房东的一套公寓又旧, 房租又贵,

   _____。

B. Complete the dialogues using 最好.

EXAMPLE: a: 我想選哲學做專業。
          我想选哲学做专业。

          b: 你最好選別的專業, 學哲學找工作不容易。
          你最好选别的专业, 学哲学找工作不容易。

1. a: 住我隔壁的人天天吵得我睡不好覺。
   住我隔壁的人天天吵得我睡不好觉。

   b: _____。

2. a: 這雙運動鞋是我媽媽昨天給我買的, 稍微小了點兒。
   这双运动鞋是我妈妈昨天给我买的, 稍微小了点儿。

   b: _____。

3. a: 我的專業是統計學, 但是我真的不喜歡。
   我的专业是统计学, 但是我真的不喜欢。

   b: _____。

C. Complete the dialogues or sentences using 稍微.

EXAMPLE: a: 聽說你病了?
          听说你病了?

          b: 我昨天肚子不舒服, 今天稍微好了點兒, 但是還得吃藥。
          我昨天肚子不舒服, 今天稍微好了点儿, 但是还得吃药。

▼▼▼▼▼▼▼▼▼▼▼▼▼▼▼▼▼▼▼▼▼▼▼▼▼▼▼▼▼▼▼▼▼▼▼▼▼▼▼

1. a: 這個房子有三個臥室, 離學校又近, 我覺得很理想。

   这个房子有三个卧室, 离学校又近, 我觉得很理想。

   b: 但是每個月的租金 $1500, _____。我們再多看兩
   家吧。

   但是每个月的租金 $1500, _____。我们再多看两
   家吧。

2. a: 這條褲子樣子好, 價錢也不貴, 買了吧?!

   这条裤子样子好, 价钱也不贵, 买了吧?!

   b: 我也覺得不錯, 不過_____。放進洗衣機一洗, 烘
   乾機一烘, 肯定更小。

   我也觉得不错, 不过_____。放进洗衣机一洗, 烘
   干机一烘, 肯定更小。

3. a: 張太太做的菜真地道, 好吃極了。

   张太太做的菜真地道, 好吃极了。

   b: 她做的菜好吃是好吃, 只是_____。我喜歡吃清
   淡一點兒的。

   她做的菜好吃是好吃, 只是_____。我喜欢吃清
   淡一点儿的。

4. 我平常吃得很清淡, 這盤豆腐
   我平常吃得很清淡, 这盘豆腐

   _____。

5. 小柯一般穿三十號的牛仔褲, 這條對他來說
   小柯一般穿三十号的牛仔裤, 这条对他来说

   _____。

▼▼▼▼▼▼▼▼▼▼▼▼▼▼▼▼▼▼▼▼▼▼▼▼▼▼▼▼▼▼▼▼▼▼▼▼

6. 媽媽想買一台新的洗衣機, 這台
   妈妈想买一台新的洗衣机, 这台

_____。

7. 小林要一條洗澡的浴巾, 這條是洗臉用的,
   小林要一条洗澡的浴巾, 这条是洗脸用的,

_____。

D. Answer the questions using ...的話 / ...的话.

EXAMPLE: a: 我要租一間房子, 你可以給我一點建議嗎?
             我要租一间房子, 你可以给我一点建议吗?

         b: 如果你想省錢的話, 可以租離學校遠一點的房子。
            <u>如果你想省钱的话, 可以租离学校远一点的房子</u>。

1. 小王: 小李, 附近哪個飯館比較好?
   小王: 小李, 附近哪个饭馆比较好?

   小李: _____。

2. a: 今天晚上我們做什麼好?
      今天晚上我们做什么好?

   b: _____。

3. a: 你覺得我應該選什麼專業? 醫學還是文學?
      你觉得我应该选什么专业? 医学还是文学?

   b: _____。

E. Complete the dialogues or sentences using 最...不過了 / 最...不过了.

EXAMPLE:　a: 你說我買房子在什麼地方買才理想?

　　　　　　　你说我买房子在什么地方买才理想?

　　　　　　b: <u>你那麼喜歡水, 要是能住在河邊最理想不過了。</u>

　　　　　　　<u>你那么喜欢水, 要是能住在河边最理想不过了。</u>

1. a: 我畢業以後, 做什麼最合適?

　　　我毕业以后, 做什么最合适?

　　b: _____, _____。

2. a: 去參加表姐的生日晚會, 帶什麼東西好?

　　　去参加表姐的生日晚会, 带什么东西好?

　　b: _____, _____。

3. a: 選什麼課對將來找工作最有用?

　　　选什么课对将来找工作最有用?

　　b: _____, _____。

F. Fill in the blanks with either 以後 / 以后 *or* 的時候 / 的时候.

1. 他每次看球賽_____, 都會激動地大喊大叫。

　　他每次看球赛_____, 都会激动地大喊大叫。

2. 小林從購物中心出來了_____, 才想起來忘了買衛生紙。

　　小林从购物中心出来了_____, 才想起来忘了买卫生纸。

3. 小張打算大學畢業_____到日本去旅行。

　　小张打算大学毕业_____到日本去旅行。

4. 選專業_____, 一定要考慮自己的興趣。

　　选专业_____, 一定要考虑自己的兴趣。

5. 我每次在中國餐館叫菜＿＿＿＿＿＿, 都得告訴服務員別放味精。

   我每次在中国餐馆叫菜＿＿＿＿＿＿, 都得告诉服务员别放味精。

6. 林雪梅每天回宿舍＿＿＿＿＿＿, 第一件事情就是給小柯打電話。

   林雪梅每天回宿舍＿＿＿＿＿＿, 第一件事情就是给小柯打电话。

G. *Complete the dialogues with appropriate verbs and directional complements.*

1. a: 如果明天你的同學過生日開舞會, 你打算帶什麼東西去?

   如果明天你的同学过生日开舞会, 你打算带什么东西去?

   b: ＿＿＿＿＿＿＿＿＿＿＿＿＿＿＿＿＿＿＿＿＿＿＿＿＿＿。

2. a: 你一上課就從書包裏拿出什麼東西來?

   你一上课就从书包里拿出什么东西来?

   b: ＿＿＿＿＿＿＿＿＿＿＿＿＿＿＿＿＿＿＿＿＿＿＿＿＿＿。

3. a: 要是教室裏的椅子不夠, 你怎麼辦?

   要是教室里的椅子不够, 你怎么办?

   b: ＿＿＿＿＿＿＿＿＿＿＿＿＿＿＿＿＿＿＿＿＿＿＿＿＿＿。

4. a: 要是你的宿舍吵得你受不了, 你怎麼辦?

   要是你的宿舍吵得你受不了, 你怎么办?

   b: ＿＿＿＿＿＿＿＿＿＿＿＿＿＿＿＿＿＿＿＿＿＿＿＿＿＿。

5. a: 你去找朋友。他住在四層, 但是電梯 (diàntī: elevator) 壞了, 你怎麼辦?

   你去找朋友。他住在四层, 但是电梯 (diàntī: elevator) 坏了, 你怎么办?

   b: ＿＿＿＿＿＿＿＿＿＿＿＿＿＿＿＿＿＿＿＿＿＿＿＿＿＿。

V. TRANSLATION

A. Translate the sentences using complements linked to the main verbs with the descriptive complement particle 得.

1. My teacher speaks quickly.

2. His younger sister sings very well.

3. We had a great time at Little Wang's place last night.

4. She was so busy that she forgot to have dinner.

5. That little boy laughed so hard that his stomach hurt.

B. Translate the passage into English.

(Traditional Characters)

　　王先生有一棟樓房要出租。樓房有三層。他希望把房子租給研究生。一層有三房一廳, 帶傢俱。二層有兩個臥房, 一個客廳, 不過, 不帶傢俱。三層王先生自己住。他認為住在三層稍微安靜一點。

　　王先生的房子離學校比較遠, 沒有車的學生肯定對他的房子沒有興趣。他的房租也很貴, 而且還不包水電, 要是賺的錢不多的話, 最好也別租他的房子。喜歡做飯的人, 租王先生的房子也不太理想, 因為一、二層都沒有廚房。

(Simplified Characters)

　　王先生有一栋楼房要出租。楼房有三层。他希望把房子租给研究生。一层有三房一厅, 带家具。二层有两个卧房, 一个客厅, 不过, 不带家具。三层王先生自己住。他认为住在三层稍微安静一点。

▼▼

王先生的房子离学校比较远, 没有车的学生肯定对他的房子没有兴趣。他的房租也很贵, 而且还不包水电, 要是赚的钱不多的话, 最好也别租他的房子。喜欢做饭的人, 租王先生的房子也不太理想, 因为一、二层都没有厨房。

C. Translate the passage into Chinese.

My adviser lived very close to the stadium. Whenever there was a basketball game, there were a lot of fans yelling and screaming in front of his house. He could not stand it. His research was also affected. He decided to move. The place he rented recently was behind a grove of trees. It was furnished, and the utilities were included. He felt the place was most ideal for him.

D. Translate the passage into Chinese using appropriate directional complements.

Yesterday I went to the shopping center to get my sister a birthday gift. Right after I walked into the house, my sister ran down the stairs and wanted to see what I had brought back. She pulled over a chair and sat next to me. I took out a pair of jeans and a T-shirt to show her. She picked them up, took a look, and said, "Please take them back (退回: tuì huí) to the store. I don't like them." I was really angry at her.

▼ ▼

房 屋 出 租	房 屋 出 租
近Northgate mall	$180-$350
三房兩廳	有共用電話
兩個廁所	及電視CABLE，近公車站
有冰箱，洗衣機	有意者請電：
月租：$1375	682 ****
有意請電：425 ****	

(See the Alternate Character Appendix for simplified characters.)

VI. COMPOSITION

請寫一個出租房子的廣告。

请写一个出租房子的广告。

You plan to find a roommate to share your apartment. Write a flier briefly describing your place and explaining specifically what kind of roommate you are looking for.

第七課 ▲ 男朋友

I. LISTENING COMPREHENSION

A. *Listen to the audio for the Textbook and answer the questions.*

1. What are Tom and Tianhua's hobbies?

2. What is the major reason for their fights?

3. Will Tianming try to mediate?

4. What will Tianming do this coming weekend?

B. *Listen to the audio for the Workbook.*

1. Listen to the passage and answer the questions.
   a. What are Little Wang's two ways to cheer himself up?

   b. Do the two methods work for Little Wang?

   c. Which of the two methods do you prefer? Why?

2. Listen to the passage and answer the questions.
   a. How do we know Little Zhang used to drink a lot?

   b. What incident made him quit drinking?

3. Listen to the passage and answer the questions.
   a. According to the passage, what are some of the things that people consider when they choose a college?

   b. What attracts people to small towns or big cities to study?

   c. Which part of the passage do you disagree with? Why?

▼▼▼

II. SPEAKING EXERCISES

A. Practice asking and answering the questions with a partner before class.

1. 什麼讓王老師的心情很好？
   什么让王老师的心情很好？

2. 什麼讓高姐姐的心情不好？
   什么让高姐姐的心情不好？

3. 小張對什麼有興趣？
   小张对什么有兴趣？

4. 湯姆對什麼樣的電視節目有興趣？
   汤姆对什么样的电视节目有兴趣？

5. 你覺得班上同學誰的性格比較開朗？
   你觉得班上同学谁的性格比较开朗？

6. 你家裏誰的脾氣比較急躁？
   你家里谁的脾气比较急躁？

7. 你心情不好的時候做什麼？
   你心情不好的时候做什么？

8. 你平常晚上回家以後先做什麼再做什麼？
   你平常晚上回家以后先做什么再做什么？

B. Practice speaking on the following topics.

1. 請談一談自己的興趣與愛好(àihǎo)。
   请谈一谈自己的兴趣与爱好(àihǎo)。

2. 請談一談你選男、女朋友的標準。
   请谈一谈你选男、女朋友的标准。

3. Your friend tries to persuade you to go on a blind date with someone, so he or she tries to present the person in the best possible light, telling you about the person's hobbies and interests, special skills, personality, etc. You, however, are wary. You have a lot of questions about that person that you would like your friend to answer.

▼▼

III. READING COMPREHENSION

A. Read the passage and answer the questions.

(Traditional Characters)

　　張天明的父母結婚已經二十八年了, 這麼多年他們一直相處得很好, 從來沒爭吵 (zhēngchǎo) 過。他們倆的性格和興趣有很多相同的地方, 比如 (bǐrú) 他們都很開朗, 都很愛交朋友, 也都愛吃中國菜, 差不多每個週末都要找一家中國餐館吃上一頓。還有, 他們都愛旅行, 最近幾年他們一起去過世界 (shìjiè) 各地不少的國家 (guójiā)。不過張先生是個籃球迷, 而張太太對體育一點興趣都沒有, 却 (què) 特別喜歡看喜劇 (xǐjù)。晚上的電視如果又有籃球比賽又有喜劇的話, 張太太就只好讓張先生看, 自己給朋友打電話聊天。可是有的時候張先生為了讓太太高興, 也只好不看球賽, 陪太太一起看喜劇。

(Simplified Characters)

　　张天明的父母结婚已经二十八年了, 这么多年他们一直相处得很好, 从来没争吵 (zhēngchǎo) 过。他们俩的性格和兴趣有很多相同的地方, 比如 (bǐrú) 他们都很开朗, 都很爱交朋友, 也都爱吃中国菜, 差不多每个周末都要找一家中国餐馆吃上一顿。还有, 他们都爱旅行, 最近几年他们一起去过世界 (shìjiè) 各地不少的国家 (guójiā)。不过张先生是个篮球迷, 而张太太对体育一点兴趣都没有, 却 (què) 特别喜欢看喜剧 (xǐjù)。晚上的电视如果又有篮球比赛又有喜剧的话, 张太太就只好让张先生看, 自己给朋友打电话聊天。可是有的时候张先生为了让太太高兴, 也只好不看球赛, 陪太太一起看喜剧。

Questions (True/False):

(　) 1. Zhang Tianming's parents got married at age twenty-eight.

(　) 2. They are more similar than different in terms of personality and interests.

(　) 3. Every weekend they try a different type of ethnic food.

(　) 4. Mr. and Mrs. Zhang like to watch different TV programs.

(　) 5. When there's a conflict, Mr. Zhang always gives in to Mrs. Zhang.

(　) 6. Mr. Zhang makes Mrs. Zhang call her friends whenever there's a basketball game on TV.

(　) 7. When they dine out, they like to eat Chinese food.

(　) 8. Mr. Zhang sometimes watches comedies to keep Mrs. Zhang company.

▼▼

Open-ended Question:

9. Can you think of a compromise which will allow Mr. Zhang and Mrs. Zhang both to watch their favorite programs?

B. Read the passage and answer the question.

(Traditional Characters)

　　我的情緒常會受音樂的影響。聽古典音樂時, 心情特別平靜 (píngjìng); 聽搖滾樂時, 就感覺比較激動。但是我的同屋跟我不一樣, 覺得聽古典音樂很沒意思, 搖滾樂又太吵。你呢?

(Simplified Characters)

　　我的情绪常会受音乐的影响。听古典音乐时, 心情特别平静 (píngjìng); 听搖滚乐时, 就感觉比较激动。但是我的同屋跟我不一样, 觉得听古典音乐很没意思, 搖滚乐又太吵。你呢?

C. Read the following passage and answer the questions.

(Traditional Characters)

　　放假的時候, 小林原來打算先去聽一個搖滾樂的音樂會, 再去波士頓看戲。可是他的女朋友想先去看戲再去聽音樂會。兩個人說著說著就吵起架來了。而且越吵越屬害, 最後兩個人鬧翻了, 小林的女朋友氣得不跟小林說話了。小林回家以後覺得挺後悔的。

(Simplified Characters)

　　放假的时候, 小林原来打算先去听一个搖滚乐的音乐会, 再去波士顿看戏。可是他的女朋友想先去看戏再去听音乐会。两个人说着说着就吵起架来了。而且越吵越厉害, 最后两个人闹翻了, 小林的女朋友气得不跟小林说话了。小林回家以后觉得挺后悔的。

Questions:

1. What was Little Lin's original plan?

▼▼

2. What was his girlfriend's plan?

3. Did they carry out either plan? Why or why not?

D. Take a look at the ad for an online dating service and answer the true/false questions. The name and the birthday have been changed in order to protect the privacy of the individual.

姓名	王小梅	星座	双子座
性别	🚹	出生年月	1976年6月14日
身高	165 cm	体重	48 kg
所在城市	北京	老家	海淀
国籍	中国	血型	O型
婚姻状况	未婚	体型	保密
休息日	双休六七	月收入	保密
学历	大学专科	毕业学校	北京医科大学
兄妹情况	兄妹两人以上	专业	眼科
工作情况	在职	从事职业	医生
吸烟	不吸		
喝酒	偶尔		
住房	与父母同住	汽车	有买车计划
擅长（爱好）	听音乐、跑步		
性格自介	活泼开朗,外向,温柔体贴,不拘小节,害羞,老实,敏感,快言快语		

(See the Alternate Character Appendix for traditional characters.)

Questions (True/False):

( ) 1. She lives in Beijing with her parents.

( ) 2. She doesn't have any siblings.

( ) 3. She's never been married.

( ) 4. She graduated from a medical school.

( ) 5. She gets one day off from work every week.

( ) 6. She smokes.

( ) 7. She owns a car.

( ) 8. She considers herself outgoing.

▼▼

E. As in the United States, newspapers and magazines in the People's Republic of China and Taiwan carry personal advertisements. The following is taken from a mainland Chinese magazine. Read the advertisement and answer the questions.

安琪小姐 大专学历，24 岁，未婚，出身于北京一高知家庭，身高 1.67 米，知书达理，端庄美丽，温柔善良，聪慧能干，身材健美。爱好体育，擅长烹调及室内设计。能说一口流利地道的英语（托福成绩 617 分），现在国内一家外商独资公司工作。欲寻一位有事业心，真诚善良，品德高尚，具有硕士以上学历的海外男士为侣（以在美加为宜）。有意者请寄简历、全身近照、电话号码及婚姻状况证明。来信请寄：100083　中国北京市海淀区暂安处一号魏淑珍转安琪小姐收。

(See the Alternate Character Appendix for traditional characters.)

Questions:

1. Circle the name of the person advertising.

2. How old is she?

3. Where is she from?

4. What are some of her attributes? List at least two.

5. What level of education does she have?

6. Where does she work?

7. What kind of person is she looking for?

F. *Suppose you want to place a personal ad in a magazine. The following is a personal information form that you need to fill out. Fill in the blanks.*

留学人员征婚需填表格

姓 名		性 别		出生日期		民 族	
籍 贯		身 高		相 貌		学 历	
爱 好		职 业		护照号		所在国	
居留身份				婚姻状况			
有无子女				身体状况			
通讯地址						电 话	
其它情况							
要求对方							

(See the Alternate Character Appendix for traditional characters.)

G. *Read the story and answer the questions.*

(Traditional Characters)

東床快婿(1)

　　中國東晉的時候 (344–405) 有個大官(2)姓郗(3), 是一個太傅(4), 有一天他叫他的學生給宰相(5)送一封信, 請宰相幫他選一個女婿。宰相回答 (huídá) 説, "我有很多學生住在我家東邊的屋子裏, 您去選吧。"郗太傅的學生去東邊的屋子看了以後回來報告説,"宰相的學生都很不錯, 聽説我來給您選女婿, 個個都很客氣, 站起來打招呼, 只有一個年輕人躺在東邊的一張床上, 好像沒看見我。" 郗太傅説,"這個人好!"於是他去看那個年輕人。原來他就是後來成為(6)有名書法家(7)的王羲之(8), 郗太傅就把女兒嫁(9)給了王羲之。現在中國人把女婿也叫做"東床", 就是從這個故事來的。

(1) (女)婿((nǚ)xù): (literary) son-in-law

(2) 官(guān): official

(3) 郗(Xī): Chinese surname

(4) 太傅(tàifù): Grand Master; tutor to the crown prince

(5) 宰相(zǎixiàng): prime minister

(6) 成為(chéngwéi): to become

(7) 書法家(shūfǎjiā): calligrapher

(8) 王羲之(Wáng Xīzhī): person's name

(9) 嫁(jià): to marry

(Simplified Characters)

东床快婿(1)

　　中国东晋的时候 (344-405) 有个大官(2)姓郗(3), 是一个太傅(4), 有一天他叫他的学生给宰相(5)送一封信, 请宰相帮他选一个女婿。宰相回答 (huídá)说, "我有很多学生住在我家东边的屋子里, 您去选吧。" 郗太傅的学生去东边的屋子看了以后回来报告说, "宰相的学生都很不错, 听说我来给您选女婿, 个个都很客气, 站起来打招呼, 只有一个年轻人躺在东边的一张床上, 好像没看见我。" 郗太傅说, "这个人好!" 于是他去看那个年轻人。原来他就是后来成为(6)有名书法家(7)的王羲之(8),后来郗太傅就把女儿嫁(9)给了王羲之。现在中国人把女婿也叫做"东床", 就是从这个故事来的。

(1) (女)婿((nǚ)xù): (literary) son-in-law

(2) 官(guān): official

(3) 郗(Xī): Chinese surname

(4) 太傅(tàifù): Grand Master; tutor to the crown prince

(5) 宰相(zǎixiàng): prime minister

(6) 成为(chéngwéi): to become

▼▼▼▼▼▼▼▼▼▼▼▼▼▼▼▼▼▼▼▼▼▼▼▼▼▼▼▼▼▼▼▼

(7)　书法家(shūfǎjiā): calligrapher

(8)　王義之(Wáng Xīzhī): person's name

(9)　嫁(jià): to marry

Questions:

1.　Why did Xi Taifu send his student to the prime minister?

2.　What did the prime minister tell Xi's student?

3.　What did Xi's student tell him about one particular young man?

4.　Why do you think Xi picked Wang Xizhi?

IV. GRAMMAR & USAGE

A. *Complete the following dialogues using* 聽起來好像 / 听起来好像.

EXAMPLE:　a: 你不是説想找小柯教你怎麼做功課嗎?
　　　　　　　　你不是说想找小柯教你怎么做功课吗?

　　　　　　b: 我跟他提了一下, <u>聽起來他好像不太願意幫忙</u>。
　　　　　　　　我跟他提了一下, <u>听起来他好像不太愿意帮忙</u>。

1.　a: 球賽快要開始了, 你覺得小張會不會來?
　　　　球赛快要开始了, 你觉得小张会不会来?

　　b: 我剛才給他打電話,
　　　　我刚才给他打电话,

　　_____。

2.　a: 我早上跟小林説了幾句話, _____。他怎麼了?
　　　　我早上跟小林说了几句话, _____。他怎么了?

b: 我聽說他跟他女朋友鬧翻了. 詳細情況怎麼樣, 我也不太清楚.

    我听说他跟他女朋友闹翻了. 详细情况怎么样, 我也不太清楚.

3. a: 那個女孩說話＿＿＿＿＿＿＿＿＿＿＿＿＿＿。她跟小梅是姐妹嗎?

    那个女孩说话＿＿＿＿＿＿＿＿＿＿＿＿＿＿。她跟小梅是姐妹吗?

b: 對, 沒錯, 她是小梅的妹妹。

    对, 没错, 她是小梅的妹妹。

B. Complete the following dialogues using the conditional 才.

EXAMPLE: a: 這套運動服, 樣子、顏色都很不錯, 你為什麼不買? (名牌)

            这套运动服, 样子、颜色都很不错, 你为什么不买? (名牌)

       b: <u>名牌的我才買</u>。

         <u>名牌的我才买</u>。

1. a: 我們一起去聽音樂會, 好嗎? (你請客)

    我们一起去听音乐会, 好吗? (你请客)

b: ＿＿＿＿＿＿＿＿＿＿＿＿＿＿＿＿＿＿＿＿。

2. a: 你打算申請上研究所嗎? (找不到工作)

    你打算申请上研究所吗? (找不到工作)

b: ＿＿＿＿＿＿＿＿＿＿＿＿＿＿＿＿＿＿＿＿。

3. a: 小姐, 你想租什麼樣的房子? (有空調)

    小姐, 你想租什么样的房子? (有空调)

b: ＿＿＿＿＿＿＿＿＿＿＿＿＿＿＿＿＿＿＿＿。

C. Complete the following dialogues using 先...再...

EXAMPLE: a: 你现在去餐厅吃饭吗? (做完功课 / 去吃饭)

            你现在去餐厅吃饭吗? (做完功课 / 去吃饭)

▼▼

     b: <u>不, 我先做完功課, 再去吃飯</u>。

        <u>不, 我先做完功课, 再去吃饭</u>。

1. a: 你明年暑假打算做什麼? (實習 / 出國旅行)

     你明年暑假打算做什么? (实习 / 出国旅行)

     b: _____。

2. a: 你覺得這套公寓, 我應該租嗎? (問清楚包不包水電 / 考慮)

     你觉得这套公寓, 我应该租吗? (问清楚包不包水电 / 考虑)

     b: _____。

3. a: 你大學畢業以後, 打算申請上研究所還是找工作? (工作兩年 / 上研究所)

     你大学毕业以后, 打算申请上研究所还是找工作? (工作两年 / 上研究所)

     b: _____。

D. *Complete the following dialoguesusing* V 得出來 / V 得出来 *or* V 不出來 / V 不出来.

EXAMPLE: a: 指導教授今天好像心情不太好。

        指导教授今天好像心情不太好。

     b: <u>是嗎? 我看不出來</u>。

       <u>是吗? 我看不出来</u>。

1. 這個問題非常難, 我想了很久, _____, 你還是去問老師吧。

   这个问题非常难, 我想了很久, _____, 你还是去问老师吧。

2. a: 喂?

   喂?

b: 是小張吧?

是小张吧?

a: 哎, 你怎麼知道是我?

哎, 你怎么知道是我?

b: 你的聲音我很熟悉,

你的声音我很熟悉,

_____。

3. a: 這肯定不是你做的菜。這麼好吃!

这肯定不是你做的菜。这么好吃!

b: 怎麼不是我做的? 就是我做的。

怎么不是我做的? 就是我做的。

a: 你做的菜又油又難吃,

你做的菜又油又难吃,

_____。

E. *Based on the information given, use* 以來 / 以来 *or* 以後 / 以后 *to complete the passage.*

(Traditional)

　　小李現在是大學三年級的學生。他上大學_____, 一直在學漢語。這個學期結束_____, 他準備搬到校外去住。他計劃大學畢業_____, 出國留學。

(Simplified)

　　小李现在是大学三年级的学生。他上大学_____, 一直在学汉语。这个学期结束_____, 他准备搬到校外去住。他计划大学毕业_____, 出国留学。

▼▼▼

F. Complete the dialogues using 從來 / 从来.

EXAMPLE:　a: 你吃過芥蘭牛肉嗎?
　　　　　　　你吃过芥兰牛肉吗?

　　　　　　b: <u>我從來沒吃過</u>, 不過聽說很好吃。
　　　　　　　<u>我从来没吃过</u>, 不过听说很好吃。

1. a: 你看過大學籃球比賽嗎?
　　　你看过大学籃球比赛吗?

　　b: 我對球賽沒有興趣,
　　　我对球赛没有兴趣, _____。

2. a: 聽說附近新開了一家購物中心, 你知道不知道在什麼地方?
　　　听说附近新开了一家购物中心, 你知道不知道在什麼地方?

　　b: 不知道, _____。

3. a: 大家都說會中文對將來找工作很有幫助。你選過中文課嗎?
　　　大家都说会中文对将来找工作很有帮助。你选过中文课吗?

　　b: _____,
　　　不過, 下個學期我打算選一門中文課。
　　　不过, 下个学期我打算选一门中文课。

G. Complete the sentences based on the illustrations.

1. 難怪他沒胃口吃東西, 原來
　　难怪他没胃口吃东西, 原来

_____。

2. 難怪教室裏又熱又悶, 原來
　　难怪教室里又热又闷, 原来

_____。

3. 難怪購物中心的人那麼多, 原來

   难怪购物中心的人那么多, 原来

_____。

4. 難怪哥哥常常睡不好覺, 原來

   难怪哥哥常常睡不好觉, 原来

_____。

V. TRANSLATION

A. Translate the passages into English.

1.

(Traditional Characters)

　　每天翻開報紙都有體育新聞。記者把前一天各隊比賽的情況都寫出來。除此之外, 還介紹當天有什麼好看的球賽。

(Simplified Characters)

　　每天翻开报纸都有体育新闻。记者把前一天各队比赛的情况都写出来。除此之外,　还介绍当天有什么好看的球赛。

2.

(Traditional Characters)

　　柯先生跟柯太太剛買了一棟房子, 四房兩廳、三個厠所。兩個人搬進去才住了一個月, 就發現房子太大, 電費特別貴。柯先生建議租出去一個房間, 可以有一點租金。柯太太不同意, 因為她不願意跟租房子的人打交道。沒想到柯先生瞞著柯太太在報上登了一個出租廣告。後來柯太太知道了, 非常不高興, 兩個人差點鬧翻。柯先生非常後悔。

(Simplified Characters)

柯先生跟柯太太刚买了一栋房子, 四房两厅、三个厕所。两个人搬进去才住了一个月, 就发现房子太大, 电费特别贵。柯先生建议租出去一个房间, 可以有一点租金。柯太太不同意, 因为她不愿意跟租房子的人打交道。没想到柯先生瞒着柯太太在报上登了一个出租广告。后来柯太太知道了, 非常不高兴, 两个人差点闹翻。柯先生非常后悔。

B. *Translate the sentences into Chinese.*

1. Not until his roommate finished watching the basketball game did Tom fall asleep.

2. Anderson always watches TV before doing his homework.

3. Mr. Zhang and Mrs. Zhang are very different in terms of interests.

C. *Translate the passages into Chinese.*

1. Zhang Tianming thought for a long time. He decided to talk to his roommate to ask him not to make so much noise when he watched ball games. If his roommate wouldn't listen, Zhang Tianming would move out right away.

2. No wonder she was in a very bad mood today. It turns out that she just broke up with her boyfriend. They had been dating since high school. Both of them are outgoing and are easy to get along with. After thinking it over, no one knows why they had a falling out.

3. You'd better not talk to him. He is in a bad mood today. I am not sure about the situation in detail, but I heard that he just had a falling out with his boss, and in addition, he also broke up with his girlfriend. He has such a short temper. No wonder no one is willing to deal with him.

VI. COMPOSITION

Describe the attributes you look for in an ideal girlfriend or boyfriend.

第八課 ▲ 電影和電視的影響
第八课 ▲ 电影和电视的影响

I. LISTENING COMPREHENSION

A. Listen to the audio for the Textbook and answer the questions.

1. What was on TV while Zhang Tianming was waiting for Lisa?

2 According to Lisa, who should be responsible for children's behavior?

3. Did they go to see a movie? Why or why not?

4. Why did the woman shoot her boyfriend's daughter?

B. Listen to the audio for the Workbook.

1. Listen to the passage and answer the questions.
   a. What are kids who watch a lot of TV called?

   b. What do kids do to make their parents give them more TV time?

2. Listen to the passage and answer the questions.
   a. Why is the programming on this channel so different from others?

   b. Why has it become so popular?

   c. Who can take advantage of this kind of programming?

3. Listen to the passage and answer the questions.
   a. What was reported in the newspaper?

   b. What was responsible for it?

II. SPEAKING EXERCISES

A. Practice asking and answering the questions with a partner before class.

1. 你最喜歡看什麼電視節目? 為什麼?
   你最喜欢看什么电视节目? 为什么?

2. 你常常一邊做功課一邊聽音樂嗎? 為什麼?
   你常常一边做功课一边听音乐吗? 为什么?

3. 什麼情況常常會引起火災?
   什么情况常常会引起火灾?

4. 美國晚上多半幾點播全國(quánguó)電視新聞?
   美国晚上多半几点播全国(quánguó)电视新闻?

B. Practice speaking on the following topics.

1. 請你談一談你最喜歡的電視節目。
   请你谈一谈你最喜欢的电视节目。

2. 你覺得電視電影對人有沒有影響? 為什麼?
   你觉得电视电影对人有没有影响? 为什么?

III. READING COMPREHENSION

A. Read the passage and answer the questions.

(Traditional Characters)

　　小柯的專業是新聞, 原來打算大學畢業以後去電視台播新聞, 可是引起他父母的反對。小柯的父母認為他長得帥, 性格開朗, 應該去演電影。可是小柯不喜歡當演員 (yǎnyuán), 想來想去還是去電視台申請播新聞的工作。電視台的老闆覺得小柯說話跟小孩一樣, 建議他去做兒童節目。可是小柯最怕小孩吵, 不願意天天跟小孩打交道。最後, 小柯只好聽他父母的話, 去演電影了。

▼ ▼

(Simplified Characters)

　　小柯的专业是新闻, 原来打算大学毕业以后去电视台播新闻, 可是引起他父母的反对。小柯的父母认为他长得帅, 性格开朗, 应该去演电影。可是小柯不喜欢当演员 (yǎnyuán), 想来想去还是去电视台申请播新闻的工作。电视台的老板觉得小柯说话跟小孩一样, 建议他去做儿童节目。可是小柯最怕小孩吵, 不愿意天天跟小孩打交道。最后, 小柯只好听他父母的话, 去演电影了。

Questions:

1. What did Little Ke plan to do after he graduated? Why?

2. What did Little Ke's parents suggest that he do? Why?

3. What did the people at the TV station suggest?

4. What does Little Ke do nowadays?

B. Read the passage and answer the questions.

(Traditional Characters)

　　現在打開電視什麼節目都有, 不過我覺得最有意思的是有一些電視台只播一種節目。比如說, 有的電視台只播新聞, 這種電視台, 只要是新聞就播。有的只播卡通片, 除了卡通, 還是卡通, 別的都不播。另外還有的電視台只播讓人看了笑, 看了高興的喜劇片。不過不是每個人都可以看得到這些電視台播的節目。因為播這些節目的都是有綫電視台, 每個月得付點錢才能看到。

(Simplified Characters)

　　现在打开电视什么节目都有, 不过我觉得最有意思的是有一些电视台只播一种节目。比如说, 有的电视台只播新闻, 这种电视台, 只要是新闻就播。有的只播卡通片，除了卡通，还是卡通，别的都不播。另外还有的电视台只播让人看了笑，看了高兴的喜剧片。不过不是每个人都可以看得到这些电视台播的节目。因为播这些节目的都是有线电视台，每个月得付点钱才能看到。

Questions:

1. What three kinds of TV programming are mentioned?

2. Who can enjoy these TV programs?

C. *Answer the first three questions by circling the relevant information on the newspaper clipping. Answer the fourth question in English.*

立体电影　独家放映
燎原电影院小厅
《驯狮三郎》
放映时间：1：30　3：00
4：30　6：00　7：30（双片）
长寿路600号　电话：2539254

(See the Alternate Character Appendix for traditional characters.)

Questions:

1. Circle the name of the theater.
2. Circle the name of the movie.
3. Circle the address of the theater.
4. How many showings are there in the morning?

D. *As in the United States, newspapers in China carry TV and movie listings. The following is taken from a Shanghai newspaper.*

今明电视

4月11日　星期一
中央电视台·五频道
23:35　4集连续剧:特区警察
③④
上海电视台·八频道
10:17　包青天:真假状元(1)
23:01　故事片:风雨相思雁
上海电视台·十四频道
0:20　杨贵妃(28)
东方电视台·廿频道
21:54　台湾电视连续剧:末
代皇孙(54)
上海教育电视台(26频道)
19:59　音乐专题:军歌声声
4月12日　星期二
中央电视台·五频道
20:05　14集连续剧:还是那
条街⑤
上海电视台·八频道
20:10　包青天:真假状元(2)
上海电视台·十四频道
23:38　杨贵妃(29)
东方电视台·廿频道
21:53　末代皇孙(55)
上海教育电视台(26频道)
20:13　七彩讲坛　话剧《冰山
情》

(See the Alternate Character Appendix for traditional characters.)

Questions:

1. What dates is the viewing guide for?

2. How many TV channels are available for the residents of Shanghai?

3. If you are interested in a music program, which channel should you watch?

E. Read the story and answer the questions.

(Traditional Characters)

自相矛盾

　　從前有個人在市場上賣矛 (1) 和盾 (2)。他拿起他的盾對人說:"你們看我的盾!我的盾是世界上最好的,什麼矛都刺不穿 (3) 它。"然後,他又拿起他的矛說:"你們再來看我的矛!我的矛是世界上最屬害的,什麼盾它都能刺穿。"大家聽了他的話,都覺得十分好笑。有個人問他:"如果你說的都是真的,你的矛是世界上最屬害的,什麼盾都能刺穿,你的盾是世界上最好的,什麼矛都刺不穿它,那用你的矛來刺你的盾,結果會怎麼樣呢?"那個人聽了,就很快地收起他的矛和盾,離開了。

(1)　矛 (máo): spear
(2)　盾 (dùn): shield
(3)　刺穿 (cì chuān): to pierce through

(Simplified Characters)

自相矛盾

　　从前有个人在市场上卖矛 (1) 和盾 (2)。他拿起他的盾对人说:"你们看我的盾!我的盾是世界上最好的,什么矛都刺不穿 (3) 它。"然后,他又拿起他的矛

▼▼

说："你们再来看我的矛！我的矛是世界上最厉害的，什么盾它都能刺穿。"
大家听了他的话，都觉得十分好笑。有个人问他："如果你说的都是真的，你
的矛是世界上最厉害的，什么盾都能刺穿，你的盾是世界上最好的，什么矛都
刺不穿它，那用你的矛来刺你的盾，结果会怎么样呢？"那个人听了，就很快地
收起他的矛和盾，离开了。

(1) 矛 (máo): spear
(2) 盾 (dùn): shield
(3) 刺穿 (cì chuān): to pierce through

Questions:

1. What did the person say about his spear and shield?

2. Did people believe what he said? Why or why not?

3. What did the person do after hearing people's comments?

4. What do you think the title means?

IV. GRAMMAR AND USAGE

A. Fill in the blanks with 的, 地, *or* 得.

1. 小湯脾氣十分急躁，做什麼事都做＿＿＿很快，可是不見得都做＿＿＿很好。
   小汤脾气十分急躁，做什么事都做＿＿＿很快，可是不见得都做＿＿＿很好。

2. 這兒＿＿＿環境很好，你可以安安靜靜＿＿＿在這兒學習。
   这儿＿＿＿环境很好，你可以安安静静＿＿＿在这儿学习。

3. 被打破＿＿＿那面鏡子是他爸爸送給他＿＿＿畢業禮物。
   被打破＿＿＿那面镜子是他爸爸送给他＿＿＿毕业礼物。

4. 別著急，慢慢兒＿＿＿吃，時間來得及。
   别着急，慢慢儿＿＿＿吃，时间来得及。

5. 那個小男孩模仿電視記者報新聞模仿＿＿＿像極了。
   那个小男孩模仿电视记者报新闻模仿＿＿＿像极了。

▼▼▼▼▼▼▼▼▼▼▼▼▼▼▼▼▼▼▼▼▼▼▼▼▼▼▼▼▼▼▼▼▼

6. 指導教授認為小夏選＿＿＿專業不太理想, 建議小夏再好好兒＿＿＿考慮考慮。

   指导教授认为小夏选＿＿＿专业不太理想, 建议小夏再好好儿＿＿＿考虑考虑。

7.

(Traditional Characters)

　　　今天電影院上演＿＿＿是一部法國＿＿＿藝術片, 演＿＿＿很不錯, 小張看＿＿＿很高興。出了電影院, 他慢慢＿＿＿走回家。他一邊走, 一邊模仿電影裏＿＿＿人物。他越模仿, 越覺得有意思, 高興＿＿＿笑起來, 旁邊＿＿＿人都覺得他很奇怪。

(Simplified Characters)

　　　今天电影院上演＿＿＿是一部法国＿＿＿艺术片, 演＿＿＿很不错, 小张看＿＿＿很高兴。出了电影院, 他慢慢＿＿＿走回家。他一边走, 一边模仿电影里＿＿＿人物。他越模仿, 越觉得有意思, 高兴＿＿＿笑起来, 旁边＿＿＿人都觉得他很奇怪。

B. Use 一邊…一邊… / 一边…一边… **and the illustrations to complete the sentences.**

EXAMPLE: 他喜歡一邊聽音樂, 一邊唱歌。
　　　　　他喜欢一边听音乐, 一边唱歌。

1. 請不要 ＿＿＿＿＿＿＿＿＿＿＿＿＿＿＿＿＿＿, 太危險了。
   请不要 ＿＿＿＿＿＿＿＿＿＿＿＿＿＿＿＿＿＿, 太危险了。

2. 毛毛的媽媽常常
   毛毛的妈妈常常＿＿＿＿＿＿＿＿＿＿＿＿＿＿＿。

3. 王先生每天早上都是＿＿＿＿＿＿＿＿＿＿＿＿＿。

C. Answer the questions using 偶爾 / 偶尔.

EXAMPLE: a: 你真的一點肉都不吃嗎?
　　　　　　你真的一点肉都不吃吗?

　　　　　b: 偶爾也吃一點兒。
　　　　　　偶尔也吃一点儿。

▼▼▼▼▼▼▼▼▼▼▼▼▼▼▼▼▼▼▼▼▼▼▼▼▼▼▼▼▼▼▼▼▼▼▼▼▼

1. a: 你平常去不去體育場看球賽?

   你平常去不去体育场看球赛?

   b: _____。

2. a: 你喝不喝咖啡?

   b: _____。

3. a: 美國的電視裏常播紀錄片嗎?

   美国的电视里常播纪录片吗?

   b: _____。

4. What are some of the things that you do or the indulgences that you allow yourself occasionally? How often do you go out to expensive restaurants and the movies, visit relatives, tidy up your room, and write to or call your high school friends?

List four examples in Chinese.

a. _____

b. _____

c. _____

d. _____

D. Complete the sentences using 引起.

EXAMPLE: 學校禮堂常演外國藝術片, <u>為了引起學生看電影的興趣</u>, 電影票一張只要一塊錢。

學校礼堂常演外国艺术片, <u>为了引起学生看电影的兴趣</u>, 电影票一张只要一块钱。

1. 他們兩個人交往不到三個月就想住在一起, _____。
(家長 ／ 反對)

他们两个人交往不到三个月就想住在一起, _____。
(家长 ／ 反对)

▼▼▼

2. 為了＿＿＿＿＿＿＿＿＿＿＿＿＿, 漢語老師常常教唱中文歌。(學生 ／ 興趣)

　　为了＿＿＿＿＿＿＿＿＿＿＿＿＿, 汉语老师常常教唱中文歌。(学生 ／ 兴趣)

3. 味精、鹽對身體健康有沒有好處, ＿＿＿＿＿＿＿＿＿＿＿。(大家 ／ 爭論)

　　味精、盐对身体健康有没有好处, ＿＿＿＿＿＿＿＿＿＿＿。(大家 ／ 争论)

E. Rewrite the sentences using 反而.

EXAMPLE: 他平常什麼都管, 今天這麼重要的事, 他反而不管了。

　　　　　 他平常什么都管, 今天这么重要的事, 他反而不管了。

1. 這是他的錯, 他不但不怪自己,

　　这是他的错, 他不但不怪自己, ＿＿＿＿＿＿＿＿＿＿＿＿＿。

2. 小王比小張晚半年上大學,

　　小王比小张晚半年上大学, ＿＿＿＿＿＿＿＿＿＿＿＿＿。

3. 我以為在日本買日本電視會便宜一些, 沒想到

　　我以为在日本买日本电视会便宜一些, 没想到＿＿＿＿＿＿＿＿＿＿＿。

F. Complete the sentences using 難免 ／ 难免.

EXAMPLE: 兩個人生活在一起, 難免會吵架。

　　　　　 两个人生活在一起, 难免会吵架。

1. 他第一次離開家, ／ 他第一次离开家,

　　＿＿＿＿＿＿＿＿＿＿＿＿＿＿＿＿＿＿＿＿＿＿＿＿。

2. 看球賽一激動, ／ 看球赛一激动,

　　＿＿＿＿＿＿＿＿＿＿＿＿＿＿＿＿＿＿＿＿＿＿＿＿。

3. 兒童看電視, ／ 儿童看电视,

　　＿＿＿＿＿＿＿＿＿＿＿＿＿＿＿＿＿＿＿＿＿＿＿＿。

G. Complete the sentences using 就是...也...

EXAMPLE: a: 今天天氣這麼冷, 你就別去看電影了。

　　　　　 今天天气这么冷, 你就别去看电影了。

b: 電影非看不可，就是天氣冷我也要去。

電影非看不可, 就是天氣冷我也要去。

1. a: 你父母反對你和小梅在一起, 你就不要再跟她交往下去了。

你父母反对你和小梅在一起, 你就不要再跟她交往下去了。

b: 我愛小梅, 小梅愛我,

我爱小梅, 小梅爱我,

_____。

2. a: 這部藝術片真的沒什麼意思。我不想看了。

这部艺术片真的没什么意思。我不想看了。

b: 別忘了, 我們看完了還得寫文章呢！

别忘了, 我们看完了还得写文章呢！

_____。

3. a: 這個牌子的衣服太貴了, 你買別的吧！

这个牌子的衣服太贵了, 你买别的吧！

b: 這個牌子的衣服質量好,

这个牌子的衣服质量好,

_____。

H. Complete the dialogues using 還是 ／ 还是.

EXAMPLE: a: 這雙鞋樣子挺好的, 買吧。

这双鞋樣子挺好的, 买吧。

b: 可是價錢稍微貴了一點兒, 還是等打折的時候買吧。

可是價錢稍微貴了一点儿, 还是等打折的时候买吧。

1. a: 我有點兒不舒服, 想先回家。

我有点儿不舒服, 想先回家。

b: 我看你病得挺屬害的,

我看你病得挺厉害的,

_____。

2. a: 媽, 我看完這個卡通片再做功課, 好嗎?

妈, 我看完这个卡通片再做功课, 好吗?

b: 你今天的功課那麽多,

你今天的功课那么多,

_____。

3. a: 你們去聽音樂會吧。別管我。

你们去听音乐会吧。别管我。

b: 你別老在家憋著, 憋久了對身體不好,

你别老在家憋着, 憋久了对身体不好,

_____。

I. Complete the dialogues between A and B using the words provided in parentheses.

A and B are friends studying in the same college. One day, A wanted to ask B to go to see a documentary film together. A came to B's room and was overwhelmed by how messy B's room was.

a: 我的天啊! 你的房間怎麽亂七八糟的?

我的天啊! 你的房间怎么乱七八糟的?

b: _____, _____。
(难免 / 难免)

a: 我看你是找藉口。好了, 好了, 不說這些了。學校礼堂正在演一部纪录片, 你
想去看嗎?

我看你是找借口。好了, 好了, 不说这些了。学校礼堂正在演一部纪录片, 你
想去看吗?

b: 不想, _____。
(還是...吧 / 还是...吧)

a: 我請客, 怎麼樣?

我请客, 怎么样?

b: _____。

(就是...也...)

中　視

08000122.xx
05:30 我們兩家都是人
06:00 新天地無用之
　　　 銀河戰警
06:30 早安! 您的氣象新聞
08:30 快樂生活王　(普)
09:00 文茜小妹大　(普)
10:00 戲說乾隆　(普)
11:00 親親你是我的寶貝
12:00 中視午間新聞
13:00 神醫俠侶　(普)
14:30 奈何花　(普)
15:30 黃色手帕　(普)
16:30 機獸新世紀　|
17:00 七龍珠　(普)
17:30 網球王子　(普)
17:57 大小同心ABC　(普)
18:00 大家來說笑　(普)
19:00 中視新聞全球報導
20:00 神醫俠侶　(普)
21:30 我們兩家都是人
22:00 世界非常奇妙　(普)
22:30 文茜小妹大　(普)
23:30 黃色手帕　(普)
00:30 中視夜線新聞
01:30 我的秘密花園　(普)
02:30 午夜我們兩家都是人
03:00 午夜文茜小妹大
04:00 午夜MIT台灣誌

A program guide for a TV station in Taiwan. How many times each day does the station provide news broadcasting?

(See the Alternate Character Appendix for simplified characters.)

▼▼

J. Connecting Sentences

1. Connect the sentences and make them a cohesive paragraph by deleting unneeded subjects and rewriting the sentences as needed.

> a. 我爸爸是一個醫生。
>
>   我爸爸是一个医生。
>
> b. 我爸爸每天早上八點去醫院。
>
>   我爸爸每天早上八点去医院。
>
> c. 我爸爸中午十二點在醫院吃午飯。
>
>   我爸爸中午十二点在医院吃午饭。
>
> d. 我爸爸下午六點才回家。
>
>   我爸爸下午六点才回家。

2. Connect the sentences and make them a cohesive paragraph by deleting unneeded subjects and rewriting the sentences as needed.

> a. 天華是大學一年級的新生。
>
>   天华是大学一年级的新生。
>
> b. 天華剛辦完註冊手續。
>
>   天华刚办完注册手续。
>
> c. 天華現在準備搬進新生宿舍。
>
>   天华现在准备搬进新生宿舍。

3. Connect the sentences and make them a cohesive paragraph by deleting unneeded subjects, replacing subjects with pronouns, and rewriting the sentences as needed.

> a. 那個小男孩玩火柴引起了火災。
>
>   那个小男孩玩火柴引起了火灾。

b. 那個小男孩不但不後悔。

　　那个小男孩不但不后悔。

c. 那個小男孩反而還怪大人給他火柴。

　　那个小男孩反而还怪大人给他火柴。

V. TRANSLATION

A. Translate the passage into English.

(Traditional Characters)

　　最近電視裏播的新聞不是誰威脅炸誰, 就是誰開槍打了誰; 不是哪兒有火災, 就是哪兒有水災, 讓人看了心情非常不好。難怪有些人一點電視新聞都不願意看。

(Simplified Characters)

　　最近电视里播的新闻不是谁威胁炸谁, 就是谁开枪打了谁; 不是哪儿有火灾, 就是哪儿有水灾, 让人看了心情非常不好。难怪有些人一点电视新闻都不愿意看。

B. Translate the passages into Chinese.

1. The movies shown in the auditorium are mostly documentaries. Occasionally, the auditorium also shows commercial movies.

2. Children nowadays watch too much TV. As soon as they have nothing to do, many children sit on the sofa and watch TV. Children like to imitate characters in the TV programs, and it's unavoidable that children are influenced by all the junk on TV. Parents shouldn't blame TV stations but should blame themselves for not educating their children to select good TV shows. They should take responsibility for their own actions as well as for their children's conduct.

3. Recently, there has been more news on students bringing guns to school and threatening their teachers and classmates. Parents not only blame the school for not being able to educate children well, but also blame the media for having a bad influence on children. However, many parents have never thought that they themselves are mostly responsible for their children's behavior.

VI. COMPOSITION

1. 請談一談你最喜歡的電視節目。
   请谈一谈你最喜欢的电视节目。

2. 談電視電影對兒童的影響。

   谈电视电影对儿童的影响。

Here is a list of all of the China Central TV (CCTV) channels. Can you identify the news, sports, children's, and music channels?

(See the Alternate Character Appendix for traditional characters.)

第九課 ▲ 旅行

I. LISTENING COMPREHENSION

A. *Listen to the audio for the Textbook and answer the questions.*

1. Why does Zhang Tianming want to go to China?

2. Will Zhang Tianming travel alone? How do you know?

3. Will this be the first time that Zhang Tianming and Lisa will travel together? How do you know?

4. Which route will be Lisa's choice if they go to China?

B. *Listen to the audio for the Workbook.*

1. Listen to the passage and answer the questions.
   a. Why didn't Mrs. Li take a walk with Mr. Li?

   b. Why did Mrs. Li quarrel with Mr. Li?

   c. Who was the woman?

2. Listen to the passage and answer the questions (True/False).
   ( ) a. Little Gao went to New York for fun.
   ( ) b. Little Gao's wife and children went to New York with him.
   ( ) c. Little Gao went to his aunt's house for dinner.
   ( ) d. Little Gao didn't want to spend any more time with his aunt.

II. SPEAKING EXERCISES

A. *Practice asking and answering the questions with a partner before class.*

1. 你是從哪兒來的？
   你是从哪儿来的？

2. 你是在什麼地方出生的?

   你是在什么地方出生的?

3. 你是在什麼地方長大的?

   你是在什么地方长大的?

4. 你去過中國嗎?

   你去过中国吗?

5. 快放寒假 / 暑假了, 你打算做什麼?

   快放寒假 / 暑假了, 你打算做什么?

6. 出國旅行以前應該準備一些什麼東西, 辦一些什麼事情?

   出国旅行以前应该准备一些什么东西, 办一些什么事情?

B. *Practice speaking on the following topics.*

1. 要是你有錢有時間的話, 你打算去什麼地方旅行? 為什麼?

   要是你有钱有时间的话, 你打算去什么地方旅行? 为什么?

2. 請談一談你最近的一次旅行。

   请谈一谈你最近的一次旅行。

▼ ▼

III. READING COMPREHENSION

A. Read the passage and answer the question.

(Traditional Characters)

　　小李脾氣不好, 常跟人吵架。跟別人一起看電視的時候, 老換頻道, 結果
什麼節目都沒看完, 反而怪電視節目不好。出門旅行, 他都是讓別人幫他訂票、
辦手續。他不但不謝謝人家, 反而不是說機票太貴, 就是怪航空公司的路線
不合適。難怪大家都怕跟他打交道。

(Simplified Characters)

　　小李脾气不好, 常跟人吵架。跟别人一起看电视的时候, 老换频道, 结果
什么节目都没看完, 反而怪电视节目不好。出门旅行, 他都是让别人帮他订票、
办手续。他不但不谢谢人家, 反而不是说机票太贵, 就是怪航空公司的路线
不合适。难怪大家都怕跟他打交道。

Question:

　　What three incidents are cited to exemplify Little Li's unpopularity?

B. Read the passage and answer the questions.

(Traditional Characters)

　　柯林以前一放假就跟林雪梅開車去玩兒, 不是去東海岸就是去西海
岸 (hǎi'àn), 都玩膩了。這次他們要坐飛機到中國去旅行。他們一個月以前就辦
好了護照, 兩個星期前又去中國領事館辦好了簽證。上飛機那天路上汽車太
多, 所以他們花了兩個小時才到飛機場。柯林怕時間來不及, 一著急, 怎麼找
也找不到機票和護照了。天氣不熱, 可是他滿頭大汗 (hàn, sweat)。林雪梅看了他
一眼, 笑著問:"你手上拿的是什麼?"柯林一看, 也笑了, 原來護照和機票都在
他手上呢。

(Simplified Characters)

　　柯林以前一放假就跟林雪梅开车去玩儿, 不是去东海岸就是去西海岸 (hǎi'àn), 都玩腻了。这次他们要坐飞机到中国去旅行。他们一个月以前就办好了护照, 两个星期前又去中国领事馆办好了签证。上飞机那天路上汽车太多, 所以他们花了两个小时才到飞机场。柯林怕时间来不及, 一着急, 怎么找也找不到机票和护照了。天气不热, 可是他满头大汗 (hàn, sweat)。林雪梅看了他一眼, 笑着问: "你手上拿的是什么?" 柯林一看, 也笑了, 原来护照和机票都在他手上呢。

Questions (True/False):

(　) 1.　Ke Lin and Lin Xuemei have taken a lot of car trips together.

(　) 2.　Every year Ke Lin and Lin Xuemei travel overseas.

(　) 3.　It took Ke Lin a week to get his visa.

(　) 4.　It took Ke Lin and Lin Xuemei a long time to get to the airport.

(　) 5.　Ke Lin forgot where he had put his passport and plane ticket.

(　) 6.　Ke Lin perspired profusely because he was dressed too warmly.

(　) 7.　Lin Xuemei wasn't as worried as Ke Lin was.

C. Answer the questions based on the itinerary given.

高老師的旅行日程:

高老师的旅行日程:

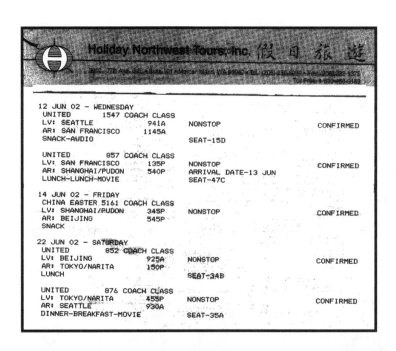

▼▼

1. 他的飛機票是跟旅行社訂的, 還是跟航空公司訂的?
   他的飞机票是跟旅行社订的, 还是跟航空公司订的?

2. 他坐哪一家航空公司的飛機?
   他坐哪一家航空公司的飞机?

3. 他是哪一天離開美國的? 是哪一天回美國來的?
   他是哪一天离开美国的? 是哪一天回美国来的?

4. 他去中國的時候, 在哪兒轉機?
   他去中国的时候, 在哪儿转机?

5. 他從東京回美國的班機號碼 / 航班(hángbān)號是多少?
   他从东京回美国的班机号码 / 航班(hángbān)号是多少?

D. *Read the newspaper ad for a travel agency and answer the questions.*

(See the Alternate Character Appendix for simplified characters.)

Questions:

1. In which city is the travel agency located?

2. Can it make a domestic reservation for you?

3. What other services does it provide?

4. When can you call the agency for services?

E. Tourist hotels in mainland China, Taiwan, and Hong Kong often advertise in newspapers and magazines. The following is taken from a Chinese publication. Read it and answer the questions.

京伦饭店位于北京市中心，

无论是商务旅行还是旅游观光均十分便利。

乘车前往北京国际机场只需三十分钟，

乘车前往天安门广场仅十分钟，

毗邻中国国际贸易中心、商务区及大使馆区。

(See the Alternate Character Appendix for traditional characters.)

Questions:

1. Circle the name of the hotel.

2 Where is the hotel located?

3. What might attract guests to stay in this hotel? List at least two things.

▼▼▼▼▼▼▼▼▼▼▼▼▼▼▼▼▼▼▼▼▼▼▼▼▼▼▼▼▼▼▼▼▼▼▼▼▼

F. *Before making a hotel reservation, guests often want to know the rate, the services available, etc.*
The following brochure is available in the lobby of a hotel in Taipei. Read it and answer the questions.

房 價 表

	NT$
單 人 房	7,600
雙 人 房 （一大床）.	7,900
雙 人 房 （二單床）.	7,900
精 緻 套 房	13,000
景 隅 套 房	17,000
行 政 套 房	18,000
豪 華 套 房	30,000
×××× 總 統 套 房	40,000
加 床	800

■ 住宿遷出時間：中午12點

● 上列價格自2004年1月1日起生效，金額以新台幣
計費並已包含5%加值營業稅。

● 10%服務費另計。

● 價格有所異動時，不再另行通知。

● 提供賓士轎車往返機場的接送服務。

● 可接受的信用卡：
美國運通卡(AE)、大來卡(Diners)、萬事達卡(Mater)
威士卡(Visa)、JCB卡、聯合信用卡。

(See the Alternate Character Appendix for simplified characters.)

Questions:

1. What is the rate for a single room per night?

2. What is the checkout time?

3. Does the hotel provide shuttle service to the airport?

G. Read the story and answer the questions.

(Traditional Characters)

井(1)底之蛙(2)

　　莊子(3)是中國古代的一位哲學家。有一次, 他給別人說了一個故事: 很久
很久以前, 在一口(4)老井裏住著一隻青蛙。一天青蛙在井邊見到了一隻從東海

來的大鱉(5)。青蛙對大鱉說:"你看, 我住的地方多好啊, 世界上沒有比我的井更好的地方了。如果我想玩, 就可以跳到井邊玩, 玩膩了, 就回到井裏休息一下。這多方便啊!"青蛙問大鱉為什麼不進來看看呢?

大鱉聽了青蛙的話, 就到井裏去看了看。覺得井裏不像青蛙說的那麼好, 又小又黑, 一點兒意思也沒有, 就對青蛙說:"你見過大海嗎?鬧水災的時候, 海水不會多很多; 很長時間不下雨, 海水也不會少很多。住在大海裏才真的快樂啊!"青蛙聽了非常不好意思, 它這才知道自己知道的太少了。

(1) 井(jǐng): well
(2) (青)蛙 (qīngwā): frog
(3) 莊子(Zhuāngzǐ): Zhuangzi
(4) 口 (kǒu): measure word for a well
(5) 鱉(biē): soft-shell turtle

(Simplified Characters)

井(1)底之蛙(2)

庄子(3)是中国古代的一位哲学家。有一次, 他给别人说了一个故事: 很久很久以前, 在一口(4)老井里住着一只青蛙。一天青蛙在井边见到了一只从东海来的大鳖(5)。青蛙对大鳖说:"你看, 我住的地方多好啊, 世界上没有比我的井

▼▼▼

更好的地方了。如果我想玩, 就可以跳到井边玩, 玩腻了, 就回到井里休息一下。这多方便啊!" 青蛙问大鳖为什么不进来看看呢?

大鳖听了青蛙的话, 就到井里去看了看。觉得井里不像青蛙说的那么好, 又小又黑, 一点儿意思也没有, 就对青蛙说: "你见过大海吗? 闹水灾的时候, 海水不会多很多; 很长时间不下雨, 海水也不会少很多。住在大海里才真的快乐啊!" 青蛙听了非常不好意思, 它这才知道自己知道的太少了。

(1) 井 (jǐng): well

(2) (青)蛙 (qīngwā): frog

(3) 庄子 (Zhuāngzǐ): Zhuangzi

(4) 口 (kǒu): measure word for a well

(5) 鳖 (biē): soft-shell turtle

Questions:

1. Where did the frog live?

2. Where did the turtle come from?

3. What did the frog brag about to the turtle?

4. What did the frog invite the turtle to do?

5. What did the turtle tell the frog?

6. How did the frog react to what the turtle said about the ocean?

7. What kind of person can be compared to the "frog in the well"?

IV. GRAMMAR & USAGE

A. Use 除非..., 否则 / 否则... *and the illustrations to complete the following dialogues.*

1. 售貨員: 小姐, 這套運動服, 你穿合適極了, 買吧! 買吧!

   售货员: 小姐, 这套运动服, 你穿合适极了, 买吧! 买吧!

客人: _____,
_____。

2. 房東: 這兒的環境好, 房租也不太貴, 你怎麼不租呢?
   房东: 这儿的环境好, 房租也不太贵, 你怎么不租呢?

   房客: _____,
   _____。

3. 小王: 小李, 你陪我看電視怎麼樣? 一個人看沒意思。
   小王: 小李, 你陪我看电视怎麼样? 一个人看没意思。

   小李: _____,
   _____。

B. *Suppose you are a landlord and you are renting to a very irresponsible tenant. You are at a point where you have to issue ultimatums. Convince him or her that you mean business. Be sure to use* 除非..., 否則 / 否則...

EXAMPLE: 我知道是你把房間裏的鏡子打破的, <u>除非你買一個新鏡子</u>, <u>否則</u> <u>你就得搬出去</u>。

我知道是你把房间里的镜子打破的, <u>除非你买一个新镜子</u>, <u>否则</u> <u>你就得搬出去</u>。

1. 你兩個月沒付房租了,
   你两个月没付房租了,

   _____,
   _____。

2. 你聽的搖滾樂太吵,
   你听的摇滚乐太吵,

   _____,
   _____。

▼ ▼

3. 你怎麼可以在房間裏吸煙？

   你怎么可以在房间里吸烟？

   _____,

   _____。

C. Are you an easy-going person? Are you always happy to accommodate others' desires and wishes?

Suppose you are such a person and respond to the following questions using question words such as 哪兒／哪儿 *within the pattern QW..., QW...*

EXAMPLE: a: 我們今天晚上看哪個體育節目？

                我们今天晚上看哪个体育节目？

            b: <u>你想看哪個我們就看哪個</u>。

               <u>你想看哪个我们就看哪个</u>。

1. a: 我明天什麼時候來好？

   我明天什么时候来好？

   b: _____。

2. a: 吃了飯你想去哪兒散步？

   吃了饭你想去哪儿散步？

   b: _____。

3. a: 暑假咱們坐哪一家航空公司的飛機去墨西哥？

   暑假咱们坐哪一家航空公司的飞机去墨西哥？

   b: _____。

4. a: 搬了新家以後，你打算買什麼顏色的地毯呢？

   搬了新家以后，你打算买什么颜色的地毯呢？

   b: _____。

▼▼

D. Complete the dialogues using 不是…就是…

EXAMPLE: a: 你週末都做些什麼？

               你周末都做些什么？

         b: <u>我週末不是打球就是看球賽</u>。

           <u>我周末不是打球就是看球赛</u>。

1. a: 你想學什麼專業？

     你想学什么专业？

    b: _____。

2. a: 你畢業以後打算做什麼？

     你毕业以后打算做什么？

    b: _____。

3. a: 你們家平常吃什麼青菜？

     你们家平常吃什么青菜？

    b: _____。

E. Complete the sentences using 難怪／难怪.

EXAMPLE: 最近電視裏的卡通片對兒童的影響越來越不好, …

                最近电视里的卡通片对儿童的影响越来越不好, …

      → 最近電視裏的卡通片對兒童的影響越來越不好, <u>難怪很多家長不</u><u>讓他們的孩子看卡通片</u>。

          最近电视里的卡通片对儿童的影响越来越不好, <u>难怪很多家长不</u><u>让他们的孩子看卡通片</u>。

1. 醫生告訴小王少吃油, 多運動, …

   医生告诉小王少吃油, 多运动, …

    → _____。

▼▼

2.　他脾氣急躁, 偶爾還喝醉酒打人, ...

　　他脾气急躁, 偶尔还喝醉酒打人, ...

　　→ _____

3.　南京夏天熱得叫人受不了, ... (Hint: Nanjing's nickname is "Big Furnace.")

　　南京夏天热得叫人受不了, ...

　　→ _____

F.　Use 既然...就... ***and the illustrations to complete the dialogues.***

a:　天氣這麼好, 咱們出去走走。

　　天气这么好, 咱们出去走走。

b:　不行, 我不太舒服。

a:　是嗎? <u>既然你不舒服, 咱們就不出去了</u>。

　　是吗? <u>既然你不舒服, 咱们就不出去了</u>。

1.　a:　對不起, 我吃素, 我不能吃芥蘭牛肉。

　　　　对不起, 我吃素, 我不能吃芥兰牛肉。

　　b:　沒關係 / 没关系,

　　_____,

　　_____。

2.　a:　我覺得搖滾樂太吵了，能不能聽聽別的?

　　　　我觉得摇滚乐太吵了, 能不能听听别的?

　　b:　沒問題 / 没问题,

　　_____,

　　_____。

3.　兒子:　媽, 當醫生得整天跟病人打交道, 我不願意。我想選別的專業。

　　儿子:　妈, 当医生得整天跟病人打交道, 我不愿意。我想选别的专业。

母親 / 母亲: 行、行、行,

_____,

_____。

4. 弟弟: 哥, 我功課做完了。

    弟弟: 哥, 我功课做完了。

    哥哥: _____,

    _____。

G. *Answer the questions using* 然後 / 然后.

EXAMPLE: a: 明天是你的生日, 打算怎麼過?

        明天是你的生日, 打算怎么过?

        b: 我打算先去餐館吃一頓, 然後去跳舞。

        我打算先去餐馆吃一顿, 然后去跳舞。

1. a: 出國旅行得辦哪些手續?

    出国旅行得办哪些手续?

    b: _____, _____。

2. a: 要是有錢, 你打算去哪些國家旅行?

    要是有钱, 你打算去哪些国家旅行?

    b: _____, _____。

3. a: 再過幾天就放假了, 你有什麼計劃?

    再过几天就放假了, 你有什么计划?

    b: _____, _____。

H. *Complete the sentences using* 多…少…

EXAMPLE: 我父親常說一個人應該多做事, 少說話。

        我父亲常说一个人应该多做事, 少说话。

▼▼

1. 為了身體健康, 我們應該＿＿＿＿＿＿＿＿＿＿＿＿＿＿＿＿＿。

   为了身体健康, 我们应该＿＿＿＿＿＿＿＿＿＿＿＿＿＿＿＿＿。

2. 想要把漢語學好, 學生得＿＿＿＿＿＿＿＿＿＿＿＿＿＿＿＿＿。

   想要把汉语学好, 学生得＿＿＿＿＿＿＿＿＿＿＿＿＿＿＿＿＿。

3. 毛毛最近書看得太少, 卡通看得太多, 媽媽讓他＿＿＿＿＿＿＿＿＿。

   毛毛最近书看得太少, 卡通看得太多, 妈妈让他＿＿＿＿＿＿＿＿＿。

V. TRANSLATION

A. *Translate the passage into Chinese.*

Lisa doesn't like to watch television. Unless there's something especially good on, she won't watch TV. Zhang Tianming is different. He'll watch whatever is on TV.

B. *Translate the brief exchange into Chinese.*

Zhang Tianming: Since you don't like watching TV, let's go and see a movie.

Lisa: Great. Afterwards, we can go to that little restaurant next to the theater and eat.

Zhang Tianming: The food there is very bad. Let's go to Chinatown to have some Chinese food.

▼ ▼

C. Translate the telephone conversation into Chinese.

Little Zhang: Eastern Travel Agency? I need to book a plane ticket.

Travel Agent: Where are you going?

Little Zhang: I am flying from Chicago to Korea, and will change planes there. Then I'll fly from Korea to Hong Kong.

Travel Agent: How many tickets do you want to purchase?

Little Zhang: One.

Travel Agent: We will mail the ticket to you right away.

Little Zhang: Thanks.

D. Translate the sentences into Chinese. Be sure to use the correct Chinese word order.

1. You have to listen to the tape before coming to class.

2. My roommate is going to visit his aunt in Nanjing.

3. They plan to go dancing after they finish their homework.

4. He went to pick up his adviser at the airport in his father's car.

5. Little Wang gave her boyfriend a ride to the bus stop. (送)

▼ ▼

E. Translate the passages into Chinese.

1. The airport is a long way from here. I'm afraid that there is not enough time. We must leave right away.

2. Generally speaking, if you want to travel abroad, you must first get your passport from the post office, and get your visa from the consulate. Then, after you decide which route that you are going to take, you book your plane ticket.

VI. COMPOSITION

1. 你要去中國旅行, 請你把需要辦的事情以及需要準備的東西寫出來。

   你要去中国旅行, 请你把需要办的事情以及需要准备的东西写出来。

2. 記(jì)一次有意思的旅行。

   记(jì)一次有意思的旅行。

第十課 ▲ 在郵局
第十课 ▲ 在邮局

第十课 ▲ 在邮局

I. LISTENING COMPREHENSION

A. Listen to the audio for the Textbook and answer the questions.

1. Why were Lisa and Tianming so surprised when they stepped into the post office?

2. What did Lisa and Tianming do at the post office?

3. Did Lisa and Tianming meet with Steve in Hong Kong as planned? Why or why not?

4. Why did Steve go to a post office in Taipei?

B. Listen to the audio for the Workbook.

1. Listen to the conversation and answer the questions.
   a. Where did the conversation take place?

   b. What did the man do when he was there?

   c. How much money did the man spend?

2. Listen to the passage and answer the questions.
   a. Why did Mr. Wang go to Hong Kong?

   b. Why did he return so soon?

   c. How did people find out that he was coming back?

3. Dictation: Write down Haitian's letter to his aunt in Chinese.

▼▼▼

4. Listen to Haitian's aunt's reply. Transcribe it in Chinese.

II. SPEAKING EXERCISES

A. Practice asking and answering the questions with a partner before class.

1. 美國的郵局什麼時候辦公？
   美国的邮局什么时候办公？

2. 中國郵局有哪些服務是美國郵局沒有的？
   中国邮局有哪些服务是美国邮局没有的？

3. 如果你要寄一個很重要的包裹，你怎麼寄？
   如果你要寄一个很重要的包裹，你怎么寄？

4. 你的老家有什麼特產？
   你的老家有什么特产？

B. Practice speaking on the following topics.

1. 請談一談出國旅行的時候應該注意哪些事情，怎麼樣才能讓家人放心。
   请谈一谈出国旅行的时候应该注意哪些事情，怎么样才能让家人放心。

2. 請談一談美國郵局的辦公時間，他們有什麼樣的服務，服務怎麼樣？
   请谈一谈美国邮局的办公时间，他们有什么样的服务，服务怎么样？

III. READING COMPREHENSION

A. Read the passage and answer the questions. (True/False)

(Traditional Characters)

　　張天明在南京認識了一個朋友，叫大亮。大亮快三十歲了，還沒有女朋友。
上個月大亮在互聯網 (hùliánwǎng: Internet) 上認識了一個叫麗麗的女孩子，覺得跟她很合得來。麗麗住在西安。大亮每天都給她發電子郵件 (e-mail), 也常常和她在網上聊天, 可是每次給她打電話都打不通。上個週末, 大亮帶了不少南京特產和糖果什麼的, 坐飛機去西安看麗麗。好不容易找到了麗麗, 可是沒想到麗麗原來是個男的!

(Simplified Characters)

张天明在南京认识了一个朋友, 叫大亮。大亮快三十岁了, 还没有女朋友。上个月大亮在互联网(hùliánwǎng: Internet) 上认识了一个叫丽丽的女孩子, 觉得跟她很合得来。丽丽住在西安。大亮每天都给她发电子邮件 (e-mail), 也常常和她在网上聊天, 可是每次给她打电话都打不通。上个周末, 大亮带了不少南京特产和糖果什么的, 坐飞机去西安看丽丽。好不容易找到了丽丽, 可是没想到丽丽原来是个男的!

Questions (True/False):

( ) 1. Da Liang lives in Nanjing.
( ) 2. Da Liang uses his computer often
( ) 3. Da Liang had never talked to Lili.
( ) 4. Da Liang sent Lili a package last weekend.
( ) 5. Da Liang didn't realize that Lili had a boyfriend.

B. *Read the passage and answer the question.*

(Traditional Characters)

航空郵簡比航空信便宜一些。航空信是寫完信以後, 把信紙放進信封然後寄出去。航空郵簡只有一張紙, 寫完以後, 不需要信封就可以寄出去。

(Simplified Characters)

航空邮简比航空信便宜一些。航空信是写完信以后, 把信纸放进信封然后寄出去。航空邮简只有一张纸, 写完以后, 不需要信封就可以寄出去。

Question:
What are the differences between the two items in question?

▼ ▼

C. Read the passage and answer the questions.

(Traditional Characters)

以前中國的郵局也叫郵電局。電是電話, 電報, 也就是說除了寄信, 寄包裹以外, 他們也有電話及電報的服務。所以如果要打電話, 特別是打國際長途電話, 也可以去郵電局。不過現在中國的郵局不叫郵電局了, 叫郵政局。因為有電話的家庭多了, 有手機的人也多了, 電話的服務就從郵局分出去了。

在美國, 送信的人有的走路, 有的開車。在中國, 送信的多半都是騎自行車。

(Simplified Characters)

以前中国的邮局也叫邮电局。电是电话, 电报, 也就是说除了寄信, 寄包裹以外, 他们也有电话及电报的服务。所以如果要打电话, 特别是打国际长途电话, 也可以去邮电局。不过现在中国的邮局不叫邮电局了, 叫邮政局。因为有电话的家庭多了, 有手机的人也多了, 电话的服务就从邮局分出去了。

在美国, 送信的人有的走路, 有的开车。在中国, 送信的多半都是骑自行车。

Questions:

1. Nowadays, what service is no longer in demand in the Chinese post offices? Why?

2. How do letter carriers in the United States deliver mail?

這是北京的一家郵局。他們現在辦公嗎?
这是北京的一家邮局。他们现在办公吗?

這是台北的一家郵局。什麼時候可以去那兒買郵票, 寄包裹呢?

这是台北的一家邮局。什么时候可以去那儿买邮票, 寄包裹呢?

D. Read the passage and answer the questions.

(Traditional Characters)

　　我昨天收到一張明信片, 上面只寫了我家的地址, 沒寫是誰寄的。我看著看著就笑了起來。原來這是姑媽三年以前去墨西哥旅行的時候寄給我的。姑媽和我都以為這張明信片早就寄丟了。沒想到, 長途旅行了三年以後卻平平安安地寄到了我家。

(Simplified Characters)

　　我昨天收到一张明信片, 上面只写了我家的地址, 没写是谁寄的。我看着看着就笑了起来。原来这是姑妈三年以前去墨西哥旅行的时候寄给我的。

▼▼▼▼▼▼▼▼▼▼▼▼▼▼▼▼▼▼▼▼▼▼▼▼▼▼▼▼▼▼▼▼▼

姑妈和我都以为这张明信片早就寄丢了。没想到, 长途旅行了三年以后却平平安安地寄到了我家。

Questions:

1. Who sent the postcard?

2. Why did the person start to smile after she looked at the postcard?

3. When was she supposed to receive the postcard?

E. Read the passage and answer the questions.

(Traditional Characters)

　　小林一向對人不錯,大家都很喜歡他。最近他隔壁搬來了一個新同學小高。沒想到卻跟小林相處得不太好。小林喜歡安靜, 偶爾聽聽古典音樂。小高對球賽特別有興趣, 常常一邊看球賽, 一邊喝酒。每次看完球賽, 小高都醉得很屬害, 常常激動得又喊又叫, 吵得小林睡不好覺。球賽的第二天, 小高都會很後悔地向小林說對不起。小林想搬家。可是找房子不容易, 不是房租太貴, 就是離學校太遠。沒辦法, 只好不搬。後來有一天, 小高不見了。原來他又喝醉了, 不小心把房東車子的窗戶打破了, 只好趕緊搬走。現在小林不怕有人吵他睡覺, 也不必搬家了。

(Simplified Characters)

　　小林一向对人不错,大家都很喜欢他。最近他隔壁搬来了一个新同学小高。没想到却跟小林相处得不太好。小林喜欢安静, 偶尔听听古典音乐。小高对球赛特别有兴趣, 常常一边看球赛, 一边喝酒。每次看完球赛, 小高都醉得很厉害, 常常激动得又喊又叫, 吵得小林睡不好觉。球赛的第二天, 小高都会很后悔地向小林说对不起。小林想搬家。可是找房子不容易, 不是房租太贵, 就是离学校太远。没办法, 只好不搬。后来有一天, 小高不见了。原来他又喝醉了, 不小心把房东车子的窗户打破了, 只好赶紧搬走。现在小林不怕有人吵他睡觉, 也不必搬家了。

Questions:

1. Why didn't Little Lin get along with Little Gao?

2. Was Little Gao remorseful for what he did to Little Lin? How do you know?

3. Why didn't Little Lin move away?

4. What caused Little Gao to leave?

F. 小柯去了一趟郵局, 下邊是郵局給他的收據。請看一看收據的正反兩面
(zhèngfǎn liǎngmiàn), 然後回答下面的是非題。

小柯去了一趟邮局, 下边是邮局给他的收据。请看一看收据的正反两面
(zhèngfǎn liǎngmiàn), 然后回答下面的是非题。

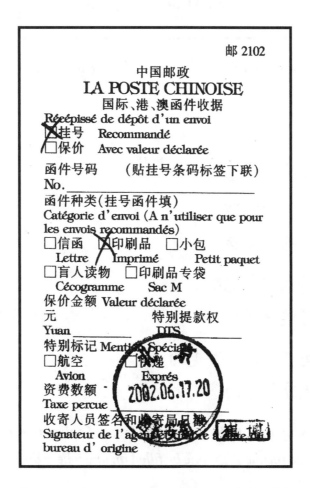

(See the Alternate Character Appendix for traditional characters.)

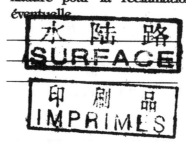

说明：
Indications：

1. 凭此据可在一年以内办理
   查询。
   La réclamation sera admise à
   la présentation de ce
   réécépissé dans le délai d'un
   an à compter du lendemain
   du jour de dépôt de l'envio.

2. 请将收件人名址填入下列
   格内以备查询。
   Veuillez inscrire, ci-après,
   le nom et l'adresse du desti-
   nataire pour la réclamation
   éventuelle.

(See the Alternate Character Appendix for traditional characters.)

是非题 (True/False):

( ) 1. 小柯寄的是信。

( ) 2. 小柯寄的是陸空聯運。
       小柯寄的是陆空联运。

( ) 3. 小柯寄的時候沒買保險。
       小柯寄的时候没买保险。

( ) 4. 小柯是從南京把東西寄走的。
       小柯是从南京把东西寄走的。

G. One must fill out a form in order to send registered mail. Look at the sample of such a form used in Taiwan. Where should the recipient's name be filled in, and where does the sender sign or place his or her chop?

中　華　郵　政
掛　號　郵　件　收　件　回　執

| 郵件種類 | 號碼 | （由郵局收寄
人員填寫） |

投　遞　記　要　｜　收件人姓名地址
（請寄件人填寫）

（供查詢時填寫）　｜　（請填收件人寫）　｜　□□□－□□

附上原掛號收據影印本一件　請查收
該機構收發單位代收訖
君收訖
經查上述郵件已於　年　月　日妥投
掛號郵件壹件
收件人蓋章
年　月　日收到第
投遞士戳
年　月　日　郵　局
號
先小
生姐

| 投　遞　後　郵　戳 | 收　寄　局　郵　戳 |

(See the Alternate Character Appendix for simplified characters.)

IV. GRAMMAR & USAGE

A. *Rewrite the following sentences using* V ＋ 著 ＋ V ＋ 著 / V ＋ 着 ＋ V ＋ 着.

EXAMPLE:　　他一直看電視, 後來在沙發上睡著了。

他一直看电视, 后来在沙发上睡着了。

→ <u>他看電視, 看著看著在沙發上睡著了。</u>

<u>他看电视, 看着看着在沙发上睡着了。</u>

1. 他喝酒, 後來唱起歌來了。

   他喝酒, 后来唱起歌来了。

   → _____。

2. 姑媽排隊買郵票, 排了不久就輪到她了。

   姑妈排队买邮票, 排了不久就轮到她了。

   → _____。

3. 小林聽音樂聽得很高興, 後來跳起舞來了。

   小林听音乐听得很高兴, 后来跳起舞来了。

   → _____。

4. 王教授的家離學校不遠, 我們一邊說話一邊走, 很快就到了。

   王教授的家离学校不远, 我们一边说话一边走, 很快就到了。

   → _____。

B. Complete the sentences using the resultative complements provided.

EXAMPLE: 小王下個月出國旅行, 飛機票旅行社已經幫他訂好了。(好)

                  小王下个月出国旅行, 飞机票旅行社已经帮他订好了。(好)

1. 表哥寄了一個包裹, 可是地址寫錯了, 結果_____。(丟)

   表哥寄了一个包裹, 可是地址写错了, 结果_____。(丢)

2. 張先生和張太太吵架, 把屋子裏的鏡子_____。(破)

   张先生和张太太吵架, 把屋子里的镜子_____。(破)

3. 小李天天反復練習寫漢字, 要不然他怕_____。(錯)

   小李天天反复练习写汉字, 要不然他怕_____。(错)

4. 那本書很有意思, 我很喜歡, 買回來以後, 很快就_____。(完)

   那本书很有意思, 我很喜欢, 买回来以后, 很快就_____。(完)

C. Complete the sentences using 卻/却.

EXAMPLE: a: 南京今年的夏天怎麼樣? 熱死了吧?!

          南京今年的夏天怎么样? 热死了吧?!

▼▼

    b: 老聽別人說南京的夏天熱得很, 沒想到今年<u>卻挺涼快的</u>。

      老听别人说南京的夏天热得很, 没想到今年<u>却挺凉快的</u>。

1. a: 學校禮堂演的那個紀錄片, 你看了覺得怎麼樣?

    學校礼堂演的那个纪录片, 你看了觉得怎么样?

    b: 我一直以為紀錄片沒意思, 但是這一部

      我一直以为纪录片没意思, 但是这一部

    _____。

2. a: 你看, 小梅身上穿的那件衣服是名牌, 質量肯定好。

    你看, 小梅身上穿的那件衣服是名牌, 质量肯定好。

    b: 名牌是名牌, 可是質量

      名牌是名牌, 可是质量

    _____。

3. a: 奇怪, 小陳今天怎麼只點了兩盤素菜?

    奇怪, 小陈今天怎么只点了两盘素菜?

    b: 是啊! 他一向喜歡吃肉, 今天

      是啊! 他一向喜欢吃肉, 今天

    _____。

D. Fill in the blanks with 一直 or 一向.

1. 從上大學以來, 他_____住在學校宿舍裏。

   从上大学以来, 他_____住在学校宿舍里。

2. 他出門旅行_____不寫明信片, 不買特產。

   他出门旅行_____不写明信片, 不买特产。

3. 小張跟他的女朋友鬧翻了以後, 心情_____很受影響。

   小张跟他的女朋友闹翻了以后, 心情_____很受影响。

▼▼▼▼▼▼▼▼▼▼▼▼▼▼▼▼▼▼▼▼▼▼▼▼▼▼▼▼▼▼▼▼▼▼▼▼▼

4. 學校禮堂＿＿＿＿＿演藝術片或者紀錄片, 從來不演商業片。

   学校礼堂＿＿＿＿＿演艺术片或者纪录片, 从来不演商业片。

5. 林先生到波士頓上研究所以來, ＿＿＿＿＿不太適應那兒的生活。

   林先生到波士顿上研究所以来, ＿＿＿＿＿不太适应那儿的生活。

6. 我＿＿＿＿＿不喜歡做菜, 只要有人做, 我就不做。

   我＿＿＿＿＿不喜欢做菜, 只要有人做, 我就不做。

E. *Complete the dialogue using the five words provided. Each word may be used only once.*

(Traditional)

趕快, 趁, 一向, 肯定, 正好

a: 快放假了, 出國旅行的人越來越多。我打算去英國旅行, 但是我的簽證和護照都還沒辦呢。

b: 你得＿＿＿＿＿辦, 要不然＿＿＿＿＿來不及。

a: 我最近＿＿＿＿＿特別忙。沒空跑來跑去辦這些事。

b: 那這樣吧, ＿＿＿＿＿這兩天我不太忙, 我幫你辦, 怎麼樣?

a: 那太好了。你做事情＿＿＿＿＿可靠, 我放心。

(Simplified)

赶快, 趁, 一向, 肯定, 正好

a: 快放假了, 出国旅行的人越来越多。我打算去英国旅行, 但是我的签证和护照都还没办呢。

b: 你得＿＿＿＿＿办, 要不然＿＿＿＿＿来不及。

a: 我最近＿＿＿＿＿特别忙。没空跑来跑去办这些事。

b: 那这样吧, ＿＿＿＿＿这两天我不太忙, 我帮你办, 怎么样?

a: 那太好了。你做事情＿＿＿＿＿可靠, 我放心。

▼▼

V. TRANSLATION

A. Translate the passage into Chinese.

Before they knew it, Zhang Tianming and his girlfriend arrived at the post office. The people at the post office spoke the Nanjing dialect (南京話／南京话) to Zhang Tianming. Zhang Tianming couldn't understand it. It never occurred to him that he wouldn't understand Chinese.

B. Translate the dialogue into Chinese.

Zhang Tianming:　Are you tired from walking?

Lisa:　　　　　　A little.

Zhang Tianming:　The summer in Nanjing is so hot. No wonder people say Nanjing is like a furnace.

Lisa:　　　　　　Actually, it's not that terrible. Where else do you want to go sightseeing?

Zhang Tianming:　Wherever is not hot.

C. Translate the passage into Chinese.

On my way to school, I went to the post office to send some parcels to my friends. There were a lot of people. I had to stand in line, and I waited and waited and fell asleep.

D. Translate the sentences into Chinese. Pay attention to the relationship between the attributives and 的.

1. Post offices in China do not process passport applications.

2. The house he rented is very close to the track field.

3. The TV program we saw last night was a documentary film.

4. The person sitting on the sofa is my roommate Little Zhang.

5. The person who played with matches and caused the fire turned out to be a little boy.

E. Translate the sentences using 趁.

1. Let's ask the landlord to buy a new air conditioner while he is in a good mood.

2. While your parents are watching the basketball game, let's take a walk in the park.

3. While you have some free time right now, could I trouble you to mail this package for me?

4. Hurry! Buy a sports outfit while it is on sale.

F. *Translate the passage into Chinese.*

Chinese New Year will soon be here. I have a lot of errands to run. It is my turn to buy groceries this time. Yesterday, I took the opportunity (when I had some free time) to go shopping. No matter where I went, I had to stand in line and wait. After I finished shopping, I went to the post office on my way home to mail some postcards to my friends in China. I hope my cards won't get lost in the mail.

VI. COMPOSITION

1. 你剛從美國坐飛機到中國去旅行, 請寫一封信給你的中文老師, 告訴他你一路上都很順利。不要忘了寫信封。

   你刚从美国坐飞机到中国去旅行, 请写一封信给你的中文老师, 告诉他你一路上都很顺利。不要忘了写信封。

信封

風景明信片 ／风景明信片

2. The following is background information for a phone conversation between you and your travel agent. Compose a conversation in Chinese based on the information.

You phone your travel agent and tell him or her that you need to change the itinerary for your trip to China. You first repeat your original travel plan, including the dates, places, and activities. Then you ask him or her to re-book your airline tickets and hotel reservations since you need to depart two days earlier and add a stop at Shanghai to visit your old roommate, whom you haven't seen for more than two years. You might get re-routed due to seat availability, the travel agent says, and you probably will pay penalties for these late changes. He or she reminds you to have all travel documents ready before your departure and not to make any more changes. Compose this conversation with the proper telephone etiquette.

▼ ▼

3. The following is background information for a conversation in a post office in China. Compose a conversation in Chinese based on the information.

Your mother asks you to go to the post office to pick up a package, buy stamps, and mail a parcel to your aunt in France. After you arrive, you first make sure that you are at the right window for the services you need. Then you ask the clerk how much the parcel weighs, how much postage you need to put on it, and how long it will take for the parcel to get to France. The clerk asks about the contents of the parcel and what kind of shipping you prefer. You buy ten $0.60 stamps from the clerk and tell him or her that you need to pick up a package. The clerk asks you to sign the receipt and wants to see a photo ID. Because you don't have an ID on you, you have to come back for the package tomorrow. The clerk tells you that the post office is only open from 8:00 AM to 12:00 PM tomorrow.

第十一課 ▲ 一封信

I. LISTENING COMPREHENSION

A. Listen to the audio for the Textbook and answer the questions.

1. How many places had Tianming and Lisa been to on their sightseeing trip at the time of the letter?

2. What do they like about the Temple of Confucius?

3. Why are they most impressed with the Sun Yat-sen Mausoleum?

4. Which city are they heading to next?

B. Listen to the audio for the Workbook.

1. Listen to the conversation between Zhang Tianming and his cousin, and answer the multiple-choice questions.

    (   ) a. The dialogue took place
        1) in a restaurant.
        2) outside a movie theater.
        3) in a park.
        4) outside a restroom.

    (   ) b. Zhang Tianming and his cousin got separated because
        1) his cousin went boating without him.
        2) there were too many people in the park.
        3) his cousin went shopping without him.
        4) his cousin didn't want to be seen with foreigners.

    (   ) c. Zhang Tianming's cousin wouldn't let him stand in a queue because
        1) Zhang Tianming talked too much and was not very attentive.
        2) Zhang Tianming frequently needed to use the restroom.
        3) Zhang Tianming was too conspicuously foreign.
        4) Zhang Tianming was too lazy and gave up too easily.

2. Listen to the passage and answer the multiple-choice questions.

(　) a. The speaker is very likely a

　　1) government official.

　　2) host of a radio program.

　　3) host of a TV program.

　　4) concerned teacher.

(　) b. The weather has been

　　1) very seasonable.

　　2) very hot.

　　3) very cold.

　　4) neither too hot nor too cold.

(　) c. The speaker asks the audience to pay attention to

　　1) his and his family's health.

　　2) his level of activity.

　　3) his food intake.

　　4) his environment.

(　) d. The audience should

　　1) tune in more often.

　　2) relax more.

　　3) play with children more often.

　　4) drink more water and avoid going out frequently.

(　) e. Children

　　1) should have three to four hours of play time every day.

　　2) should have at least three or four friends.

　　3) shouldn't play between noon and four o'clock.

　　4) shouldn't have three to four hours of play time.

(　) f. One shouldn't

　　1) eat too much.

　　2) exercise in hot weather.

　　3) drink cold water immediately after exercising.

　　4) take a cold shower immediately after exercising.

(　) g. Old people should

　　1) go out more.

　　2) eat more fruit and vegetables.

　　3) be with children.

　　4) watch less TV.

3. Listen to the passage and answer the multiple-choice questions.

(   ) a. The speaker is a

     1) history teacher.

     2) tour guide.

     3) telephone repairman.

     4) government official.

(   ) b. A gòngyuàn is a(n)

     1) amusement park in Nanjing.

     2) public telephone booth.

     3) complex where examinations were held.

     4) room for officials to relax.

(   ) c. Kējǔ kǎoshì was a(n)

     1) imperial civil service examination.

     2) physical examination.

     3) final examination.

     4) mid-term examination.

(   ) d. Examinations were held

     1) everywhere.

     2) at a special place.

     3) at a different place every time.

     4) at a different place every year.

(   ) e. The cubicles did not have doors because the proctors

     1) felt it was too hot in Nanjing.

     2) had them taken down for repair.

     3) wanted to see what the candidates were doing.

     4) could hear better when the candidates asked questions.

II. SPEAKING EXERCISES

A. Practice asking and answering the questions with a partner before class.

1. 你遊覽過哪些名勝古蹟？

     你游览过哪些名胜古迹？

2. 你對美國哪一個城市的印象最深？為什麼？

     你对美国哪一个城市的印象最深？为什么？

3. 你覺得你的老家有什麼吸引人的地方？

你觉得你的老家有什么吸引人的地方？

4. "人老珠黃"是什麼意思？

"人老珠黄"是什么意思？

B. *Practice speaking on the following topic.*

請你介紹一下美國的一個名勝古蹟。

请你介绍一下美国的一个名胜古迹。

III. READING COMPREHENSION

A. *Read the passage and answer the questions.*

(Traditional Characters)

我們的校園有山有水，環境好，風景美，每棟建築都別具風格，常常有許多遊客來遊覽。難怪有人說我們的校園比公園更吸引人。可是學校的教授認為遊客太多，難免會影響學生學習。他們建議只讓遊客週末進校園，這個建議引起了一些爭論。

(Simplified Characters)

我们的校园有山有水，环境好，风景美，每栋建筑都别具风格，常常有许多游客来游览。难怪有人说我们的校园比公园更吸引人。可是学校的教授认为游客太多，难免会影响学生学习。他们建议只让游客周末进校园，这个建议引起了一些争论。

Questions:

1. What attracts tourists to the campus? List at least three things.

2. What is the faculty's concern?

3. What does the faculty suggest?

4. Do you think the suggestion will work? Why or why not?

B. Read the passage and answer the questions. (True/False)

(Traditional)

爸爸媽媽:

　　沒想到西安的旅館裏也可以發電子郵件, 真是太方便了。西安沒有上海那麼大, 可是名勝古蹟特別多, 建築也別具風格。西安最吸引人的地方是中國第一個皇帝 (1) 的陵墓。那個皇帝真是個奇怪的人, 他讓成千上萬個泥人 (2) 跟他葬在一起。那些泥人看起來就像真人一樣。另外, 我們在華清池聽到不少楊貴妃的故事。聽說她是當時中國最美的女人, 可是卻很胖。看來麗莎的看法有道理: 女孩子不一定要瘦才漂亮。要是楊貴妃還活著, 麗莎說不定要去找她做朋友呢。姑媽說過幾天有個重要的節日, 要我們後天回南京。

　　　　敬祝

安好！

　　　　　　　　　　　　　　　　　　　　　　　天明

(1) 皇帝(huángdì): emperor
(2) 泥人(nírén): terracotta figures

(Simplified)

爸爸妈妈:

　　没想到西安的旅馆里也可以发电子邮件, 真是太方便了。西安没有上海那么大, 可是名胜古迹特别多, 建筑也别具风格。西安最吸引人的地方是中国第一个皇帝 (1) 的陵墓。那个皇帝真是个奇怪的人, 他让成千上万个泥人 (2) 跟他葬在一起。那些泥人看起来就像真人一样。另外, 我们在华清池听到不少杨贵妃的故事。听说她是当时中国最美的女人, 可是却很胖。看来丽莎的看法有道理: 女孩子不一定要瘦才漂亮。要是杨贵妃还活着, 丽莎说不定要去找她做朋友呢。姑妈说过几天有个重要的节日, 要我们后天回南京。

敬祝

安好！

天明

(1) 皇帝(huángdì): emperor
(2) 泥人(nírén): terracotta figures

Questions (True/False):

( ) 1. Zhang Tianming had to go to the post office to mail the letter.

( ) 2. Most likely Zhang Tianming stayed at a hotel when he was in Xi'an.

( ) 3. According to Zhang Tianming, Xi'an is similar to Shanghai, although smaller.

( ) 4. Zhang Tianming thinks China's first emperor must have been a most remarkable man.

( ) 5. Among all the tourist spots in Xi'an, Zhang Tianming seemed to like Huaqing Springs the most.

( ) 6. Lisa is interested in maintaining her slim figure.

( ) 7. In Xi'an, Lisa befriended a Chinese girl.

( ) 8. Zhang Tianming and Lisa were going to be back in Nanjing in a couple of days.

C. *Read the description of Nanjing and answer the questions. (True/False)*

(Traditional Characters)

南京

在中國歷史上, 南京曾經是好幾個朝代 (1) 的國都 (2), 所以市內和郊區 (3) 都有很多歷史古蹟。城裏有一條河, 叫秦淮河, 雖然現在只是一條不太吸引人的小河, 可是它很有名。兩百年前, 秦淮河兩岸曾經是南京最熱鬧的地方之一。一到晚上, 河上到處都是船, 船上的遊客有的喝酒做詩, 有的看唱歌跳舞, 非常熱鬧。在中國文學史上, 不少詩人作家曾被秦淮河所吸引, 並且寫了一些跟秦淮河有關的書、詩詞和文章。

▼▼

(1)　朝代 (cháodài): dynasty

(2)　國都 (guódū): capital of the country

(3)　郊區 (jiāoqū): outskirts; suburbs

(Simplified Characters)

南京

　　在中国历史上, 南京曾经是好几个朝代 (1) 的国都 (2), 所以市内和郊区 (3) 都有很多历史古迹。城里有一条河, 叫秦淮河, 虽然现在只是一条不太吸引人的小河, 可是它很有名。两百年前, 秦淮河两岸曾经是南京最热闹的地方之一。一到晚上, 河上到处都是船, 船上的游客有的喝酒做诗, 有的看唱歌跳舞, 非常热闹。在中国文学史上, 不少诗人作家曾被秦淮河所吸引, 并且写了一些跟秦淮河有关的书、诗词和文章。

(1)　朝代 (cháodài): dynasty

(2)　国都 (guódū): capital of the country

(3)　郊区 (jiāoqū): outskirts; suburbs

Questions (True/ False):

(　　) 1.　兩百年前秦淮河兩岸有很多學校。

　　　　　兩百年前秦淮河兩岸有很多学校。

(　　) 2.　歷史上不少詩人作家到秦淮河岸邊賣他們寫的書。

　　　　　历史上不少诗人作家到秦淮河岸边卖他们写的书。

(　　) 3.　秦淮河在歷史上很有名, 是因為不少詩人作家都在文章裏提到它。

　　　　　秦淮河在历史上很有名, 是因为不少诗人作家都在文章里提到它。

(　　) 4.　歷史上的秦淮河是很多人喜歡去的地方。

　　　　　历史上的秦淮河是很多人喜欢去的地方。

(　　) 5.　中國歷史上有不少皇帝在南京住過。

　　　　　中国历史上有不少皇帝在南京住过。

D. Many travel agencies post fliers and ads on the Internet. The following is a list of local tours in Nanjing offered by a travel agency. Circle the ones that are mentioned in this lesson.

☎ 南京中山陵
☎ 句容茅山
☎ 南京中华门
☎ 南京郑和墓
☎ 南京朝天宫
☎ 南京秦淮风光带
☎ 南京中山植物园
☎ 南京紫霞湖
☎ 南京紫金山天文台
☎ 南京栖霞山
☎ 南京玄武湖
☎ 南京桂子山石柱林
☎ 南京汤山风景区
☎ 南京长江大桥
☎ 南京明孝陵
☎ 南京总统府
☎ 南京莫愁湖
☎ 南京雨花台
☎ 南京固城湖
☎ 南京长江二桥

(See the Alternate Character Appendix for traditional characters.)

E. Read the story and answer the questions. (True/False)

(Traditional Characters)

東施效(1)顰(2)

　　中國古代有一個美女叫西施 (3), 大家都認為她長得非常美。西施的隔壁住著一個叫東施 (4) 的女人, 她看見西施那麼好看, 聽見別人都說西施漂亮,

非常羨慕 (5)。有一天, 西施病了, 皺 (6) 著眉頭 (7), 從東施的家門前走過。東施
看見了,覺得西施皺著眉頭的樣子非常好看,就模仿西施的樣子,整天皺著眉頭。
大家見了她, 不是趕緊關上門不出來了, 就是趕緊走開了。

　　東施只知道西施皺眉的樣子好看, 可是她不知道為什麼西施皺眉好看。
請你們猜猜"東施效顰"這句話的意思是什麼?

(1)　效(xiào): to imitate; (literary) 模仿, 仿效
(2)　顰(pín): to knit one's eyebrows; (literary) 皺眉
(3)　西施(Xīshī): a person's name
(4)　東施(Dōngshī): a person's name
(5)　羨慕(xiànmù): to envy; envious
(6)　皺(zhòu): to wrinkle; to furrow
(7)　眉頭(méitóu): eyebrows

(Simplified Characters)

东施效 (1) 颦 (2)

　　中国古代有一个美女叫西施 (3), 大家都认为她长得非常美。西施的隔壁
住着一个叫东施 (4) 的女人, 她看见西施那么好看, 听见别人都说西施漂亮,
非常羡慕 (5)。有一天, 西施病了, 皱 (6) 着眉头 (7), 从东施的家门前走过。东施
看见了,觉得西施皱着眉头的样子非常好看,就模仿西施的样子,整天皱着眉头。
大家见了她, 不是赶紧关上门不出来了, 就是赶紧走开了。

　　东施只知道西施皱眉的样子好看, 可是她不知道为什么西施皱眉好看。
请你们猜猜 "东施效颦" 这句话的意思是什么?

(1)　效(xiào): to imitate; (literary) 模仿, 仿效
(2)　颦(pín): to knit one's eyebrows; (literary)皱眉
(3)　西施(Xīshī): person's name
(4)　东施(Dōngshī): person's name
(5)　羡慕(xiànmù): to envy; envious
(6)　皱(zhòu): to wrinkle; to furrow
(7)　眉头(méitóu): eyebrows

▼▼

Questions (True/False):

(   ) 1.   大家都説西施好看。

             大家都说西施好看。

(   ) 2.   東施希望自己和西施一樣好看。

             东施希望自己和西施一样好看。

(   ) 3.   西施皺眉頭的樣子很好看。

             西施皱眉头的样子很好看。

(   ) 4.   東施皺眉的樣子一點兒不好看。

             东施皱眉的样子一点儿不好看。

(   ) 5.   東施不知道西施為什麼好看。

             东施不知道西施为什么好看。

(   ) 6.   這個故事是叫人不要隨便地模仿別人。

             这个故事是叫人不要随便地模仿别人。

E. Nanjing is an important metropolis in the lower Yangtze valley. Its long history and rich cultural tradition have left many historic sights in the city and the suburbs, making Nanjing one of the major tourist cities in China. Read the passage taken from a tourist brochure about the Sun Yat-sen Mausoleum and circle the answers to the questions.

(Traditional Characters)

中山陵

     中山陵, 是偉大的革命先行者(gémìng xiānxíngzhě)孫中山先生的陵墓, 建于南京東郊(dōngjiāo)景色秀麗(jǐngsè xiùlì)的紫金山南麓(nánlù)。

     孫中山先生, 原名孫文,號逸仙, 1866年11月12日生于廣東香山縣(今中山縣)翠亨村, 1925年(民國14年)3月12日逝世(shìshì)于北京。

     為了紀念孫中山先生的豐功偉績(fēnggōngwěijì), 在他逝世以後, 為他建造了這座雄偉壯麗(xióngwěizhuànglì)的陵墓。

(Simplified Characters)

中山陵

　　中山陵, 是伟大的革命先行者(géming xiānxíngzhě)孙中山先生的陵墓, 建于南京东郊(dōngjiāo)景色秀丽(jǐngsè xiùlì)的紫金山南麓(nánlù)。

　　孙中山先生, 原名孙文, 号逸仙, 1866年11月12日生于广东香山县(今中山县)翠亨村, 1925年(民国14年)3月12日逝世(shìshì)于北京。

　　为了纪念孙中山先生的丰功伟绩(fēnggōngwěijì), 在他逝世以后, 为他建造了这座雄伟壮丽(xióngwěizhuànglì)的陵墓。

Questions:

1. 中山陵在南京的什麽地方?
   中山陵在南京的什么地方?

2. 孙中山原来的名字是什麽?
   孙中山原来的名字是什么?

3. 孙中山的出生地原来的名字是什麽?
   孙中山的出生地原来的名字是什么?

4. 那個地方現在叫什麽?
   那个地方现在叫什么?

IV. GRAMMAR & USAGE

A. *Fill in the blanks with either* 以來 / 以来 *or* 來/来.

1. 柯林上大學＿＿＿＿＿＿, 一直是白天上課, 晚上打工。
   柯林上大学＿＿＿＿＿＿, 一直是白天上课, 晚上打工。

2. 十年＿＿＿＿＿＿, 他一直在同一家航空公司工作。

3. 自從當記者＿＿＿＿＿＿, 小王每個月都得出差好幾次。
   自从当记者＿＿＿＿＿＿, 小王每个月都得出差好几次。

4. 兩個星期＿＿＿＿＿＿, 姑媽遊覽了十多個名勝古蹟。
   两个星期＿＿＿＿＿＿, 姑妈游览了十多个名胜古迹。

5. 柯林自從愛上林雪梅＿＿＿＿＿＿, 整天吃不下飯, 睡不好覺。
   柯林自从爱上林雪梅＿＿＿＿＿＿, 整天吃不下饭, 睡不好觉。

B. *Fill in the blanks with either* 才 *or* 就.

1. 一般人大學念四年畢業, 我弟弟念了五年＿＿＿＿畢業。
   一般人大学念四年毕业, 我弟弟念了五年＿＿＿＿毕业。

2. 小張每次買東西都得買三、四個鐘頭, 沒想到今天一個鐘頭＿＿＿＿買完了。
   小张每次买东西都得买三、四个钟头, 没想到今天一个钟头＿＿＿＿买完了。

3. 郵局的服務員跟我說我寄給我指導教授的掛號信兩天＿＿＿＿會到, 但是我的老師四天＿＿＿＿收到。
   邮局的服务员跟我说我寄给我指导教授的挂号信两天＿＿＿＿会到, 但是我的老师四天＿＿＿＿收到。

4. 別的同學租房子都很容易, 一下子＿＿＿＿找到了合適的房子。可是我找了三個星期＿＿＿＿找到合適的。
   别的同学租房子都很容易, 一下子＿＿＿＿找到了合适的房子。可是我找了三个星期＿＿＿＿找到合适的。

5. 小林的表弟說好八點鐘來飛機場接小林, 但是他差不多九點鐘＿＿＿到。

   小林的表弟说好八点钟来飞机场接小林, 但是他差不多九点钟＿＿＿到。

C. Rearrange the order of the attributes (note the addition of 的).

EXAMPLE: 　　好、一種、酒、他喜歡喝 → <u>他喜歡喝的一種好酒</u>

　　　　　好、一种、酒、他喜欢喝 → <u>他喜欢喝的一种好酒</u>

1. 從圖書館借、昨天、書、舊、一本

   从图书馆借、昨天、书、旧、一本

   → ＿＿＿＿＿＿＿＿＿＿＿＿＿＿＿＿＿＿＿＿＿＿

2. 一件、衣服、新、媽媽給我做

   一件、衣服、新、妈妈给我做

   → ＿＿＿＿＿＿＿＿＿＿＿＿＿＿＿＿＿＿＿＿＿＿

3. 秘密、一個、小、他告訴我

   秘密、一个、小、他告诉我

   → ＿＿＿＿＿＿＿＿＿＿＿＿＿＿＿＿＿＿＿＿＿＿

4. 可怕的、電視裏播、那個、故事

   可怕的、电视里播、那个、故事

   → ＿＿＿＿＿＿＿＿＿＿＿＿＿＿＿＿＿＿＿＿＿＿

D. Complete the following dialogues using 催.

EXAMPLE: a: 去機場的車快開了, 可是小李還在化妝。

　　　　　　去机场的车快开了, 可是小李还在化妆。

　　　　 b: <u>催她快一點兒</u>。

　　　　　　<u>催她快一点儿</u>。

1. a: 你的孩子每天睡得早嗎?

　　你的孩子每天睡得早吗?

　 b: 不, 我每天得＿＿＿＿＿＿＿＿＿＿＿＿＿＿＿＿＿＿。

2. a: 快過新年了, 你們卡片寄了沒有?

　　 快过新年了, 你们卡片寄了没有?

　　b: 還沒有。我先生還沒寫完呢。我得＿＿＿＿＿＿＿＿＿＿＿＿＿＿＿＿＿。

　　 还没有。我先生还没写完呢。我得＿＿＿＿＿＿＿＿＿＿＿＿＿＿＿＿＿。

3. a: 這家餐館的生意真好。

　　 这家餐馆的生意真好。

　　b: 可不是嗎? 要是你吃得太慢, 老闆會＿＿＿＿＿＿＿＿＿＿＿＿＿＿。

　　 可不是吗? 要是你吃得太慢, 老板会＿＿＿＿＿＿＿＿＿＿＿＿＿＿。

4. a: 飛機馬上就要起飛了, 你能不能開快一點兒?

　　 飞机马上就要起飞了, 你能不能开快一点儿?

　　b: 我開得已經夠快的了。別＿＿＿＿＿＿＿＿＿＿＿＿＿＿, 來得及。

　　 我开得已经够快的了。别＿＿＿＿＿＿＿＿＿＿＿＿＿＿, 来得及。

E. Complete the following dialogues using 忍不住.

EXAMPLE: a: 你不是不喜歡吃魚嗎? 怎麼今天吃起魚來了?

　　　　　 你不是不喜欢吃鱼吗? 怎么今天吃起鱼来了?

　　　　b: 沒辦法, 我餓死了! <u>忍不住吃了兩口</u>。

　　　　　 没办法, 我饿死了! <u>忍不住吃了两口</u>。

1. a: 那個小孩長得確實很可愛。

　　 那个小孩长得确实很可爱。

　　b: 可不是嗎? 大家都＿＿＿＿＿＿＿＿＿＿＿＿＿＿＿。(多看兩眼)

　　 可不是吗? 大家都＿＿＿＿＿＿＿＿＿＿＿＿＿＿＿。(多看两眼)

2. a: 昨天咱們學校的籃球隊打得真好。

　　 昨天咱们学校的篮球队打得真好。

　　b: 對。我同屋看得大喊大叫, 連我也＿＿＿＿＿＿＿＿＿＿＿＿。

　　 对。我同屋看得大喊大叫, 连我也＿＿＿＿＿＿＿＿＿＿＿＿。

▼▼▼

3. a: 這個演員演的喜劇都非常有意思。

    这个演员演的喜剧都非常有意思。

   b: 我也常看他演的戲。每次我都會

    我也常看他演的戏。每次我都会＿＿＿＿＿＿＿＿＿＿＿＿＿＿。(哈哈大笑)

F. Fill in the blanks using 跟, 對/对, *or* 向.

1. 他老＿＿＿別人借錢, 可是常常不還。(對、向)

   他老＿＿＿別人借钱, 可是常常不还。(对、向)

2. 他＿＿＿我要王老師的電話號碼, 可是我沒有。(對、跟)

   他＿＿＿我要王老师的电话号码, 可是我没有。(对、跟)

3. 他現在的車是＿＿＿我買的。(跟、對)

   他现在的车是＿＿＿我买的。(跟、对)

4. 小張每次買東西都會＿＿＿售貨員要收據。(向、對)

   小张每次买东西都会＿＿＿售货员要收据。(向、对)

G. List in English four places or occasions that fit the descriptions.

1. 人山人海:

   a)＿＿＿＿＿＿＿＿＿＿＿＿＿＿＿   b)＿＿＿＿＿＿＿＿＿＿＿＿＿＿＿

   c)＿＿＿＿＿＿＿＿＿＿＿＿＿＿＿   d)＿＿＿＿＿＿＿＿＿＿＿＿＿＿＿

2. 別具風格 / 别具风格:

   a)＿＿＿＿＿＿＿＿＿＿＿＿＿＿＿   b)＿＿＿＿＿＿＿＿＿＿＿＿＿＿＿

   c)＿＿＿＿＿＿＿＿＿＿＿＿＿＿＿   d)＿＿＿＿＿＿＿＿＿＿＿＿＿＿＿

3. 十分壯觀 / 十分壮观:

   a)＿＿＿＿＿＿＿＿＿＿＿＿＿＿＿   b)＿＿＿＿＿＿＿＿＿＿＿＿＿＿＿

   c)＿＿＿＿＿＿＿＿＿＿＿＿＿＿＿   d)＿＿＿＿＿＿＿＿＿＿＿＿＿＿＿

▼▼

H. Foreign travelers are asked to fill out an entry card and a departure card when they enter or leave China. Chinese citizens have to do the same. However, they need to fill them out in Chinese characters. Take a look of the two cards and see how much you could fill in if you were Chinese.

入境登记卡（边防检查）

中国公民（含港澳台）填写
请使用中文填写，内请划 ✓

| 姓 名 | | 男 □ 女 □ | 官方使用 |

证件号码

签注号码

签注签发地

船名/车次/航班号

来自何地

国内住址

出生日期 年 月 日

国籍（地区）
中国 □（香港 □ 澳门 □ 台湾 □ ）

入境事由（只能填写一项）
会议/商务 □　访问 □　观光/休闲 □
探亲访友 □　就业 □　学习 □
返回常住地 □　定居 □　其他 □

证件种类

以上申明真实完整。如有不实填报，愿承担由此引起的一切法律责任。

签名

入境日期 年 月 日

出入境管理局监制 公安部

J(03.12)

出境登记卡（边防检查）

中国公民（含港澳台）填写
请使用中文填写，内请划 ✓

姓 名　　男 □ 女 □　官方使用

证件号码

出生日期 年 月 日

国籍（地区）中国 □（香港 □ 澳门 □ 台湾 □ ）

航班号 车次 船名

前往何地

国内住址

出境事由（只能填写一项）
会议/商务 □　访问 □　观光/休闲 □
探亲访友 □　就业 □　学习 □
返回常住地 □　定居 □　其他 □

证件种类

以上申明真实完整。如有不实填报，愿承担由此引起的一切法律责任。

签名

出境日期 年 月 日

出入境管理局监制 公安部

J(03.12)

(See the Alternate Character Appendix for traditional characters.)

▼▼▼

V. TRANSLATION

Translate the passages into Chinese.

1. Tomorrow is my father's birthday. My mother had been repeatedly urging me to go shopping for a sweater. This afternoon I didn't have any classes, so I took the opportunity to go shopping. There were huge crowds of people in the shopping center, which made me realize what "crowded" really meant. After two hours, I succeeded in buying a sweater. On my way home, I went to the post office to pick up a package for my father. It was a book sent by my aunt to my father.

2. Several days ago we went to a park. It was a Sunday. There were huge crowds of people in the park. First, we went boating on the lake. Then, we took a walk in the woods. We liked the trees there very much. There was also a very old, very interesting temple in the park. It had a unique architectural style. Our friend Anderson liked the temple very much. He looked at the temple for a long time, and wasn't willing to leave. We had to urge him again and again. Finally, he reluctantly left (the temple) with us.

    (別具風格, 戀戀不捨, 人山人海)

    (别具风格, 恋恋不舍, 人山人海)

This is a sign posted at the Beijing Capital Airport.

(See the Alternate Character Appendix for traditional characters.)

VI. COMPOSITION

你最喜歡去什麼地方旅遊？為什麼？

你最喜欢去什么地方旅游？为什么？

第十二課　▲　中國的節日
第十二课　▲　中国的节日

I. LISTENING COMPREHENSION

A. Listen to the audio for the Textbook and answer the questions.

1. What is the pouch for?

2. Why did the poet commit suicide?

3. What are the major holidays in China?

B. Listen to the audio for the Workbook.

1. Listen to the story and answer the multiple-choice questions.

（　）a. Zhang Tianming's aunt took him to
    1) pay respects to his grandparents at their tombs.
    2) go mountain climbing.
    3) buy fresh flowers and fruit.
    4) clean the family cottage on the mountain.

（　）b. On the fifth day of the fourth month on the lunar calendar Chinese people
    1) visit their grandparents.
    2) clean their houses thoroughly.
    3) go hiking with family members.
    4) pay respects to their deceased ancestors.

（　）c. Zhang Tianming's aunt took him to the mountain because
    1) the weather was very good that day.
    2) there were very few people on the mountain.
    3) it was a rare opportunity since Zhang Tianming lived in America.
    4) mountain climbing was Zhang Tianming's passion.

2. Listen to the story and answer the multiple-choice questions.

（　）a. When Ke Lin went to Lin Xuemei's home for the first time, it was
    1) during the Mid-Autumn Festival.
    2) during the Spring Festival.
    3) Christmas Day.
    4) New Year's Eve.

(   ) b. Ke Lin ate the whole fish because

      1)   he didn't like the other dishes.

      2)   there was only one main course.

      3)   it was very good.

      4)   he wanted to please the host.

(   ) c. Ke Lin kept sweeping the floor because

      1)   he felt bad and wanted to pick up the mess.

      2)   the floor was very greasy.

      3)   Lin Xuemei's mother asked him to.

      4)   Lin Xuemei was angry with him.

(   ) d. Lin Xuemei kept staring at Ke Lin because

      1)   he was being very rude.

      2)   he was being too shy.

      3)   he had violated Chinese customs.

      4)   he had embarrassed her.

(   ) e. Chinese people always leave some of the fish uneaten on the eve of Chinese New Year because

      1)   there is too much food.

      2)   they have to offer the fish to their deceased ancestors.

      3)   it is a good omen to leave some of the fish uneaten.

      4)   they can only eat the rest of the fish next year.

II. SPEAKING EXERCISES

A. Practice asking and answering the following questions with a partner before class.

1. 你最喜歡過什麼節？為什麼？

    你最喜欢过什么节？为什么？

2. 對你來說哪個節日最重要？為什麼？

    对你来说哪个节日最重要？为什么？

3. 過什麼節你會儘可能回家和家人團圓？

    过什么节你会尽可能回家和家人团圆？

4. 中國人過春節的時候做些什麼？

    中国人过春节的时候做些什么？

5. 粽子和賽龍舟跟屈原有什麼關係？

粽子和赛龙舟跟屈原有什么关系？

B. *Practice speaking on the following topics.*

1. 請談談美國有哪些風俗習慣。

请谈谈美国有哪些风俗习惯。

2. 談談你家過感恩節(Gǎn'ēn Jié: Thanksgiving)或聖誕節(Shèngdàn Jié: Christmas)的情況。如果你家不過感恩節或聖誕節, 那請你談談你家過什麼節, 怎麼過。

谈谈你家过感恩节(Gǎn'ēn Jié: Thanksgiving)或圣诞节(Shèngdàn Jié: Christmas)的情况。如果你家不过感恩节或圣诞节, 那请你谈谈你家过什么节, 怎么过。

III. READING COMPREHENSION

A. *Read the passage and answer the questions. (True/False)*

(Traditional Characters)

　　麗莎覺得屈原的故事很動人, 她認為屈原確實是中國歷史上的偉大人物。可是張天明的想法不大一樣。他認為屈原是個憂國憂民的好官, 可是無論怎樣他也不應該自殺, 因為自殺對他的國家和人民都沒有幫助。還有, 老百姓祭祀屈原的做法也不一定好。那時中國還有不少人沒飯吃, 為什麼要把米投到江裏去呢？要是屈原還活著, 他一定會把那些米都送給老百姓。張天明把他的想法告訴了表哥, 表哥覺得他說得有道理。

(Simplified Characters)

　　丽莎觉得屈原的故事很动人, 她认为屈原确实是中国历史上的伟大人物。可是张天明的想法不大一样。他认为屈原是个忧国忧民的好官, 可是无论怎样他也不应该自杀, 因为自杀对他的国家和人民都没有帮助。还有, 老百姓祭祀屈原的做法也不一定好。那时中国还有不少人没饭吃, 为什么要把米投到江里去呢？要是屈原还活着, 他一定会把那些米都送给老百姓。张天明把他的想法告诉了表哥, 表哥觉得他说得有道理。

Questions (True/False):

(   ) 1.   Lisa was touched by the story of Qu Yuan.

(   ) 2.   Zhang Tianming's attitude toward Qu Yuan was somewhat more critical than Lisa's.

(   ) 3.   Zhang Tianming didn't agree that Qu Yuan was a good official.

(   ) 4.   Zhang Tianming thought that Qu Yuan should not have killed himself.

(   ) 5.   According to Zhang Tianming, it was a waste to throw rice into the river.

(   ) 6.   Qu Yuan often gave away his rice to poor people.

(   ) 7.   Zhang Tianming's argument sounded persuasive to his cousin.

B. Read the passage and answer the questions.

(Traditional Characters)

中國有許多風俗習慣, 比方說過春節要放鞭炮。這裏邊有一個故事。聽說很久以前, 有一個怪物 (1) 叫 "年"。"年" 到了冬天就會到各個地方找東西吃。"年" 什麼都吃, 也吃人。當時人們一聽 "年" 來了, 就爭先恐後地逃跑 (2)。有一次, 有一個老人, 又累又餓, 來到一家人的門口。那家人也沒有多少吃的東西了, 可是還是給了老人一些。老人吃著吃著, 就聽到有人大喊 "年" 來了。那家人叫老人趕緊跟他們一起走, 可是老人卻要他們放心地離開, 說他要等 "年" 來。原來老人雖然表面上看起來又累又餓, 但實際上是天上的神仙 (3), 是來幫助老百姓趕走 (4) "年" 的。老人知道 "年" 怕很大的聲音 (5),於是就放鞭炮。"年" 一聽到鞭炮聲就嚇跑 (6) 了。從那以後, 中國人過春節就開始放鞭炮了。

(1)   怪物 (guàiwù): monster

(2)   逃跑 (táopǎo): to run and escape

(3)   神仙 (shénxian): god; deity

(4)   趕走 (gǎn zǒu): to drive away

(5)   聲音 (shēngyīn): sound

(6)   嚇跑 (xià pǎo): to frighten into running away

(Simplified Characters)

中国有许多风俗习惯, 比方说过春节要放鞭炮。这里边有一故事。听说很久以前, 有一个怪物 (1) 叫 "年"。"年" 到了冬天就会到各个地方找东西吃。"年" 什么都吃, 也吃人。当时人们一听 "年" 来了, 就争先恐后地逃跑 (2)。有一次, 有一个老人, 又累又饿, 来到一家人的门口。那家人也没有多少吃的东西了。可是还是给了老人一些。老人吃着吃着, 就听到有人大喊"年"来了。那家人叫老人赶紧跟他们一起走, 可是老人却要他们放心地离开, 说他要等"年"来。原来老人虽然表面上看起来又累又饿, 但实际上, 是天上的神仙 (3), 是来帮助老百姓赶走 (4)"年"的。老人知道"年"怕很大的声音(5),于是就放鞭炮。"年"一听到鞭炮声就吓跑 (6) 了。从那以后, 中国人过春节就开始放鞭炮了。

(1) 怪物(guàiwù): monster

(2) 逃跑(táopǎo): to run and escape

(3) 神仙(shénxian): god; deity

(4) 赶走(gǎn zǒu): to drive away

(5) 声音(shēngyīn): sound

(6) 吓跑(xià pǎo): to frighten into running away

Questions:

1. What did 年 do to people?

2. Who was the old man?

3. When the old man first arrived, how was he?

4. What did the old man do after everyone went away?

5. According to this legend, how did the custom of setting off firecrackers on Chinese New Year's Eve begin?

C. Read the story and answer the questions.

(Traditional Characters)

嫦娥 (1) 奔 (2) 月

　　中國有許多關於月亮的故事, 嫦娥奔月就是其中之一。據說很久很久以前, 天上有十個太陽 (3), 大家都熱得受不了, 很多人熱死了。嫦娥的丈夫 (4) 是個有名的獵人(5), 他射下了九個太陽以後, 大地才涼快了下來。他有一種仙

丹(6), 人吃了以後能飛起來。嫦娥沒讓丈夫知道, 就把仙丹吃了, 飛到了月亮上。每當中秋節的時候, 大家常常一邊賞月, 一邊吃月餅, 有時還講嫦娥奔月的故事。下次你買月餅的時候看看盒子(7) 上面畫的是什麼?

(1) 嫦娥(Cháng'é): name of a goddess

(2) 奔(bēn): to run; to fly to

(3) 太陽(tàiyáng): sun

(4) 丈夫(zhàngfu): husband

(5) 獵人(lièrén): hunter

(6) 仙丹(xiāndān): elixir

(7) 盒子(hézi): box

(Simplified Characters)

嫦娥(1) 奔(2)月

中国有许多关于月亮的故事, 嫦娥奔月就是其中之一。据说很久很久以前, 天上有十个太阳(3), 大家都热得受不了, 很多人热死了。嫦娥的丈夫(4) 是个有名的猎人(5), 他射下了九个太阳以后, 大地才凉快了下来。他有一种仙丹(6), 人吃了以后人能飞起来。嫦娥没让丈夫知道, 就把仙丹吃了, 飞到了月亮上。每当中秋节的时候, 大家常常一边赏月, 一边吃月饼, 有时还讲嫦娥奔月的故事。下次你买月饼的时候, 看看盒子 (7) 上画的是什么?

(1) 嫦娥 (Cháng'é): name of a goddess

(2) 奔 (bēn): to run; to fly to

(3) 太阳 (tàiyáng): sun

(4) 丈夫 (zhàngfu): husband

(5) 猎人 (lièrén): hunter

(6) 仙丹 (xiāndān): elixir

(7) 盒子 (hézi): box

Questions:

1. Why did so many people die from the heat?

2. Why could Chang'e fly to the moon?

3. What do Chinese people do to celebrate the Mid-Autumn Festival?

D. Read the story and answer the questions.

(Traditional Characters)

只許州官放火 (1), 不許百姓點燈

很久以前有一個官, 他的名字叫田登 (2), 可他不讓別人叫他的名字。他覺得別人叫他的名字就是對他不尊敬 (3)。因為"登"和"燈"念起來一樣, 所以大家都不能說"燈", 只能說"火", 也不能說"點燈", 因為"點燈"聽上去好像他的名字"田登", 只能說"放火"。元宵節的時候, 大家都要點燈, 田登就發告示 (4), 說要"放火三日"因為他是個官, 所以老百姓都沒有辦法, 只能生氣地說 : "只許州官放火, 不許百姓點燈。"

(1)　放火: to set fire; to commit arson
(2)　田登(Tián Dēng): person's name
(3)　尊敬(zūnjìng): to respect
(4)　告示(gàoshì): announcement

(Simplified Characters)

只许州官放火 (1), 不许百姓点灯

很久以前有一个官, 他的名字叫田登 (2), 可他不让别人叫他的名字。他觉得别人叫他的名字就是对他不尊敬 (3)。因为"登"和"灯"念起来一样, 所以大家都不能说"灯", 只能说"火", 也不能说"点灯", 因为"点灯" 听上去好像他的名字"田登", 只能说"放火"。元宵节的时候, 大家都要点灯, 田登就发告示 (4), 说要"放火三日"。因为他是个官, 所以老百姓都没有办法, 只能生气地说 : "只许州官放火, 不许百姓点灯。"

(1)　放火: to set fire; to commit arson
(2)　田登(Tián Dēng): a person's name
(3)　尊敬(zūnjìng): to respect
(4)　告示(gàoshì): announcement

Questions:

1. Why didn't the official let people address him by his own name?

2. What did his name sound like?

▼▼▼

3. What did the announcement say? What did it really mean?

4. What did the commoners mean by 只許州官放火, 不許百姓點燈 / 只许州官放火, 不许百姓点灯?

IV. GRAMMAR & USAGE

A. *Match the festivals in the left column with the activities associated with them in the right column by drawing a line between the two.*

1.	春節 春节	a.	吃月餅, 賞月 吃月饼, 赏月
2.	端午節 端午节	b.	吃餃子、魚, 放鞭炮 吃饺子、鱼, 放鞭炮
3.	中秋節 中秋节	c.	吃粽子, 賽龍舟 吃粽子, 赛龙舟
4.	元宵節 元宵节	d.	吃元宵, 賞燈 吃元宵, 赏灯

B. *Complete the dialogues using V +* 著玩 / V +着玩 *or* 忙著 V / 忙着 V.

1. a: 哎, 你唱歌唱得真好聽, 應該在學校的晚會上唱兩首(shǒu)。
    哎, 你唱歌唱得真好听, 应该在学校的晚会上唱两首(shǒu)。

    b: 不行, 不行, 我只是在家_____, 一上台就唱不出來了。
    不行, 不行, 我只是在家_____, 一上台就唱不出来了。

2. a: 你打球打得好極了, 能教教我嗎?
    你打球打得好极了, 能教教我吗?

    b: 哪裏, 哪裏, 我_____, 如果你們真想學, 得跟我
    的老師學。
    哪里, 哪里, 我_____, 如果你们真想学, 得跟我
    的老师学。

3. a: 這些天小柯怎麼一直沒到那個中國餐館去吃飯？他忙什麼呢？

    這些天小柯怎么一直没到那个中国餐馆去吃饭？他忙什么呢？

  b: 他＿＿＿＿＿＿＿＿＿＿＿＿＿＿，沒有時間出來吃飯。(寫文章)

    他＿＿＿＿＿＿＿＿＿＿＿＿＿＿，没有时间出来吃饭。(写文章)

B. Complete the dialogues using 根本.

1. a: 你覺得小李和他的女朋友在一起合適嗎？

    你觉得小李和他的女朋友在一起合适吗？

  b: 小李和他的女朋友性格、興趣等等都不同，＿＿＿＿＿＿＿＿＿。

    小李和他的女朋友性格、兴趣等等都不同，＿＿＿＿＿＿＿＿＿。

2. a: 你吃過粽子嗎？好吃嗎？

    你吃过粽子吗？好吃吗？

  b: 我不知道好吃不好吃，＿＿＿＿＿＿＿＿＿＿＿＿。

3. a: 聽說這個牌子的衣服質量好。

    听说这个牌子的衣服质量好。

  b: 誰說的？＿＿＿＿＿＿＿＿＿＿＿＿＿＿＿，千萬別買。

    谁说的？＿＿＿＿＿＿＿＿＿＿＿＿＿＿＿，千万别买。

C. Complete the sentences by using ...之一.

EXAMPLE: 中國是世界上人口最多的國家之一。

           中国是世界上人口最多的国家之一。

1. 北京是＿＿＿＿＿＿＿＿＿＿＿＿＿＿＿＿＿。

2. 端午節／端午节是＿＿＿＿＿＿＿＿＿＿＿＿＿。

3. 夫子廟／夫子庙是＿＿＿＿＿＿＿＿＿＿＿＿。

過什麼節戴荷包？／过什么节戴荷包？

D. Complete the dialogues using 儘可能／尽可能.

EXAMPLE:　a: 請你最好在今天晚上八點以前把這篇文章看完。

　　　　　　请你最好在今天晚上八点以前把这篇文章看完。

　　　　　b: <u>我儘可能在八點鐘以前看完</u>。

　　　　　　<u>我尽可能在八点钟以前看完</u>。

1. a: 小姐, 飛機票麻煩你幫我訂最便宜的。

　　小姐, 飞机票麻烦你帮我订最便宜的。

　b: 你放心, _____。

2. a: 明天有十幾個人来家过端午节, 你最好多包一些粽子。

　　明天有十几个人来家过端午节, 你最好多包一些粽子。

　b: 行, _____。

3. a: 醫生説味精吃多了對身體不好。

　　医生说味精吃多了对身体不好。

　b: 好吧, _____。

E. Complete the sentences using potential complements.

EXAMPLE:　a: 我這兩條毯子放到你的櫃子裏去好嗎？(放/下)

　　　　　　我这两条毯子放到你的柜子里去好吗？(放/下)

b: 對不起, 我的櫃子裏東西太多, <u>放不下</u>。

對不起, 我的柜子里东西太多, <u>放不下</u>。

1. a: 快過元宵節了, 應該買點元宵吃。(買/到)

快过元宵节了, 应该买点元宵吃。(买/到)

b: 可是我們這兒沒有中國店, _____。

可是我们这儿没有中国店, _____。

2. a: 老師用中文上課, 你覺得怎麼樣? (聽/懂)

老师用中文上课, 你觉得怎么样? (听/懂)

b: _____。

3. a: 我買了二十個月餅, 你們儘可能多吃幾個。(吃/完)

我买了二十个月饼, 你们尽可能多吃几个。(吃/完)

b: _____。

過什麼節吃月餅? / 过什么节吃月饼?

F. Use the words and phrases to complete the story, and answer the question posted at the end of the story in English.

(Traditional Characters)

最後, 可是, 於是, 突然, 以後, 有一天, 從那以後

▼▼▼▼▼▼▼▼▼▼▼▼▼▼▼▼▼▼▼▼▼▼▼▼▼▼▼▼▼▼▼▼▼▼▼▼

　　　很久很久以前, 宋國有一個農人 (1), 每天都要到地裏幹活 (2)。＿＿＿＿＿＿,
他又去地裏幹活, 看見一隻兔子 (3) 在地裏很快地跑著, ＿＿＿＿＿＿兔子撞 (4)
到一棵樹上。他走到樹下, 發現兔子死了, ＿＿＿＿＿＿他把死兔子拿到市場上去
賣了很多錢。回家＿＿＿＿＿＿, 他想：這比我每天在地裏幹活好多了, 又舒服,
錢又多。＿＿＿＿＿＿他就天天坐在樹下, 等別的兔子再來撞死。＿＿＿＿＿＿再也
沒有兔子撞到樹上, ＿＿＿＿＿＿這個農人在樹下餓死了。

(1)　農人(nóngrén): farmer

(2)　幹活(gàn huó): to work

(3)　兔子(tùzi): rabbit

(4)　撞(zhuàng): to bump into

這就是"守株 (shǒu zhū) 待兔"的故事。請你猜猜"守株待兔"是什么意思?

(Simplified Characters)

最后, 可是, 于是, 突然, 以后, 有一天, 从那以后

　　　很久很久以前, 宋国有一个农人 (1), 每天都要到地里干活 (2)。＿＿＿＿＿＿,
他又去地里干活, 看见一只兔子 (3) 在地里很快地跑着, ＿＿＿＿＿＿兔子撞 (4)
到一棵树上。他走到树下, 发现兔子死了, ＿＿＿＿＿＿他把死兔子拿到市场上去
卖了很多钱。回家＿＿＿＿＿＿, 他想：这比我每天在地里干活好多了, 又舒服,
钱又多。＿＿＿＿＿＿他就天天坐在树下, 等别的兔子再来撞死。＿＿＿＿＿＿再也
没有兔子撞到树上, ＿＿＿＿＿＿这个农人在树下饿死了。

(1)　农人(nóngrén): farmer

(2)　干活(gàn huó): to work

(3)　兔子(tùzi): rabbit

(4)　撞(zhuàng): to bump into

这就是"守株 (shǒu zhū) 待兔"的故事。请你猜猜"守株待兔"是什么意思?

G. Use time and place expressions to string the sentences together into one paragraph. Replace unneeded subjects with pronouns to complete the narrative.

a.　小林昨天上午九點去接小王來家裏過端午節。

　　小林昨天上午九点去接小王来家里过端午节。

▼▼▼▼▼▼▼▼▼▼▼▼▼▼▼▼▼▼▼▼▼▼▼▼▼▼▼▼▼▼▼▼▼▼▼▼▼▼▼

b. 小林給小王戴上荷包。

小林给小王戴上荷包。

c. 小林和小王一邊聊天，一邊包粽子。

小林和小王一边聊天，一边包粽子。

d. 小林和小王中午十二點吃很多粽子。

小林和小王中午十二点吃很多粽子。

e. 小林和小王去河邊看賽龍舟。

小林和小王去河边看赛龙舟。

f. 小林下午四點送小王回家。

小林下午四点送小王回家。

V. TRANSLATION

A. *Translate the passage into English.*

(Traditional Characters)

     很多歷史上的偉大人物都有著憂國憂民的愛國精神。他們不圖當大官，賺大錢，只希望老百姓能過好日子。

(Simplified Characters)

     很多历史上的伟大人物都有着忧国忧民的爱国精神。他们不图当大官，赚大钱，只希望老百姓能过好日子。

▼▼

B. Translate the passage into Chinese.

For many Americans, Thanksgiving (感恩節 ／ 感恩节 Gǎn'ēnjié) is one of the most important holidays. It is on the fourth Thursday in November. It's a day of family reunion. People who work or study away from home (外地) try their best to go home to celebrate the holiday.

C. Translate the passage into Chinese using the phrases provided.

There are many parks in Beijing. Zhongshan Park is one of them. In addition to all types of architecture, there are many trees and flowers in the park. One day I went to Zhongshan Park with a friend of mine. My friend seemed uninterested in it. I asked him, "You don't think the park is interesting?" He said, "It's not that. I'm tired." I asked, "How come you're tired? You just got to the park." He said, "Probably it has to do with the fact that I went to bed really late last night." I said, "Then let's leave early. Try to go to bed as early as possible tonight."

...之一, 各種各樣的, 好像, 跟...有關係, 儘可能

...之一, 各种各样的, 好像, 跟...有关系, 尽可能

D. Translate the passage into Chinese. Be sure to use potential complements where appropriate in your translation.

Zhang Tianming invited his friend Little Li to celebrate Chinese New Year with his family. Zhang Tianming's mother prepared an elaborate dinner. Little Li really liked the food. He said to Tianming's mom that he wouldn't be able to find such great food anywhere else. Tianming's mom asked him to have some more food. Little Li said that he couldn't possibly finish that much food.

E. Translate the passage into Chinese using the phrases provided.

吸引, 印象, 戀戀不捨

吸引, 印象, 恋恋不舍

This past summer during summer vacation, I traveled to Charleston (查爾斯敦 / 查尔斯敦 Chá'ěrsīdūn), South Carolina (南卡). Charleston is a tourist city (旅遊城市 / 旅游城市) on the southeastern coast of America. Every year it attracts many tourists. It has not only beautiful scenery but also a good climate. Charleston's architecture cannot be said to be grand, but it has its own characteristics, especially buildings along the seacoast. Those buildings, and the big trees, left a deep impression on me. I went sightseeing there for three days. I left reluctantly on the fourth day.

VI. COMPOSITION

1. Describe how you and your family celebrate the New Year.

2. Include the following items in your composition about a holiday (or festival) of your choice.

...之一, 儘可能, ...跟...有關係, 把 structure

...之一, 尽可能, ...跟...有关系, 把 structure

過春節的時候, 門上貼什麼? / 过春节的时候, 门上贴什么?

Why is this character upside-down?

第十三課 ▲ 談體育
第十三课 ▲ 谈体育

A. Listen to the audio for the Textbook and answer the questions.

1. Why did Zhang Tianming call Anderson?

2. Who won the ball game last night?

3. Who played extremely well for Michigan?

4. What is the point of sports, according to Zhang Tianming?

B. Listen to the audio for the Workbook.

1. Listen to the passage and answer the questions.
   a. How old is Mr. Li?

   b. How is his health?

   c. What kind of exercise does he do on weekdays?

   d. What exercise does he do on weekends?

   e. What embarrassed Mr. Li?

2. Listen to the passage and answer the questions.
   a. How good is Tianming's school's football team?

   b. How are their star players?

   c. Why are the faculty and other students fed up with the players?

   d. What does the school plan to do to change the players' behavior?

▼▼▼▼▼▼▼▼▼▼▼▼▼▼▼▼▼▼▼▼▼▼▼▼▼▼▼▼▼▼▼▼▼▼▼▼▼

3. Listen to the passage and answer the questions.

    a. What was Mr. Ke's top priority while he was in college?

    b. Why was he too busy to study?

    c. What did he do later on to improve his career opportunities?

II. SPEAKING EXERCISES

A. Practice asking and answering the following questions with a partner before class.

1. 學校開學已經多久了？
   学校开学已经多久了？

2. 你什麼時候會覺得寂寞？
   你什么时候会觉得寂寞？

3. 奧林匹克運動會多久辦一次？
   奥林匹克运动会多久办一次？

4. 什麼樣的人才能當學校籃球隊的隊員？
   什么样的人才能当学校篮球队的队员？

B. Practice speaking on the following topics.

1. 你喜歡體育嗎？你為什麼(不)喜歡體育？
   你喜欢体育吗？你为什么(不)喜欢体育？

2. 你認為體育比賽的目的是什麼？是為了給國家爭榮譽嗎？
   你认为体育比赛的目的是什么？是为了给国家争荣誉吗？

3. 談談一個人可以怎麼為他的學校爭榮譽。
   谈谈一个人可以怎么为他的学校争荣誉。

4. 談談在什麼情況下你的父母為你感到驕傲。
   谈谈在什么情况下你的父母为你感到骄傲。

▼▼▼▼▼▼▼▼▼▼▼▼▼▼▼▼▼▼▼▼▼▼▼▼▼▼▼▼▼▼▼▼▼▼▼▼

III. READING COMPREHENSION

A. *Read this excerpt from Anderson's basketball training diary and answer the questions.*

(Traditional Characters)

　　每次比賽以前, 教練都告訴隊員儘可能表現得好一點。如果比賽贏了, 應該高興, 可是千萬不要驕傲。如果比賽輸了, 也沒關係, 不要感到失望, 下次再來。

(Simplified Characters)

　　每次比赛以前, 教练都告诉队员尽可能表现得好一点。如果比赛赢了, 应该高兴, 可是千万不要骄傲。如果比赛输了, 也没关系, 不要感到失望, 下次再来。

世界青棒賽	
昨天戰績	
義大利勝南 非	6:0
日　本勝荷　蘭	4:2
巴拿馬勝澳　洲	12:2
美　國勝德　國	10:4
古　巴勝南　韓	3:2

哪些隊贏了？／哪些队赢了？

(See the Alternate Character Appendix for simplified characters.)

Questions (True/False):
(　　) 1. The coach always wants his team to try its best.
(　　) 2. To the coach, winning is everything.
(　　) 3. The players feel that there's a next time if they fail.

B. *Read the passage and answer the questions.*

(Traditional Characters)

　　張天明學校的美式足球隊打贏了決賽, 成為今年的全國冠軍。今天晚上成千上萬的人上街慶祝。他們覺得這不但是這個學校的光榮, 也是整個城市

的光榮。張天明雖然住在校外, 可是外面的慶祝活動還是吵得他沒法準備明
天的考試。他本來也覺得這場比賽很精彩, 也為自己學校的勝利 (shènglì) 感到
驕傲, 可是現在, 他開始覺得那場決賽要是輸了也沒什麼不好。他知道, 如
果他把這個想法告訴上街慶祝的人們, 説不定他們會把他扔到河裏去。

(Simplified Characters)

　　张天明学校的美式足球队打赢了决赛, 成为今年的全国冠军。今天晚上
成千上万的人上街庆祝。他们觉得这不但是这个学校的光荣, 也是整个城市
的光荣。张天明虽然住在校外, 可是外面的庆祝活动还是吵得他没法准备明
天的考试。他本来也觉得这场比赛很精彩, 也为自己学校的胜利 (shènglì) 感到
骄傲,　可是现在, 他开始觉得那场决赛要是输了也没什么不好。他知道, 如
果他把这个想法告诉上街庆祝的人们, 说不定他们会把他扔到河里去。

Questions (True/False):

(　) 1. Zhang's school won the championship.

(　) 2. All of the people celebrating on the street were students.

(　) 3. Zhang couldn't study because of the noise from the street.

(　) 4. From the very beginning, Zhang hoped that his school would lose the championship.

(　) 5. Zhang didn't watch the final game.

(　) 6. Zhang knew that people on the street would not agree with him.

C. *Read the passage and answer the questions.*

(Traditional Characters)

　　那個運動員最近打破了好幾個世界記錄, 老家的父母為他取得這麼好的
成績感到十分光榮。馬上就要過春節了, 他們打算趁兒子回家過年的時候,
再好好慶祝慶祝。沒想到兒子拍電報回來説得出國參加國際比賽, 不能回家
過春節了, 這讓兩位老人家有些失望。

(Simplified Characters)

　　那个运动员最近打破了好几个世界记录, 老家的父母为他取得这么好的
成绩感到十分光荣。马上就要过春节了, 他们打算趁儿子回家过年的时候,

再好好庆祝庆祝。没想到儿子拍电报回来说得出国参加国际比赛, 不能回家过春节了, 这让两位老人家有些失望。

Questions:

1. What did the athlete accomplish recently?

2. When did his parents expect him to be home?

3. What spoiled his parents' plan?

D. Read the passage and answer the questions.

(Traditional Characters)

　　喜歡體育的人非常多, 有男的, 有女的, 有老人, 也有小孩。有的人每天都要運動, 否則就覺得不舒服, 他們一有機會就去打球或者跑步；有的人自己並不怎麼喜歡運動, 可是他們喜歡看體育比賽, 尤其是球賽, 如籃球, 足球等。每當有重大的比賽時, 這些球迷就會想辦法買票去體育場看比賽, 有些球迷還會跟他們喜歡的球隊去外地或者外國看比賽。有些球迷脾氣比較急躁, 如果他們的球隊打得不好, 或者輸了, 他們就會生氣鬧事 (nàoshì)。我覺得為了看球賽而打架實在沒有必要。

(Simplified Characters)

　　喜欢体育的人非常多, 有男的, 有女的, 有老人, 也有小孩。有的人每天都要运动, 否则就觉得不舒服, 他们一有机会就去打球或者跑步；有的人自己并不怎么喜欢运动, 可是他们喜欢看体育比赛, 尤其是球赛, 如篮球, 足球等。每当有重大的比赛时, 这些球迷就会想办法买票去体育场看比赛, 有些球迷还会跟他们喜欢的球队去外地或者外国看比赛。有些球迷脾气比较急躁, 如果他们的球队打得不好, 或者输了, 他们就会生气闹事 (nàoshì)。我觉得为了看球赛而打架实在没有必要。

Questions (True/False):

( ) 1.　只有學生喜歡體育。

　　　只有学生喜欢体育。

( ) 2.　喜歡體育的人都運動。

　　　喜欢体育的人都运动。

( ) 3.　喜歡看球賽的人都喜歡打球。

　　　喜欢看球赛的人都喜欢打球。

( ) 4.　有時候球票很難買，可是球迷會想辦法買。

　　　有时候球票很难买，可是球迷会想办法买。

( ) 5.　有些球迷常常跟著自己喜歡的球隊到各地去。

　　　有些球迷常常跟着自己喜欢的球队到各地去。

E. Read the passage and answer the questions.

(Traditional Characters)

　　足球可能是世界上最受歡迎的體育運動，特別是在歐洲 (1) 和南美洲 (2)。一場精彩的足球能吸引成千上萬的球迷，本地的，外地的，甚至是外國的，都趕到體育場去觀看比賽。再加上電視，一場足球賽可能有上百萬，上千萬的人看。今天我們看的足球最早是從英國開始的。可是很少有人知道，中國漢代 (206 BCE–220 CE)(3) 有一種跟足球很像的運動，我們現在還可以從古代的畫中看到當時人們踢 (4) 球的樣子。只是那時的球場，兩邊各有六個門。另一種在英國非常受歡迎的運動是馬球 (5)。馬球和足球不一樣，只有有錢人才能參加。中國古代也有馬球，這我們可以從出土的俑 (6) 看出來。後來這些運動在中國都沒有了。跟別的國家一樣，中國現在的足球也是從英國來的。

(1) 歐洲(Ōuzhōu): Europe
(2) 南美洲(Nánměizhōu): South America
(3) 漢代(Hàn Dài): Han dynasty
(4) 踢(tī): to kick

(5) 馬球: polo

(6) 俑(yǒng): figurines buried with the dead in ancient times

(Simplified Characters)

　　足球可能是世界上最受欢迎的体育运动, 特别是在欧洲 (1) 和南美洲 (2)。一场精彩的足球能吸引成千上万的球迷, 本地的, 外地的, 甚至是外国的, 都赶到体育场去观看比赛。再加上电视, 一场足球赛可能有上百万, 上千万的人看。今天我们看的足球最早是从英国开始的。可是很少有人知道, 中国汉代 (206 BCE–220 CE)(3) 有一种跟足球很像的运动, 我们现在还可以从古代的画中看到当时人们踢 (4) 球的样子。只是那时的球场, 两边各有六个门。另一种在英国非常受欢迎的运动是马球 (5)。马球和足球不一样, 只有有钱人才能参加。中国古代也有马球, 这我们可以从出土的俑 (6) 看出来。后来这些运动在中国都没有了。跟别的国家一样, 中国现在的足球也是从英国来的。

(1) 欧洲(Ōuzhōu): Europe

(2) 南美洲(Nánměizhōu): South America

(3) 汉代(Hàn Dài): Han dynasty

(4) 踢(tī): to kick

(5) 马球: polo

(6) 俑(yǒng): figurines buried with the dead in ancient times

Questions (True/False):

(　　) 1. 馬球是南美洲最受歡迎的體育運動。
　　　　 马球是南美洲最受欢迎的体育运动。

(　　) 2. 足球是英國最先開始的。
　　　　 足球是英国最先开始的。

(　　) 3. 每次看馬球比賽的球迷都上百萬。
　　　　 每次看马球比赛的球迷都上百万。

(　　) 4. 古代中國踢的足球跟現在中國踢的足球一樣。
　　　　 古代中国踢的足球跟现在中国踢的足球一样。

(   ) 5. 中國人現在踢的足球跟英國人的一樣。

中国人现在踢的足球跟英国人的一样。

F. *Like their counterparts in English-speaking countries, Chinese newspapers, especially those geared toward a large readership, cover sports extensively. There are also newspapers and magazines devoted exclusively to sports. Read the short clipping and circle the correct information.*

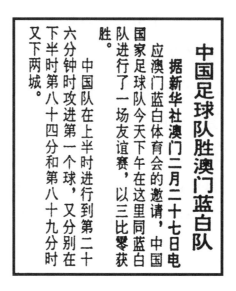

(See the Alternate Character Appendix for traditional characters.)

Questions:

1. When did the football match take place?
2. Where did it take place?
3. What are the names of the two teams involved?
4. Which team scored a goal in the first half?
5. What was the final score?
6. Which team won?

IV. GRAMMAR & USAGE

A. Complete the dialogues using 連...也/都... / 连...也/都...

EXAMPLE: a: 你的學生知道不知道中國的元宵節？(春節)

你的学生知道不知道中国的元宵节？(春节)

     b: 元宵節？不知道。<u>他們連中國的春節都不知道</u>。

元宵节？不知道。<u>他们连中国的春节都不知道</u>。

1. a: 你住的地方怎麼樣? 有沒有空調? (窗戶)

   你住的地方怎么样? 有没有空调? (窗户)

   b: 空調? 沒有。 _____。

   空调? 没有。 _____。

2. a: 你會不會做清蒸魚? (米飯)

   你会不会做清蒸鱼? (米饭)

   b: 清蒸魚? 不會做。 _____。

   清蒸鱼? 不会做。 _____。

3. a: 你去過中國南京嗎? (美國波士頓)

   你去过中国南京吗? (美国波士顿)

   b: 中國南京? 沒去過。 _____。

   中国南京? 没去过。 _____。

4. a: 你打算買新車嗎? (下個月的房租)

   你打算买新车吗? (下个月的房租)

   b: 別開玩笑了! _____。

   别开玩笑了! _____。

B. Complete the following dialogues using 反正 (regardless).

EXAMPLE: a: 隊排得那麼長, 恐怕得等很長時間, 今天別看電影了! (一定要看)

         队排得那么长, 恐怕得等很长时间, 今天别看电影了! (一定要看)

     b: 等多長時間都沒關係, <u>反正我一定要看</u>。

       等多长时间都没关系, <u>反正我一定要看</u>。

1. 妹妹:寒假姐姐和弟弟都不回家, 哥哥, 你還回家嗎?

   妹妹:寒假姐姐和弟弟都不回家, 哥哥, 你还回家吗?

   哥哥:他們回不回家我不管, _____。(要回家)

   哥哥:他们回不回家我不管, _____。(要回家)

2. a: 這套公寓對你挺合適的, 應該租。(不租)

　　　这套公寓对你挺合适的, 应该租。(不租)

　　b: 合適不合適都一樣, ＿＿＿＿＿＿＿＿＿＿＿＿＿＿＿＿。

　　　合适不合适都一样, ＿＿＿＿＿＿＿＿＿＿＿＿＿＿＿＿。

3. a: 過春節, 你得給小孩壓歲錢啊。(不給)

　　　过春节, 你得给小孩压岁钱啊。(不给)

　　b: 要給你給, ＿＿＿＿＿＿＿＿＿＿＿＿＿＿＿＿＿＿。

　　　要给你给, ＿＿＿＿＿＿＿＿＿＿＿＿＿＿＿＿＿＿。

C. *Complete the following dialogues using* 反正 *(anyway).*

EXAMPLE:　a: 那封信, 我沒掛號。

　　　　　　　那封信, 我没挂号。

　　　　　b: 沒關係, <u>反正也不重要</u>。

　　　　　　　没关系, <u>反正也不重要</u>。

1. a: 我聽說昨天的球賽精彩極了。你看了嗎?

　　　我听说昨天的球赛精彩极了。你看了吗?

　　b: ＿＿＿＿＿＿＿＿＿＿＿＿＿＿＿＿＿, 沒看也沒關係。(輸了)

　　　＿＿＿＿＿＿＿＿＿＿＿＿＿＿＿＿＿, 没看也没关系。(输了)

2. a: 咱們改了日程以後, 就沒有時間去西安了。

　　　咱们改了日程以后, 就没有时间去西安了。

　　b: ＿＿＿＿＿＿＿＿＿＿＿＿＿＿＿＿＿。(對…沒興趣 / 对…没兴趣)

3. 女兒: 爸爸, 我跟小林吹了。

　　女儿: 爸爸, 我跟小林吹了。

　　爸爸: 吹了就吹了, ＿＿＿＿＿＿＿＿＿＿＿＿＿＿＿＿＿＿＿。

　　(對…印象不好 / 对…印象不好)

▼▼▼▼▼▼▼▼▼▼▼▼▼▼▼▼▼▼▼▼▼▼▼▼▼▼▼▼▼▼

D. Complete the dialogues using 所以…是因為…／所以…是因为…

EXAMPLE: a: 你認為密西根隊為什麼贏球？(速度快, 比賽經驗豐富)

                你认为密西根队为什么赢球？(速度快, 比赛经验丰富)

        b: <u>他們所以贏球是因為他們球員的速度快, 比賽經驗豐富。</u>

           <u>他们所以赢球是因为他们球员的速度快, 比赛经验丰富。</u>

1. a: 小張為什麼那麼喜歡夫子廟？(那兒的建築別具風格)

     小张为什么那么喜欢夫子庙？(那儿的建筑别具风格)

   b: _____。

2. a: 你為什麼不申請念我們學校的研究所？(我的指導教授建議我別申請)

     你为什么不申请念我们学校的研究所？(我的指导教授建议我别申请)

   b: _____。

3. a: 大家為什麼不願意跟他交往？(脾氣急躁, 說話難聽)

     大家为什么不愿意跟他交往？(脾气急躁, 说话难听)

   b: _____。

國際比賽／国际比赛

E. Connect the sentences by deleting or replacing unneeded subjects with pronouns, and using connectives and time and place expressions.

a. 小湯去年暑假去中國旅行。

小汤去年暑假去中国旅行。

b. 小湯從美國西岸坐飛機直飛中國北京。

小汤从美国西岸坐飞机直飞中国北京。

c. 小湯遊覽了長城和香山。

小汤游览了长城和香山。

d. 小湯從北京坐火車去南京。

小汤从北京坐火车去南京。

e. 小湯遊覽了夫子廟以及中山陵。

小汤游览了夫子庙以及中山陵。

f. 小湯坐汽車到了上海。

小汤坐汽车到了上海。

g. 小湯想從上海坐飛機直飛美國西岸。

小汤想从上海坐飞机直飞美国西岸。

h. 沒有位子。

没有位子。

i. 小湯過兩天再回美國。

小汤过两天再回美国。

▼▼▼▼▼▼▼▼▼▼▼▼▼▼▼▼▼▼▼▼▼▼▼▼▼▼▼▼▼▼▼▼▼▼▼▼▼▼

V. TRANSLATION

A. Translate the telephone conversation into Chinese using the phrases provided.

V + 出來, 上 + Number, 反正, 閑著沒事

V + 出来, 上 + Number, 反正, 闲着没事

a: Oh, Little Wang, it's you. [I] didn't recognize your voice. What's up?

b: I am thinking of getting a used computer for about $100.00.

a: Why don't you buy a new one?

b: A new one costs seven or eight hundred dollars. I don't have that much money.

a: Anyway, you don't need a computer right away. You don't have much to do this week. You can go to the school computer center and look at some ads there. Then we'll talk again.

B. Translate the passages into Chinese.

1. Whenever there's a holiday, I miss my family even more. I always tell myself that since I am abroad I cannot go home anyway. On the surface, it might seem that I couldn't care less. Actually, I want to try my best to go home to reunite with my family and celebrate the holiday.

反正, 表面上, 實際上, 儘可能

反正, 表面上, 实际上, 尽可能

2. The reason we won today was because our team was faster than yours, and our team was more experienced in competition than yours. Besides, our team was less nervous than yours.

所以...是因為...

所以...是因为...

3. My brother is one of the players on the school basketball team. He is tall and strong. He can also run very fast on the court. He practices very hard every day, and hopes that one day he can earn honor for the school. The coach said that my brother plays well, but he does not have enough experience and needs to sit on the side to watch more games. My brother was a little disappointed after he heard that.

...之一, 為...爭榮譽, 失望

...之一, 为...争荣誉, 失望

▼▼▼▼▼▼▼▼▼▼▼▼▼▼▼▼▼▼▼▼▼▼▼▼▼▼▼▼▼▼▼▼▼▼▼▼▼

VI. COMPOSITION

1. 請寫一篇短文, 題目是: 我最喜歡的體育運動
   请写一篇短文, 题目是: 我最喜欢的体育运动

2. 如果你不喜歡做或看體育運動, 請寫一篇短文, 題目是:我為什麼不喜歡
   體育
   如果你不喜欢做或看体育运动, 请写一篇短文, 题目是:我为什么不喜欢
   体育

第十四課 ▲ 家庭

I. LISTENING COMPREHENSION

A. Listen to the audio for the Textbook and answer the questions.

1. Why does Zhang Tianming go home for a visit?

2. What course does Tianming's father want him to take?

3. What subjects is Tianming least interested in?

4. Will Zhang Tianming listen to his father and break up with Lisa? How do you know?

5. Why did Tianming's cousin and his family move out from his aunt's?

6. Why was Tianming's cousin always fighting with his wife?

B. Listen to the audio for the Workbook.

1. Listen to the passage and answer the true/false questions.
   ( ) a. Anderson's parents moved away last year.
   ( ) b. A holiday is coming up.
   ( ) c. He's glad that he will be able to see his siblings again.
   ( ) d. He decided that it's better that he spend the holiday with his parents.

2. Listen to the passage and answer the questions.

   a. 麗莎的表姐夫每天下班後都做什麼？
      丽莎的表姐夫每天下班后都做什么？

   _____

   b. 麗莎的表姐為什麼老是那麼忙？
      丽莎的表姐为什么老是那么忙？

   _____

c. 麗莎的表姐叫她表姐夫幫忙時, 她表姐夫會怎麼樣?
   丽莎的表姐叫她表姐夫帮忙时, 她表姐夫会怎么样?

   _____

d. 他們兩個人的關係為什麼越來越緊張?
   他们两个人的关系为什么越来越紧张?

   _____

3. Listen to the passage and answer the questions.
   a. Were Li Zhe's parents born in the United States?

   b. Why did his parents work in Chinese restaurants for more than ten years?

   c. What would they like Li Zhe to become?

   d. Why can't they understand Li Zhe's passion for philosophy?

   e. What does Li Zhe tell them?

II. SPEAKING EXERCISES

A   Practice asking and answering the following questions with a partner before class.

1. 你的興趣在哪些方面?你對什麼有興趣?
   你的兴趣在哪些方面?你对什么有兴趣?

2. 你覺得什麼樣的工作是鐵飯碗?
   你觉得什么样的工作是铁饭碗?

3. 你小時候常常跟父母告誰的狀?
   你小时候常常跟父母告谁的状?

4. 什麼叫做獨立？

　　什么叫做独立？

B. Practice speaking on the following topics.

1. 要是你的父母要你選你不感興趣的專業, 你會跟他們怎麼說？

　　要是你的父母要你选你不感兴趣的专业, 你会跟他们怎么说？

2. 要是你的父母反對你和你的男 / 女朋友在一起, 你會怎麼說？

　　要是你的父母反对你和你的男 / 女朋友在一起, 你会怎么说？

3. 你認為美國家庭和中國家庭有什麼不同？

　　你认为美国家庭和中国家庭有什么不同？

4. 請你介紹一下你的家人。

　　请你介绍一下你的家人。

老伴兒 / 老伴儿

III. READING COMPREHENSION

A. Read the passage and answer the questions.

(Traditional Characters)

　　毛毛十歲, 又聰明, 學習成績又好。每天放學回家要麼畫畫兒, 要麼彈鋼琴。他什麼事都自己做, 不用別人催, 也不用別人操心。可是他太獨立了, 不常跟別的小朋友玩, 也不願意跟大人打交道, 老師和爸爸媽媽都怕他長大以後不容易跟別人相處。

(Simplified Characters)

    毛毛十岁, 又聪明,学习成绩又好。每天放学回家要么画画儿,要么弹钢琴。他什么事都自己做, 不用别人催, 也不用别人操心。可是他太独立了, 不常跟别的小朋友玩, 也不愿意跟大人打交道, 老师和爸爸妈妈都怕他长大以后不容易跟别人相处。

Questions (True/False):

(   ) 1.   Maomao is a good student.

(   ) 2.   Maomao is not very fond of playing the piano.

(   ) 3.   Maomao is self-motivated and self-disciplined.

(   ) 4.   Maomao loves to play with others.

(   ) 5.   Maomao's lack of social skills worries his parents and teachers.

B. Read the passage and answer the questions.

(Traditional Characters)

    上個月張天明姑媽的老同事又給她介紹了一位老先生, 六十五歲。兩位老人家庭背景差不多, 生活習慣也差不多, 雙方都希望早點兒把關係定下來。姑媽不想讓婆媳關係變得更緊張, 所以想找個機會把這件事告訴表嫂。姑媽去年認識了一位老職員, 就是因為表嫂的反對而分手的。姑媽覺得這次表嫂也許不會反對。這位老先生是退休老師, 可以幫表嫂管管玲玲的功課, 還可以教玲玲畫畫。

(Simplified Characters)

    上个月张天明姑妈的老同事又给她介绍了一位老先生, 六十五岁。两位老人家庭背景差不多, 生活习惯也差不多, 双方都希望早点儿把关系定下来。姑妈不想让婆媳关系变得更紧张, 所以想找个机会把这件事告诉表嫂。姑妈去年认识了一位老职员, 就是因为表嫂的反对而分手的。姑妈觉得这次表嫂也许不会反对。这位老先生是退休老师, 可以帮表嫂管管玲玲的功课, 还可以教玲玲画画。

▼▼▼▼▼▼▼▼▼▼▼▼▼▼▼▼▼▼▼▼▼▼▼▼▼▼▼▼▼▼▼▼▼

Questions (True/False):

( ) 1. Zhang's aunt started to date a retired clerk last month.

( ) 2. Zhang's aunt would like to take their relationship to the next level.

( ) 3. Zhang's aunt's decision to date did not please her daughter-in-law.

( ) 4. Zhang's aunt hoped her daughter-in-law would approve of her new boyfriend because of Lingling.

C. Read the dialogue and answer the questions.

(Traditional Characters)

柯林： 小張, 你感恩節過得怎麼樣?

張天明： 別提了, 本來以為可以好好地跟家人過節, 沒想到和我父親吵了好幾次。

柯林： 怎麼會呢? 你不是和你父親相處得很好嗎?

張天明： 我也以為我父親知道我已經長大了, 可以對自己的行為負責任了。可是現在我才知道他也跟其他中國父母一樣, 管得那麼多, 實在讓人受不了。

柯林： 你別那麼激動, 你們為什麼事吵架?

張天明： 我爸爸不同意我只選那些我有興趣的課, 他說這樣畢業以後找工作會有問題。

柯林： 為了子女的將來, 做父親的有責任提一些建議。那也沒有什麼不對的。

張天明： 我知道, 但是他總是以為我還是一個不懂事的三歲孩子。對了, 另外他還說我不應該再和麗莎交往。他說我們兩個文化背景不同, 要考慮清楚。

柯林： 你應該跟你父親再好好地談談, 把話說清楚。不過, 說真的, 現在找工作真不容易, 我有好些同學都後悔以前沒多選一些有用的課。

張天明： 可是他也不能叫我和麗莎分手啊。

柯林： 這個問題比較麻煩。我想你應該讓他知道你和麗莎只是男女朋友，還沒有談到結婚的事。另外，你也應該抽個時間把麗莎帶回家讓你父母親看看。

(Simplified Characters)

柯林： 小张，你感恩节过得怎么样？

张天明： 别提了，本来以为可以好好地跟家人过节，没想到和我父亲吵了好几次。

柯林： 怎么会呢？你不是和你父亲相处得很好吗？

张天明： 我也以为我父亲知道我已经长大了，可以对自己的行为负责任了。可是现在我才知道他也跟其他中国父母一样，管得那么多，实在让人受不了。

柯林： 你别那么激动，你们为什么事吵架？

张天明： 我爸爸不同意我只选那些我有兴趣的课，他说这样毕业以后找工作会有问题。

柯林： 为了子女的将来，做父亲的有责任提一些建议，那也没有什么不对的。

张天明： 我知道，但是他总是以为我还是一个不懂事的三岁孩子。对了，另外他还说我不应该再和丽莎交往。他说我们两个文化背景不同，要考虑清楚。

柯林： 你应该跟你父亲再好好地谈谈，把话说清楚。不过，说真的，现在找工作真不容易，我有好些同学都后悔以前没多选一些有用的课。

张天明： 可是他也不能叫我和丽莎分手啊。

柯林：　　这个问题比较麻烦。我想你应该让他知道你和丽莎只是男女朋友，还没有谈到结婚的事。另外，你也应该抽个时间把丽莎带回家让你父母亲看看。

Questions:

1. What did Zhang Tianming and his father fight over?

2. Did Ke Lin think that Zhang's father was at fault? How do you know?

3. Why was Zhang Tianming angry with his father?

4. What did Zhang's father think of Lisa?

5. What were Ke Lin's suggestions to Zhang Tianming?

D. Lingling's mother was trying to find a new art teacher for her. Look at one of the ads she saw in a newspaper and list three kinds of lessons one could take at this art studio.

專教美術
畫家授課，耐心有序
兒童至成人
卡通，素描，水彩，油畫
國畫，電腦設計，攝影

(See the Alternate Character Appendix for simplified characters.)

E. Read the story and answer the questions.

(Traditional Characters)

破鏡重 (1) 圓

　　陳朝 (2) 有一個駙馬 (3) 叫徐德言, 因為陳朝馬上就要滅亡 (4) 了, 他怕萬一他和妻子走丟了, 就把家裏的一面鏡子分成兩半, 一半給他的妻子, 一半自己留著, 說好元宵節時, 他們在街上, 一個人買鏡子, 一個賣鏡子, 用這樣的方法來找對方 (5)。陳朝滅亡後, 徐德言的妻子真的走丟了。

　　徐德言非常想念妻子, 元宵節那天就去街上找賣鏡子的人。他看到一位老人正在賣半面鏡子, 徐德言拿出自己的半面鏡子, 兩面鏡子正好對上 (6)。原來是他的妻子讓老人替她賣鏡子找丈夫的。徐德言就這樣找到了他的妻子。

　　現在中國人常常用 "破鏡重圓" 來說夫妻分開或離婚後又團圓的情況, 就是從這個故事來的。

(1)　重 (chóng): to renew; to repeat; again

(2)　陳朝 (Chén Cháo): Chén dynasty 557–589

(3)　駙馬 (fùmǎ): emperor's son-in-law

(4) 滅亡 (mièwáng): to perish; to die out

(5) 對方 (duìfāng): the "other" side in a relationship, conversation, etc.; (here) each other

(6) 對上 (duì shang): to match

(Simplified Characters)

破镜重 (1) 圆

　　陈朝 (2) 有一个驸马 (3) 叫徐德言, 因为陈朝马上就要灭亡 (4) 了, 他怕万一他和妻子走丢了, 就把家里的一面镜子分成两半, 一半给他的妻子, 一半自己留着, 说好元宵节时, 他们在街上, 一个人买镜子, 一个卖镜子, 用这样的方法来找对方 (5)。陈朝灭亡后, 徐德言的妻子真的走丢了。

　　徐德言非常想念妻子, 元宵节那天就去街上找卖镜子的人。他看到一位老人正在卖半面镜子, 徐德言拿出自己的半面镜子, 两面镜子正好对上 (6)。原来是他的妻子让老人替她卖镜子找丈夫的。徐德言就这样找到了他的妻子。

　　现在中国人常常用 "破镜重圆" 这句话来说夫妻分开或离婚后又团圆的情况, 就是从这个故事来的。

(1) 重 (chóng): to renew; to repeat; again

(2) 陈朝 (Chén Cháo): Chén dynasty 557–589

(3) 驸马 (fùmǎ): emperor's son-in-law

(4) 灭亡 (mièwáng): to perish; to die out

(5) 对方 (duìfāng): the "other" side in a relationship, conversation, etc.; (here) each other

(6) 对上 (duì shang): to match

Questions:

1. What did Xu Deyan give his wife?

2. Why did he separate the mirror into two parts?

3. What did he ask his wife to do in case they got separated?

4. What time did they decide on to look for each other?

5. Whom did Xu Deyan meet on the street?

6. How did Xu Deyan find his wife?

7. 破鏡重圓 / 破镜重圆 is a metaphor for what?

F. In recent years, China has witnessed a new phenomenon: a proliferation of talk shows, especially on the radio. Advice columns in the print media are equally popular. Answer the questions after skimming through a fairly typical representation of such columns.

(Traditional Characters)

讓孩子吃點苦

城市裏的孩子吃得好, 穿得好, 玩得好, 讀書用功, 有的還會彈琴, 唱歌, 畫畫。做家長的很容易滿足, 好像現在的孩子什麼都有, 什麼都好。可是也有人說現在的孩子吃不了苦, 我認為説得很有道理。那怎麼讓孩子學會吃苦呢?

今年寒假, 上海一位年輕的爸爸為了教育女兒, 給了她兩個選擇, 一是1000元的紅包, 二是回老家幫助姑媽做農活。這個小女孩選擇了後者, 去經受"吃苦磨練"。我認為對這位有遠見的父親, 不妨也獎他一個紅包。

為了使今天的中國孩子在下個世紀不會輸給美國人, 日本人, 德國人 ... 做大人的要給我們的孩子上好"吃苦磨練"這一課。

(Simplified Characters)

让孩子吃点苦

城市里的孩子吃得好, 穿得好, 玩得好, 读书用功, 有的还会弹琴, 唱歌, 画画。做家长的很容易满足, 好像现在的孩子什么都有, 什么都好。可是也有人说现在的孩子吃不了苦, 我认为说得很有道理。那怎么让孩子学会吃苦呢?

▼▼▼▼▼▼▼▼▼▼▼▼▼▼▼▼▼▼▼▼▼▼▼▼▼▼▼▼▼▼▼▼▼▼▼▼

今年寒假, 上海一位年轻的爸爸为了教育女儿, 给了她两个选择, 一是 1000 元的红包, 二是回老家帮助姑妈做农活。这个小女孩选择了后者, 去经受 "吃苦磨练"。我认为对这位有远见的父亲, 不妨也奖他一个红包。

为了使今天的中国孩子在下个世纪不会输给美国人, 日本人, 德国人 ... 做 大人的要给我们的孩子上好 "吃苦磨练" 这一课。

Questions:

1. According to the article, what ability do today's children lack?

2. Why does the writer think that the father deserves an award?

IV. GRAMMAR & USAGE

A. Rewrite the following sentences using V + 起來／起来.

EXAMPLE:　　她聽到這件事很高興。她開始唱歌。

　　　　　　她听到这件事很高兴。她开始唱歌。

→ 她聽到這件事很高興, 就唱起歌來了。

她听到这件事很高兴, 就唱起歌来了。

1. 小林剛回到家。小林坐在沙發上開始看電視。

小林刚回到家。小林坐在沙发上开始看电视。

→ _____。

2. 中文課結束了。他們開始說英文。

中文课结束了。他们开始说英文。

→ _____。

3. 姑媽早上起床以後。姑媽開始洗衣服。
   姑妈早上起床以后。姑妈开始洗衣服。

→ _____。

4. 這兩天天氣一天比一天冷了。
   这两天天气一天比一天冷了。

→ _____。

5. 他戒烟以後, 一天比一天胖了。
   他戒烟以后, 一天比一天胖了。

→ _____。

B. *Complete the sentences using V＋得／不＋了.*

EXAMPLE: 她跟她先生鬧翻了, 要求離婚, 但是她先生不肯簽字, 所以短時間
<u>離不了</u>。
她跟她先生闹翻了, 要求离婚, 但是她先生不肯签字, 所以短时间
<u>离不了</u>。

1. 一般的退休年齡是六十五歲, 老張今年才五十歲,
   一般的退休年龄是六十五岁, 老张今年才五十岁,

_____。

2. 感恩節大家都回家過節, 小李得工作,
   感恩节大家都回家过节, 小李得工作,

_____。

3. 排隊划船的人很多, 可是船很少, 今天我們恐怕
   排队划船的人很多, 可是船很少, 今天我们恐怕

   _____。

C. *Rewrite the sentences using* 要.

EXAMPLE: 這件事情很重要, 我們應該好好考慮考慮。
              这件事情很重要, 我们应该好好考虑考虑。

     → <u>這件事情很重要, 我們要好好考慮考慮。</u>
         <u>这件事情很重要, 我们要好好考虑考虑。</u>

1. 天太熱, 你應該多喝水。
   天太热, 你应该多喝水。

   → _____。

2. 快比賽了, 大家應該多練球。
   快比赛了, 大家应该多练球。

   → _____。

3. 醫生说為了身體健康應該少吃油的, 多吃清淡的。
   医生说为了身体健康应该少吃油的, 多吃清淡的。

   → _____。

D. *You are concerned that if someone you know keeps acting unwisely, there will be adverse consequences. You feel obligated to warn him. Be sure to incorporate* 下去 *in your sentences.*

EXAMPLE: 他每天吃很多肉, <u>再這樣吃下去(的話), 會出問題</u>。
             他每天吃很多肉, <u>再这样吃下去(的话), 会出问题</u>。

    or 再這樣下去, 會出問題。
       再这样下去, 会出问题。

1. 他每天花很多錢,

   他每天花很多钱, _____。

2. 他每天喝很多酒, _____。

3. 張先生和張太太每天吵架,

   张先生和张太太每天吵架, _____。

E. *Rewrite the sentences using* 要不是.

EXAMPLE: 今天晚上的電視節目精彩極了, <u>要不是功課太多</u>, 我一定看下去。

今天晚上的电视节目精彩极了, <u>要不是功课太多</u>, 我一定看下去。

1. 這種牌子的化妝品質量特別好, _____, 我一定會買。

   这种牌子的化妆品质量特别好, _____, 我一定会买。

2. 我是一年級的新生, 對校園不太熟悉,

   _____,

   我的註冊手續不會辦得那麼順利。

   我是一年级的新生, 对校园不太熟悉,

   _____,

   我的注册手续不会办得那么顺利。

3. 那個房子又大又漂亮, 附近環境也好,

   _____,

   我肯定會租下來。

   那个房子又大又漂亮, 附近环境也好,

   _____,

   我肯定会租下来。

F. *It takes a while for English speakers to get used to topic-comment constructions, which are highly characteristic of Chinese. Rephrase the following sentences in more idiomatic Chinese, using topic-comment constructions.*

EXAMPLE: 我弟弟有大眼睛, 高鼻子。

我弟弟有大眼睛, 高鼻子。

→ <u>我弟弟的眼睛大、鼻子高。</u>

▼▼▼▼▼▼▼▼▼▼▼▼▼▼▼▼▼▼▼▼▼▼▼▼▼▼▼▼▼▼▼▼▼▼▼▼

1. 我們有不同的文化背景。

   我们有不同的文化背景。

   → _____。

2. 中國有很多的人口。

   中国有很多的人口。

   → _____。

3. 我父母有很大的房子。

   我父母有很大的房子。

   → _____。

4. 表哥有很多功課。

   表哥有很多功课。

   → _____。

5. a: 你看了那個電影了嗎?

   你看了那个电影了吗?

   b: 看了。那是一個沒有意思的電影。

   看了。那是一个没有意思的电影。

   → _____。

6. a: 你覺得那本書怎麼樣?

   你觉得那本书怎么样?

   b: 那是一本很好看的書。

   那是一本很好看的书。

   → _____。

G. Fill in the blanks with the words provided and translate the passage into English.

(Traditional Characters)

念不下, 看不出來, 看下去, 吃不下

▼▼▼▼▼▼▼▼▼▼▼▼▼▼▼▼▼▼▼▼▼▼▼▼▼▼▼▼▼▼▼▼▼▼▼▼

小林每次一看籃球賽就會激動得大喊大叫。要是有三、四場球賽, 他會一直＿＿＿＿＿＿。他平常很安靜, 大家都＿＿＿＿＿＿他是一個球迷。他自己也覺得奇怪, 為什麼一看球賽就＿＿＿＿＿＿書, ＿＿＿＿＿＿飯。

(Simplified Characters)

念不下, 看不出来, 看下去, 吃不下

小林每次一看篮球赛就会激动得大喊大叫。要是有三、四场球赛, 他会一直＿＿＿＿＿＿。他平常很安静, 大家都＿＿＿＿＿＿他是一个球迷。他自己也觉得奇怪, 为什么一看球赛就＿＿＿＿＿＿书, ＿＿＿＿＿＿饭。

V. TRANSLATION

A. Translate the sentences using 要不是 *and* 说不定 / 说不定.

1. You and Little Gao probably would have gotten married already if your parents hadn't objected.

2. My younger brother probably could have been a great athlete if he hadn't been so lazy.

3. I probably wouldn't have been able to graduate if it hadn't been for my adviser's help.

B. Translate the dialogue into Chinese.

Lisa: I can't go to the movies. I don't feel well. (*V* + 不了)

Tianming: What's the matter?

Lisa: As soon as I got home this afternoon, I began to have a headache.

Tianming: Have you seen a doctor?

Lisa: No, I haven't.

Tianming: Take down my doctor's number and call him. (*V* + 下來 / 下来)

Lisa: All right.

C. Translate the passage into Chinese.

You want to be independent? First of all, you should rent an apartment and move out of your parents' place. Second, you need to find a secure job and not rely on your parents to get by anymore. Third, you need to be responsible for your own conduct.

D. Translate the passage into Chinese using the phrases provided.

In China, people used to believe that men and women should get married when they have reached a certain age (男大當婚, 女大當嫁 / 男大当婚, 女大当嫁) but now I hear that the number of people, especially educated women, who remain single is rising. Some women feel that their work is more important than anything else. Others think that it is best not to have a family or children, because only in this way can one be free. I left China five or six years ago. Who'd have thought that China could have undergone such big changes (變化 / 变化: biànhuà)?

聽說, 起來, 最好, 沒想到
听说, 起来, 最好, 没想到

VI. COMPOSITION

你認為父母應該怎樣教育孩子？

你认为父母应该怎样教育孩子？

第十五課　▲　男女平等

I. LISTENING COMPREHENSION

A. Listen to the audio for the Textbook and answer the questions.

1. Why did Lisa's friend quit her job?

2. What do Zhang Tianming and Lisa agree on?

3. Who is more optimistic about the issue in question?

4. Whom should a Chinese woman have obeyed in the old society?

5. According to the author, in which period did Chinese women start to gain true equality?

B. Listen to the audio for the Workbook.

1. Look at the new words before listening to the recording:

   女籃 / 女篮 (nǚlán): short for 女子籃球 / 女子篮球, women's basketball

   男籃 / 男篮 (nánlán): short for 男子籃球 / 男子篮球, men's basketball

   a. Which team has a better record?

   b. Why do men's basketball teams in general get much more TV coverage?

   c. Why is the women's basketball coach's salary much lower than that of the men's basketball coach?

d. On the basis of the incident, do you think the school discriminates against women? Why or why not?

2. Listen to the passage and answer the questions.

   a. 中國婦女找工作是改革開放以前容易還是改革開放以後容易?
   中国妇女找工作是改革开放以前容易还是改革开放以后容易?

   b. 要是一個女的想在公司裏找一個主管的工作, 她找到的機會大不大? 為什麼?
   要是一个女的想在公司里找一个主管的工作, 她找到的机会大不大? 为什么?

   c. 報紙的廣告上, 有哪些男女不平等的現象?
   报纸的广告上, 有哪些男女不平等的现象?

3. Listen to the passage and answer the questions.
   a. What do women find so painful when they go to a ball game in a sports stadium?

   b. What do women have to do when they cannot wait any longer?

   c. What preconceptions do people have about women and sports?

   d. Why should people change their preconceptions?

▼▼▼▼▼▼▼▼▼▼▼▼▼▼▼▼▼▼▼▼▼▼▼▼▼▼▼▼▼▼▼▼▼▼▼▼▼

II. SPEAKING EXERCISES

A. Practice asking and answering the following questions with a partner before class.

1. 你家誰負責帶孩子？誰負責教育孩子？

 你家谁负责带孩子？谁负责教育孩子？

2. 你幫不幫父母分擔家務？

 你帮不帮父母分担家务？

3. "老鼠見了貓"是什麼意思？

 "老鼠见了猫"是什么意思？

4. 社會上有哪些男女不平等的現象？

 社会上有哪些男女不平等的现象？

B. Practice speaking on the following topics.

1. 你認為怎樣才算男女平等？你認為男女能平等嗎？

 你认为怎样才算男女平等？你认为男女能平等吗？

2. 談談從五十年代以來中國婦女的社會地位有什麼樣的變化。

 谈谈从五十年代以来中国妇女的社会地位有什么样的变化。

婦女外出工作 / 妇女外出工作

III. READING COMPREHENSION

A. Read the passage and answer the questions. (True/False)

(Traditional Characters)

　　現在的年輕夫婦大部份一起分擔家務, 照顧孩子。丈夫不見得一定在外邊工作賺錢, 妻子也不是非辭職回家當家庭主婦不可。很多家庭夫婦兩人一起商量怎樣解決家中的問題。可以說在家庭中男女的地位是平等的。

(Simplified Characters)

　　现在的年轻夫妇大部分一起分担家务, 照顾孩子。丈夫不见得一定在外边工作赚钱, 妻子也不是非辞职回家当家庭主妇不可。很多家庭夫妇两人一起商量怎样解决家中的问题。可以说在家庭中男女的地位是平等的。

Questions (True/False):

(   ) 1. Most young couples do not want to do housework.

(   ) 2. Husbands have to be the breadwinners.

(   ) 3. Husbands and wives have an equal say in everything regarding the household.

B. Fill in the blanks with vocabulary items from this lesson.

(Traditional Characters)

　　麗莎的姐姐是一位律師, 有很多婦女找她幫忙打官司 (sue)。不少是因為在工作上受到＿＿＿＿＿＿,和她們的男同事做同樣的工作,可是薪水卻比男同事低。麗莎的姐姐認為男女應該＿＿＿＿＿＿, 應該＿＿＿＿＿＿,社會上不應該＿＿＿＿＿＿。

(Simplified Characters)

　　丽莎的姐姐是一位律师, 有很多妇女找她帮忙打官司 (sue)。不少是因为在工作上受到＿＿＿＿＿＿,和她们的男同事做同样的工作,可是薪水却比男同事低。丽莎的姐姐认为男女应该＿＿＿＿＿＿, 应该＿＿＿＿＿＿,社会上不应该＿＿＿＿＿＿。

C. Answer the questions after reading the passage.

(Traditional Characters)

　　林雪梅的父母親非常重男輕女。他們生第一個孩子的時候, 一看是個女的, 就叫她"林招弟", 希望她能帶來一個弟弟。生第二個的時候, 沒想到又是個女的, 就把她的名字叫做"林來弟", 希望以後能生個弟弟。林雪梅是第三個孩子。出生的時候, 父母看她又是個女孩, 但是不願意再生了, 就叫她"林若男", 希望她能像個男孩一樣。

　　林雪梅的父母從小就把她當男孩: 不給她裙子 (1) 穿,只讓她穿牛仔褲。也不讓她留長頭髮 (2)。但是林雪梅從小就認為男孩能做的, 自己也都能做, 特別反對重男輕女。她認為女孩沒有什麼不好。上大學以後, 就把自己的名字從"林若男"改成"林雪梅"了。

(1)　裙子(qúnzi): skirt
(2)　頭髮(tóufa): hair (on the human head)

(Simplified Characters)

　　林雪梅的父母亲非常重男轻女。他们生第一个孩子的时候, 一看是个女的, 就叫她 "林招弟", 希望她能带来一个弟弟。生第二个的时候, 没想到又是个女的, 就把她的名字叫做 "林来弟", 希望以后能生个弟弟。林雪梅是第三个孩子, 出生的时候, 父母看她又是个女孩, 但是不愿意再生了, 就叫她 "林若男", 希望她能像个男孩一样。

　　林雪梅的父母从小就把她当男孩: 不给她裙子(1)穿, 只让她穿牛仔裤,也不让她留长头发 (2)。但是林雪梅从小就认为男孩能做的, 自己也都能做, 特别反对重男轻女。她认为女孩子没有什么不好。上大学以后, 就把自己的名字从 "林若男" 改成 "林雪梅" 了。

(1)　裙子(qúnzi): skirt
(2)　头发(tóufa): hair (on the human head)

Questions:

1.　How many brothers and sisters does Lin Xuemei have?

2. Why was her oldest sister named 招弟?

3. What is her second sister's name?

4. What does Lin Xuemei's original name mean?

5. How did Lin Xuemei get her current name?

D. Read the passage and answer the questions.

(Traditional Characters)

　　上個星期六柯林去王先生家玩。柯林覺得王先生的家庭體現了男女平等的精神。王先生結婚三年了。太太去年生了孩子以後，就把工作辭了，在家裏當家庭主婦。王先生看起來非常體貼妻子。他告訴柯林，在家他太太的地位比他高，很多事情都是太太當家作主，他得服從太太。吃飯的時候，柯林聽到王先生叫他太太"當家的"："當家的，把醋給我。""當家的，給我一杯茶。"吃完飯，趁王太太在廚房洗碗，柯林問王先生為什麼老叫太太"當家的"，王先生笑著小聲說："我把她的名字忘了。"

(Simplified Characters)

　　上个星期六柯林去王先生家玩。柯林觉得王先生的家庭体现了男女平等的精神。王先生结婚三年了。太太去年生了孩子以後，就把工作辞了，在家里当家庭主妇。王先生看起来非常体贴妻子。他告诉柯林，在家他太太的地位比他高，很多事情都是太太当家作主，他得服从太太。吃饭的时候，柯林听到王先生叫他太太"当家的"："当家的，把醋给我。""当家的，给我一杯茶。"吃完饭，趁王太太在厨房洗碗，柯林问王先生为什么老叫太太"当家的"，王先生笑着小声说："我把她的名字忘了。"

▼▼

Questions (True/False):

(　　) 1. When Mr. Wang got married, his wife was not working.

(　　) 2. Mrs. Wang had a child two years after she got married.

(　　) 3. Mr. Wang's claim of being subordinate to his wife proved to be disingenuous.

Questions (Multiple Choice):

(　　) 4. The term 當家的 ／ 当家的 means:

    a.　the one who stays home.

    b.　the one who is in charge of the household.

    c.　the one who does the housework.

(　　) 5. At the dinner table, Mr. Wang appeared quite _____ his wife.

    a.　commanding toward

    b.　considerate of

    c.　deferential to

E. A company placed this recruitment ad in the newspaper. Would you be qualified to apply? Why or why not?

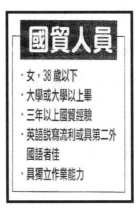

(See the Alternate Character Appendix for simplified characters.)

F. Read the story and answer the questions.

(Traditional Characters)

花木蘭的故事

　　中國古時候有一個叫花木蘭的女子。有一天, 她在家裏一邊幹活, 一邊想著父親前一天說的話。父親昨天很著急地告訴她, 他們家必須有一個人去當

兵 (1)。父親說他已經老了, 身體又不好, 可是因為木蘭沒有哥哥, 弟弟又太小, 看來父親只能自己去了。木蘭想來想去, 決定自己穿上男人的衣服替父親去當兵。

　　木蘭當了兵以後, 和男兵一樣, 男兵能做的, 她也能做, 而且做得非常好。大家都以為她是男的。幾年以後, 木蘭回到了家, 換上女人穿的衣服, 化了妝, 男兵們看了都非常驚訝 (2)。木蘭說,"兩隻兔子 (3) 在地上一起跑, 誰能看得出哪個是雌 (4) 的, 哪個是雄 (5) 的呢?"

(1)　當兵(dāng bīng): to serve in the army

(2)　驚訝(jīngyà): surprised; astonished

(3)　兔子(tùzi): rabbit

(4)　雌(cí): (of animals) female

(5)　雄(xióng): (of animals) male

(Simplified Characters)

花木兰的故事

　　中国古时候有一个叫花木兰的女子。有一天, 她在家里一边干活, 一边想着父亲前一天说的话。父亲昨天很着急地告诉她, 他们家必须有一个人去当

▼▼▼▼▼▼▼▼▼▼▼▼▼▼▼▼▼▼▼▼▼▼▼▼▼▼▼▼▼▼▼▼▼▼▼

兵 (1)。父亲说他已经很老了, 身体又不好, 可是因为木兰没有哥哥, 弟弟又太小, 看来父亲只能自己去了。木兰想来想去, 决定自己穿上男人的衣服替父亲去当兵。

　　木兰当了兵以后, 和男兵一样, 男兵能做的, 她也能做, 而且做得非常好。大家都以为她是男的。几年以后, 木兰回到了家, 换上女人穿的衣服, 化了妆, 男兵们看了都非常惊讶 (2)。木兰说,"两只兔子 (3) 在地上一起跑, 谁能看得出哪个是雌 (4) 的, 哪个是雄 (5) 的呢?"

(1)　当兵(dāng bīng): to serve in the army

(2)　惊讶(jīngyà): surprised; astonished

(3)　兔子(tùzi): rabbit

(4)　雌(cí): (of animals) female

(5)　雄(xióng): (of animals) male

Questions:

1. What did Mulan's father say to her?

2. How many brothers did Mulan have?

3. Did Mulan do a good job in the army?

4. Why were her fellow soldiers surprised when Mulan returned home?

5. How did Mulan respond to people?

IV. GRAMMAR & USAGE

A. Complete the sentences using 就拿...來說 / 就拿...来说.

EXAMPLE:　　　他對他太太非常體貼。就拿昨天來說, 他親自下廚做了幾個拿手好菜給太太吃。

　　　　　　　他对他太太非常体贴。<u>就拿昨天来说,</u> <u>他亲自下厨做了几个拿手</u><u>好菜给太太吃</u>。

1. 在社會上有許多男女不平等的現象。
   在社会上有许多男女不平等的现象。

   _____, _____。

2. 小張在學校各方面都表現得非常好。
   小张在学校各方面都表现得非常好。

   _____, _____。

3. 中國人過不同的節, 吃的東西不同。
   中国人过不同的节, 吃的东西不同。

   _____, _____。

B. *Complete the sentences using* 甚至.

EXAMPLE:　　a: 你平常看什麼電視? (看 廣告)
　　　　　　　你平常看什么电视? (看 广告)

　　　　　　b: 我什麼都看, <u>甚至連廣告都看</u>。
　　　　　　　我什么都看, <u>甚至连广告都看</u>。

1. a: 你什麼時候結婚啊?
   你什么时候结婚啊?

   b: 結婚?! 我_____。(沒有 女朋友)
   结婚?! 我_____。(没有 女朋友)

2. a: 你先生在家幫不幫你分擔家務?
   你先生在家帮不帮你分担家务?

   b: 幫我做家務事? 他_____。(不洗 碗)
   帮我做家务事? 他_____。(不洗 碗)

3. 我同屋很願意幫助別人, _____。(幫 不認識的人)
   我同屋很愿意帮助别人, _____。(帮 不认识的人)

▼▼▼▼▼▼▼▼▼▼▼▼▼▼▼▼▼▼▼▼▼▼▼▼▼▼▼▼▼▼▼▼▼▼▼▼▼▼

C. Rewrite the sentences using ...以來 ／ ...以来.

EXAMPLE:　　　從結婚到現在, 老張從來沒跟太太吵過架。

　　　　　　　从结婚到现在, 老张从来没跟太太吵过架。

　　→ 結婚以來, 老張從來沒跟太太吵過架。

　　　結婚以来, 老张从来没跟太太吵过架。

1. 從退休到現在, 王老師一直沒閒著, 不是寫文章, 就是出國旅行。

   从退休到现在, 王老师一直没闲着, 不是写文章, 就是出国旅行。

   →＿＿＿＿＿＿＿＿＿＿＿＿＿＿＿＿, 王老師一直沒閒著, 不是寫文章, 就是
   出國旅行。

   →＿＿＿＿＿＿＿＿＿＿＿＿＿＿＿＿, 王老师一直没闲着, 不是写文章, 就是
   出国旅行。

2. 那部電影從上演到現在, 已經打破美國商業片的票房記錄。

   那部电影从上演到现在, 已经打破美国商业片的票房记录。

   →＿＿＿＿＿＿＿＿＿＿＿＿＿＿＿＿, 已經打破美國商業片的票房記錄。

   →＿＿＿＿＿＿＿＿＿＿＿＿＿＿＿＿, 已经打破美国商业片的票房记录。

3. 那個公園從開放到今天, 已經吸引了成千上萬的遊客。

   那个公园从开放到今天, 已经吸引了成千上万的游客。

   →＿＿＿＿＿＿＿＿＿＿＿＿＿＿＿＿, 已經吸引了成千上萬的遊客。

   →＿＿＿＿＿＿＿＿＿＿＿＿＿＿＿＿, 已经吸引了成千上万的游客。

4. 從開學到現在, 你大概學了多少新漢字？

   从开学到现在, 你大概学了多少新汉字？

   →＿＿＿＿＿＿＿＿＿＿＿＿＿＿＿＿, 你大概學了多少新漢字？

   →＿＿＿＿＿＿＿＿＿＿＿＿＿＿＿＿, 你大概学了多少新汉字？

▼ ▼

D. Fill in the blanks with either 一樣 ／ 一样 *or* 同樣 ／ 同样*.*

1. ＿＿＿＿＿＿＿的問題不用反復討論那麼多次。

   ＿＿＿＿＿＿＿的问题不用反复讨论那么多次。

2. 雖然他們都住宿舍, 可是宿舍的設備很不＿＿＿＿＿＿＿。

   虽然他们都住宿舍, 可是宿舍的设备很不＿＿＿＿＿＿＿。

3. 她們兩姐妹的性格脾氣很不＿＿＿＿＿＿＿,一個很開朗, 另一個很不開朗。

   她们两姐妹的性格脾气很不＿＿＿＿＿＿＿, 一个很开朗, 另一个很不开朗。

4. 中國南方和北方的氣候很不＿＿＿＿＿＿＿。

   中国南方和北方的气候很不＿＿＿＿＿＿＿。

5. 小王、小李、小柯都申請了＿＿＿＿＿＿＿的研究所。

   小王、小李、小柯都申请了＿＿＿＿＿＿＿的研究所。

E. Fill in the blanks with the words provided.

(Traditional Characters)

要不是, 沒想到, 甚至, 實際上, 說不定

　　自從小李辭職以來,她的婆婆常跟他吵架。＿＿＿＿＿＿＿小李的先生在旁邊, ＿＿＿＿＿＿＿她們吵得更屬害呢。小李所以辭職是因為想待在家裏帶孩子。＿＿＿＿＿＿＿婆婆不讓小李帶, 有時候＿＿＿＿＿＿＿不讓小李跟孩子一起吃飯。婆婆說小李不是個好妻子、好母親。可是＿＿＿＿＿＿＿, 大家都知道小李是個模範妻子、模範母親, 不但體貼先生, 而且非常愛孩子。

(Simplified Characters)

要不是, 没想到, 甚至, 实际上, 说不定

　　自从小李辞职以来, 她的婆婆常跟她吵架。＿＿＿＿＿＿＿小李的先生在旁边, ＿＿＿＿＿＿＿她们吵得更厉害呢。小李所以辞职是因为想待在家里带孩子。＿＿＿＿＿＿＿婆婆不让小李带, 有时候＿＿＿＿＿＿＿不让小李跟孩子一起吃饭。婆婆说小李不是个好妻子、好母亲。可是＿＿＿＿＿＿＿, 大家都知道小李是个模范妻子、模范母亲, 不但体贴先生, 而且非常爱孩子。

▼▼▼▼▼▼▼▼▼▼▼▼▼▼▼▼▼▼▼▼▼▼▼▼▼▼▼▼▼▼▼▼▼▼▼▼▼▼

V. TRANSLATION

A. Translate the passage into Chinese. Pay attention to Chinese word order.

It's been three years since Mr. and Mrs. Wang got divorced. They fought fiercely before they parted company. Things have been much better since the divorce. Now they even joke when they speak to each other. Every year their kids spend six months with their dad and six months with their mom, but every New Year they go back together to Washington, D.C., by plane to see their grandma. Now Mr. and Mrs. Wang get along with one another much better. People all say that they were right to divorce.

B. Translate the following passage into Chinese using the phrases provided.

Equality between men and women is not an issue that could be easily resolved. Take me, for example: I think women's status is already very high. Men sometimes do not fare as well as women. Isn't it true that it's easier for women to find jobs? My wife does not agree with me. She says that in terms of position and salary, society as a whole flagrantly favors men over women. She believes that so long as people are discussing equality between men and women, it must be because inequality exists in reality. Furthermore, she says that equality between men and women may never be achieved.

就拿...來說, 明顯, 實際上

就拿...来说, 明显, 实际上

C. *Translate the passage into Chinese.*

Many people believe that women's social status has been elevated and that gender equality is slowly manifesting itself in families and in society. However, many women are not that optimistic. They feel that there is still plenty of discrimination against women.

升學 → 畢業 → 就業 / 升学 → 毕业 → 就业

VI. COMPOSITION

1. 我生活中的一位女性 (可以寫你的母親、姐姐、或者妹妹)

   我生活中的一位女性 (可以写你的母亲、姐姐、或者妹妹)

2. 我對男女平等問題的看法
   我对男女平等问题的看法

第十六課 ▲ 健康與保險

第十六课 ▲ 健康与保险

 I. LISTENING COMPREHENSION

A. Listen to the audio for the Textbook and answer the questions.

1. Why couldn't Tianming go to the movie?

2. Why didn't his aunt have the operation in Canada?

3. What is the drawback of having the operation in America?

4. Why does Lisa think the Canadians have a better health care system?

5. Why does Lisa want to meet Tianming's aunt?

B. Listen to the audio for the Workbook.

1. Listen to the passage and answer the multiple-choice questions.

( ) a. 張天明的媽媽年輕時
   　　張天明的妈妈年轻时

   1) 喜歡看電影。
      喜欢看电影。

   2) 在電影院工作。
      在电影院工作。

   3) 想當電影明星。
      想当电影明星。

( )b. 姑媽年輕的時候
姑妈年轻的时候

　　1) 沒有人買保險。
　　　沒有人买保险。

　　2) 電影公司會替明星買保險。
　　　电影公司会替明星买保险。

　　3) 很有錢，她自己買保險。
　　　很有钱，她自己买保险。

　　4) 拍武打片不能買保險。
　　　拍武打片不能买保险。

( )c. 張天明的姑媽不再拍武打片了，因為
張天明的姑妈不再拍武打片了，因为

　　1) 她的醫生説不行。
　　　她的医生说不行。

　　2) 拍武打片買不到保險。
　　　拍武打片买不到保险。

　　3) 武打片沒有意思。
　　　武打片没有意思。

　　4) 她想移民到加拿大去。

( )d. 保險公司讓張天明的姑媽在中國移民中做生意，因為
保险公司让张天明的姑妈在中国移民中做生意，因为

　　1) 她只會中文，不懂英文。
　　　她只会中文，不懂英文。

2) 中國移民喜歡買保險。

中国移民喜欢买保险。

3) 很多中國移民都知道她是誰。

很多中国移民都知道她是谁。

4) 她經常去台灣、香港和中國大陸。

她经常去台湾、香港和中国大陆。

( ) e. 張天明的姑媽現在

張天明的姑妈现在

1) 有自己的保險公司。

有自己的保险公司。

2) 出錢辦醫院。

出钱办医院。

3) 開了一家電影公司。

开了一家电影公司。

4) 教人說中國話。

教人说中国话。

2. Listen to the passage and answer the questions.

a. What phenomenon don't Chinese people understand when they first come to this country?

b. According to the passage, what kinds of insurance do Americans purchase?

c. Why do many Chinese people start buying insurance after they've been in the United States for a while?

3. Listen to the passage and answer the questions.

a. Why was David taken to the hospital?

b. What was the doctor's evaluation?

   c.   What did the doctor decide to do?

   d.   Why was David nervous?

   e.   Did he have a reason to feel nervous? Why?

II. SPEAKING EXERCISES

A. Practice asking and answering the questions with a partner before class.

1. 你家買了些什麽保險？
   你家买了些什么保险？

2. 你覺得美國的醫療保險制度有什麽問題？
   你觉得美国的医疗保险制度有什么问题？

3. 你認爲應該怎樣改革美國的醫療保險制度？
   你认为应该怎样改革美国的医疗保险制度？

4. “羊毛出在羊身上”是什麽意思？
   “羊毛出在羊身上”是什么意思？

一张保单保全家

为爱尽责　让家无忧

B. Practice speaking on the following topics.

1. 請談談美國政府應該怎麼照顧窮人。

   请谈谈美国政府应该怎么照顾穷人。

2. 請談談怎麼樣才能有健康的身體。

   请谈谈怎么样才能有健康的身体。

3. 你認為政府是不是應該給所有的人買保險? 為什麼?

   你认为政府是不是应该给所有的人买保险? 为什么?

III. READING COMPREHENSION

A. Answer the questions after reading the passage.

(Traditional Characters)

　　在美國, 子女不滿十八歲, 大部份人是父母替他們買健康保險。成年人從學校畢業或找到工作以後, 一般由公司和個人分擔保險費用。要是沒有了工作, 就得自己花錢買保險。但是美國一般的醫療保險不是什麼都管, 像眼睛和牙齒還得另外買保險。所以一家人的保險費加起來實在不少。難怪有人說在美國生不起病。以前在中國, 城市裏大部份有工作的人都是公費醫療, 生了病就到醫院去掛號看病, 醫藥費大多由政府出, 自己幾乎不花錢。改革開放以後, 中國政府慢慢地把公費醫療改變 (gǎibiàn) 成保險制度, 老百姓個人的醫療負擔也越來越重了。

(Simplified Characters)

　　在美国, 子女不满十八岁, 大部分是父母替他们买健康保险。成年人从学校毕业或找到工作以后, 一般由公司和个人分担保险费用。要是没有了工作, 就得自己花钱买保险。但是美国一般的医疗保险不是什么都管, 像眼睛和牙齿还得另外买保险。所以一家人的保险费加起来实在不少, 难怪有人说在美国生不起病。以前在中国, 城市里大部分有工作的人都是公费医疗, 生了病就到医院去挂号看病, 医药费大多由政府出, 自己几乎不花钱。改革开放以后, 中国政府慢慢地把公费医疗改变 (gǎibiàn) 成保险制度, 老百姓个人的医疗负担也越来越重了。

1. 請問, "公費" 是什麽意思?
   请问, "公费" 是什么意思?

2. 中國過去的公費醫療和美國的醫療保險有什麽不同?
   中国过去的公费医疗和美国的医疗保险有什么不同?

3. 為什麽在美國生不起病?
   为什么在美国生不起病?

B. *Read the passage and answer the questions. (True/False)*

(Traditional Characters)

　　斯蒂夫的哥哥約翰住在一個小城裏。有一天約翰突然覺得很不舒服, 頭很疼, 他覺得病得很厲害。他不相信小城裏的醫生。因為他有醫療保險, 弟弟斯蒂夫又很有錢, 不用怕付不起醫療費, 所以特地坐飛機去紐約一家非常有名的醫院看病。醫生給他檢查, 然後跟他說 "先生, 你確實有病, 是你的腦子有問題, 非做手術不可。" 約翰問: "你肯定我的腦子有問題嗎?" 醫生回答說: "要是你的腦子沒問題, 你怎麽會為了一點兒小病坐飛機來紐約看病呢?"

(Simplified Characters)

　　斯蒂夫的哥哥约翰住在一个小城里。有一天约翰突然觉得很不舒服，头很疼，他觉得病得很厉害。他不相信小城里的医生。因为他有医疗保险，弟弟斯蒂夫又很有钱，不用怕付不起医疗费，所以特地坐飞机去纽约一家非常有名的医院看病。医生给他检查，然後跟他说："先生，你确实有病，是你的脑子有问题，非做手术不可。"约翰问："你肯定我的脑子有问题吗？"医生回答说："要是你的脑子没问题，你怎么会为了一点儿小病坐飞机来纽约看病呢？"

Questions (True/False):

(　　) 1. John started to feel sick when he went to New York.

(　　) 2. John felt that only famous doctors in famous hospitals were trustworthy.

(　　) 3. John felt that if he needed it, Steven would give him financial support.

(　　) 4. John found out in New York that his illness was more serious than he had thought.

(　　) 5. The doctor didn't think it was necessary for John to come to New York.

(　　) 6. John would have the operation after consulting with the doctor.

*C. **Read the story and answer the questions. (True/False)***

(Traditional Characters)

中醫、中藥有幾千年的歷史, 出了許多有名的醫學家, 如華陀 (1), 張仲景 (2), 李時珍 (3) 等。華陀生活在公元 (4) 二世紀到三世紀,他能夠用一種藥來麻醉 (5) 病人,然後在病人身上做手術。張仲景 (公元二—三世紀) 也是漢代的醫學家, 他的《傷寒論》(6) 對中醫的發展產生了很大的影響, 在書中他提出了防病 (7) 比治病 (8) 更重要的觀點。李時珍是中國明代 (1368–1644) 的醫學家和藥物學 (9) 家。他寫了《本草綱目》(10), 對中國藥物學的發展做出了極大的貢獻 (11)。

(1)   華陀 (Huà Tuó): a person's name
(2)   張仲景 (Zhāng Zhòngjǐng): a person's name
(3)   李時珍 (Lǐ Shízhēn): a person's name
(4)   公元 (gōngyuán): "common era," i.e., CE (formerly AD) in the Western dating system
(5)   麻醉 (mázuì): anaesthetize
(6)   《傷寒論》 (Shānghán Lùn): *On Febrile Diseases*
(7)   防病 (fáng bìng): to prevent illness
(8)   治病 (zhì bìng): to treat an illness
(9)   藥物學 (yàowùxué): pharmacology
(10) 《本草綱目》 (Běncǎo Gāngmù): *Materia Medica*
(11) 貢獻 (gòngxiàn): contribution

(Simplified Characters)

中医、中药有几千年的历史, 出了许多有名的医学家, 如华陀 (1), 张仲景 (2), 李时珍 (3) 等。华陀生活在公元 (4) 二世纪到三世纪, 他能够用一种药来麻醉 (5) 病人,然后在病人身上做手术。张仲景 (公元二 — 三世纪) 也是汉代的医学家, 他的《伤寒论》(6) 对中医的发展产生了很大的影响, 在书中他提出了防病 (7) 比治病 (8) 更重要的观点。李时珍是中国明代 (1368–1644) 的医学家和药物学 (9) 家。他写了《本草纲目》(10), 对中国药物学的发展做出了极大的贡献 (11)。

(1)   华陀 (Huà Tuó): a person's name
(2)   张仲景 (Zhāng Zhòngjǐng): a person's name
(3)   李时珍 (Lǐ Shízhēn): a person's name
(4)   公元 (gōngyuán): "common era," i.e., CE (formerly AD) in the Western dating system

▼ ▼

(5) 麻醉 (mázuì): anaesthetize

(6) 《伤寒论》 (Shānghán Lùn): *On Febrile Diseases*

(7) 防病 (fang bìng): to prevent illness

(8) 治病 (zhì bìng): to treat an illness

(9) 药物学 (yàowùxué): pharmacology

(10) 《本草纲目》 (Běncǎo Gāngmù): *Materia Medica*

(11) 贡献 (gòngxiàn): contribution

Questions (True/False):

(　　) 1.　華陀和張仲景都是漢代的醫學家。

　　　　华陀和张仲景都是汉代的医学家。

(　　) 2.　華陀也很懂藥。

　　　　华陀也很懂药。

(　　) 3.　張仲景認為醫生應該儘可能讓人不生病。

　　　　张仲景认为医生应该尽可能让人不生病。

(　　) 4.　《本草綱目》和《傷寒論》一樣，都是藥物學方面的書。

　　　　《本草纲目》和《伤寒论》一样，都是药物学方面的书。

D. Read the introduction, examine the insurance card, and answer the questions.

From 1949 until a few years ago, insurance in any form was all but unknown in China. There is now a flourishing insurance industry in China. Foreign insurance companies are also trying to cash in on the potentially huge insurance market in China. One of them, the American International Group, has returned to Shanghai, where it was founded before 1949.

中國平安保險公司

西湖游船游客人身安全保险证

贰　　　　角

(See the Alternate Character Appendix for traditional characters.)

1. Who issued the card?

2. Who is it for?

3. What is it for?

4. How much does it cost?

E. Take a look at a schedule for a clinic's outpatient service and answer the questions. (True/False)

門診時間 ：
上午 8:00 ～ 12:00
下午 14:00 ～ 17:50
晚上 18:30 ～ 21:30
※ 國 定 假 日 · 照 常 門 診
※ 周 日 僅 上 午 看 診

(See the Alternate Character Appendix for simplified characters.)

(   ) 1. The clinic is open daily.

(   ) 2. The clinic is open for holidays.

(   ) 3. Patients can make appointments for Sunday afternoons.

IV. GRAMMAR & USAGE

A. Complete the sentences using V + 得/不 + 起*.*

EXAMPLE: 這件衣服太貴了, <u>我買不起</u>。
               这件衣服太贵了, <u>我买不起</u>。

1. 沒有醫療保險的人_____。
    没有医疗保险的人_____。

2. 現在大學的學費越來越貴, 很多人_____。
    现在大学的学费越来越贵, 很多人_____。

3. 那家餐館的菜價錢那麽貴, _____。
    那家餐馆的菜价钱那么贵, _____。

▼▼▼

B. Rewrite the sentences using 不如.

EXAMPLE: 這家醫院的心臟科醫生比那家醫院的有名。

這家医院的心脏科医生比那家医院的有名。

→ 那家醫院的心臟科醫生不如這家醫院的有名。

那家医院的心脏科医生不如这家医院的有名。

1. 很多人覺得國際足球比美式足球精彩。

很多人觉得国际足球比美式足球精彩。

→ _____。

2. 今年申請這個大學的人比去年少。

今年申请这个大学的人比去年少。

→ _____。

3. 我們球隊的教練比你們球隊的教練有經驗。

我们球队的教练比你们球队的教练有经验。

→ _____。

C. Rearrange the modifiers into their correct sequence.

EXAMPLE: 最有名、美國、幾個、大學

最有名、美国、几个、大学

→ 美國幾個最有名的大學

美国几个最有名的大学

1. 英國、兩個、最古老、城市

英国、两个、最古老、城市

→ _____。

2. 我吃過、一頓、最好吃、飯

我吃过、一顿、最好吃、饭

→ _____。

3. 很多、中文、經驗豐富、老師
　　很多、中文、经验丰富、老师

　　→ _____。

4. 黑、小、貓
　　黑、小、猫

　　→ _____。

5. 紅紅、圓、臉
　　红红、圆、脸

　　→ _____。

D. *Rewrite the following using* 毫無 ／ 毫无.

EXAMPLE:　　這個情況很糟糕, 我一點辦法都沒有。
　　　　　　　这个情况很糟糕, 我一点办法都没有。

　　　→ <u>這個情況很糟糕, 我毫無辦法</u>。
　　　　<u>这个情况很糟糕, 我毫无办法</u>。

1. 他這個人做事一點計劃都沒有。
　　他这个人做事一点计划都没有。

　　→ _____。

2. 那個研究生對哲學一點興趣都沒有。
　　那个研究生对哲学一点兴趣都没有。

　　→ _____。

3. 小張大學剛畢業, 一點工作經驗都沒有, 找工作肯定不容易。
　　小张大学刚毕业, 一点工作经验都没有, 找工作肯定不容易。

　　→ _____, 找工作肯定不容易。

E. *Complete the dialogues using* 至少.

EXAMPLE:　a: 你怎麼申請這個管理學院?
　　　　　　　你怎么申请这个管理学院?

▼ ▼

b: 這個管理學院雖然不太有名, 但是<u>至少學費便宜</u>。

這个管理学院虽然不太有名, 但是<u>至少学费便宜</u>。

1. a: 李先生不是一個模範丈夫。

李先生不是一个模范丈夫。

b: 李先生雖然不是一個模範丈夫, 但是＿＿＿＿＿＿＿＿＿＿＿。

李先生虽然不是一个模范丈夫, 但是＿＿＿＿＿＿＿＿＿＿＿。

2. a: 這套運動服的顏色實在難看。

这套运动服的颜色实在难看。

b: 這套運動服的顏色雖然難看, 可是＿＿＿＿＿＿＿＿＿＿＿。

这套运动服的颜色虽然难看, 可是＿＿＿＿＿＿＿＿＿＿＿。

3. a: 這個工作真沒意思, 真想辭職不幹了。

这个工作真没意思, 真想辞职不干了。

b: 千萬別辭職。這個工作雖然沒意思, 可是＿＿＿＿＿＿＿＿＿＿。

千万别辞职。这个工作虽然没意思, 可是＿＿＿＿＿＿＿＿＿＿。

F. Complete the dialogues using 畢竟／毕竟.

EXAMPLE: a: 你覺得這棟樓的設備怎麼樣?(老樓)

你觉得这栋楼的设备怎么样?(老楼)

b: 這棟樓的設備不錯, <u>但是畢竟是一棟老樓, 設備沒有新樓好</u>。

这栋楼的设备不错, <u>但是毕竟是一栋老楼, 设备没有新楼好</u>。

1. a: 聽說柯林的中文很好, 能上中國電視播中文新聞嗎?(只學了三年中文)

听说柯林的中文很好, 能上中国电视播中文新闻吗?(只学了三年中文)

b: 他的中文雖然不錯, ＿＿＿＿＿＿＿＿, ＿＿＿＿＿＿＿＿。

他的中文虽然不错, ＿＿＿＿＿＿＿＿, ＿＿＿＿＿＿＿＿。

2. a: 你新租的房子怎麼樣? 比學校的宿舍安靜吧?(公寓)

你新租的房子怎么样? 比学校的宿舍安静吧?(公寓)

b: 雖然比學校的宿舍安靜, ＿＿＿＿＿＿＿＿＿＿, ＿＿＿＿＿＿＿＿＿＿。

虽然比学校的宿舍安静, ＿＿＿＿＿＿＿＿＿＿, ＿＿＿＿＿＿＿＿＿＿。

3. a: 這條褲子質量好、颜色漂亮, 你買一條吧。(不是名牌)

这条裤子质量好、颜色漂亮, 你买一条吧。(不是名牌)

b: 這條褲子質量、颜色都不錯, ＿＿＿＿＿＿＿＿＿, ＿＿＿＿＿＿＿＿＿。

这条裤子质量、颜色都不错, ＿＿＿＿＿＿＿＿＿, ＿＿＿＿＿＿＿＿＿。

G. Which is a better choice? Note that in some cases either choice is possible, although there may be a slight difference in nuance. Explain your decision briefly in English.

1. 大家知道小王生病動手術以後, ＿＿＿＿＿＿都給他寫信。(人人、每個人)

大家知道小王生病动手术以后, ＿＿＿＿＿＿都给他写信。(人人、每个人)

2. 李哲畢業找到工作以後, 給學校的＿＿＿＿＿＿寫了一封感謝信。(人人、每個人)

李哲毕业找到工作以后, 给学校的＿＿＿＿＿＿写了一封感谢信。(人人、每个人)

3. 那個主管說了那麼多難聽的話, 讓＿＿＿＿＿＿都很不高興。(人人、每個人)

那个主管说了那么多难听的话, 让＿＿＿＿＿＿都很不高兴。(人人、每个人)

V. TRANSLATION

A. Translate the passage into Chinese using the words provided.

Many people cannot afford to see a doctor when they are ill. No wonder some people think that America's health insurance system is not as good as Canada's. In Canada, at least everybody can afford to see a doctor. However, the Canadian health care system has problems, too. Sometimes patients have to wait a long time before they can see a doctor. In addition, some people feel that medical facilities in Canada are not as good as those in the United States.

V + 不起, 不如, *V* + 得起, 至少

▼▼▼▼▼▼▼▼▼▼▼▼▼▼▼▼▼▼▼▼▼▼▼▼▼▼▼▼▼▼▼▼▼▼▼▼▼▼

B. Translate the passage into Chinese.

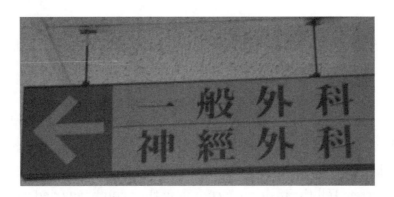

要是手受傷, 應該看哪一科?　／要是手受伤, 应该看哪一科?

(See the Alternate Character Appendix for simplified characters.)

My teacher takes good care of his health. Not only does he exercise every day, he is also very careful about what he eats. He doesn't eat oily food, and does not use even the tiniest amount of sugar. He eats a lot of fruit. Although he is not a vegetarian, he seldom eats meat. His health is very good. But it seems to me while health is very important, what meaning would life have if one could not eat good food?

C. Translate the passage into Chinese. Pay attention to the use of multiple attributives.

The narrow little river outside the town is very appealing to the town's residents. It's a great place to take a walk. There is often a pleasure boat on the river. The tourists on board all like to greet the people selling flowers and newspapers by the river. It's a sight that looks like a painting.

VI. COMPOSITION

You are having a dispute with your insurance company, which does not think the drug that your doctor prescribed (醫生開的藥 / 医生开的药) for you was necessary. Write a letter in which you explain that you owe your recovery to the drug, and that you have asked your doctor to write a supporting letter. Tell the insurance company that you have tried several times to call its representatives, but nobody was there to take your calls, and that you are very unhappy with its service.

第十七課 ▲ 教育

I. LISTENING COMPREHENSION

A. Listen to the audio for the Textbook and answer the questions.

1. Which education system does Tianming's father prefer?

2. Which part of the sister's comment indicates that the American education system has flaws?

3. What is most important in teaching?

4. What do the parents who emigrated from China think of education?

B. Listen to the audio for the Workbook.

1. Listen to the phone conversation and answer the multiple-choice questions.

   ( ) a. Little Long had not called his parents for a long time because
        1) he had forgotten to do so.
        2) he did not need money.
        3) he had been too busy.
        4) he had been away.

   ( ) b. According to Little Long, he did not do well on the examinations because
        1) he had been bar hopping.
        2) he was not interested in his classes.
        3) he had to work.
        4) he had been hanging out with his girlfriend.

   ( ) c. Little Long's mother was
        1) an immigration lawyer.
        2) a school teacher.
        3) a banker.
        4) a pensioner.

   ( ) d. She had been looking for money to
        1) fund bilingual classes and more science classes.
        2) open a private school.

       3)   enable her to go back to school.

       4)   supplement her income.

( )   e.   Little Long needed money to

       1)   pay his debt.

       2)   visit his girlfriend.

       3)   buy more books.

       4)   plan for a summer trip.

2. Listen to the description and answer the multiple-choice questions.

( )   a.   The audience of this speech is very likely

       1)   a group of tourists from abroad.

       2)   a group of championship rowers.

       3)   a group of high school students and their parents.

       4)   a group of basketball players.

( )   b.   The school is

       1)   less than a hundred years old.

       2)   more than a hundred years old.

       3)   a hundred years old.

       4)   just twenty years old.

( )   c.   The students come from

       1)   the Midwest.

       2)   fifteen states and thirty foreign countries.

       3)   local neighboring towns.

       4)   all fifty states and eighty foreign countries.

( )   d.   The school can boast of having the

       1)   most beautiful national park nearby.

       2)   most diverse student population on a campus.

       3)   best basketball team in the country.

       4)   largest conservatory of music in the country.

II. SPEAKING EXERCISES

A. Practice asking and answering the questions with a partner before class.

1. 你每天一放學回家就做什麼?

   你每天一放学回家就做什么?

2. 你覺得你自己的學習態度夠不夠認真?
   你觉得你自己的学习态度够不够认真?

3. 你覺得美國的中小學教育有什麼優點, 有什麼缺點?
   你觉得美国的中小学教育有什么优点, 有什么缺点?

4. 你覺得美國的大學教育有什麼優點, 有什麼缺點?
   你觉得美国的大学教育有什么优点, 有什么缺点?

5. "望子成龍, 望女成鳳" 是什麼意思?
   "望子成龙, 望女成凤" 是什么意思?

6. 你的童年過得怎麼樣?
   你的童年过得怎么样?

B. Practice speaking on the following topics.

1. 請談談對你影響最大的老師。
   请谈谈对你影响最大的老师。

2. 請談談什麼樣的老師才是個好老師。
   请谈谈什么样的老师才是个好老师。

▼ ▼

III. READING COMPREHENSION

A. *Read the following passage and answer the questions. (True/False)*

(Traditional Characters)

現在在中國的城市, 特別是大城市, 很多家庭只有一個孩子。這些孩子從小就吃好的, 穿好的。很多家長還花錢請老師教孩子鋼琴、英語等等。家長把大部份的時間和金錢都花在孩子身上, 把這些獨生子女當成太陽(1)一樣, 圍著(2)他們轉(3)。這些孩子要什麼, 大人就給他們什麼。有些孩子因此變得非常自私(4), 什麼事都以自己為中心, 不關心家裏人, 也不理解父母的苦心。這跟中國家庭的傳統文化完全不同。這種現象已經引起社會學家的重視。

(1) 太陽(tàiyáng): sun
(2) 圍著(wéi zhe): around
(3) 轉(zhuàn): to turn; to revolve
(4) 自私(zìsī): selfish

(Simplified Characters)

现在在中国的城市, 特别是大城市, 很多家庭只有一个孩子。这些孩子从小就吃好的, 穿好的。很多家长还花钱请老师教孩子钢琴、英语等等。家长把大部分的时间和金钱都花在孩子身上, 把这些独生子女当成太阳(1)一样, 围着(2)他们转(3)。这些孩子要什么, 大人就给他们什么。有些孩子因此变得非常自私(4), 什么事都以自己为中心, 不关心家里人, 也不理解父母的苦心。这跟中国家庭的传统文化完全不同。这种现象已经引起社会学家的重视。

(1) 太阳(tàiyáng): sun
(2) 围着(wéi zhe): around
(3) 转(zhuàn): to turn; to revolve
(4) 自私(zìsī): selfish

Questions (True/False):

( ) 1. 在中國的每個地方, 只有一個孩子的家庭很多。
在中国的每个地方, 只有一个孩子的家庭很多。

( ) 2. 除了鋼琴、英文以外, 很多家長還出錢請老師教他們的孩子別的東西。
除了钢琴、英文以外, 很多家长还出钱请老师教他们的孩子别的东西。

( ) 3. 這些家長很少把時間和金錢留給自己。
这些家长很少把时间和金钱留给自己。

▼▼▼▼▼▼▼▼▼▼▼▼▼▼▼▼▼▼▼▼▼▼▼▼▼▼▼▼▼▼▼▼▼▼

( ) 4. 很多獨生子女以爲自己最重要。

  很多独生子女以为自己最重要。

( ) 5. 中國文化要求孩子關心、體貼父母。

  中国文化要求孩子关心、体贴父母。

B. Read the passage and answer the questions.

(Traditional Characters)

　　最近十幾年來, 去中國學習的外國學生越來越多, 其中不少是去學習漢語的, 也有些學生是去學中國歷史或醫學的。當然, 外國人去中國學習不是最近才有的現象。早在唐朝(1)就有日本和韓國的學生去唐朝的國都(2)長安, 也就是現在的西安, 學習中國文化。現在, 北京、上海、南京等很多大、中城市都有外國留學生。一般來説, 如果外國學生想在中國上大學, 需要先學一到兩年的漢語, 或者參加漢語水平考試, 然後才能進入專業學習。很多外國留學生, 除了學習以外, 還經常參加各種社會活動。如參加中國電視台辦的外國人唱中國歌的比賽等等, 這些活動很受歡迎(3)。今後, 去中國學習的外國學生將會更多, 因為中國的經濟發展得很快, 中國將會變得越來越吸引人。

(1) 唐朝(Táng Cháo): Tang dynasty, 618–907 　　(2) 國都(guódū): capital
(3) 歡迎(huānyíng): welcome

(Simplified Characters)

　　最近十几年来, 去中国学习的外国学生越来越多, 其中不少是去学习汉语的, 也有些学生是去学中国历史或医学的。当然, 外国人去中国学习不是最近才有的现象。早在唐朝(1)就有日本和韩国的学生去唐朝的国都(2)长安, 也就是现在的西安, 学习中国文化。现在, 北京、上海、南京等很多大、中城市都有外国留学生。一般来说, 如果外国学生想在中国上大学, 需要先学一到两年的汉语, 或者参加汉语水平考试, 然后才能进入专业学习。很多外国留学生, 除了学习以外, 还经常参加各种社会活动。如参加中国电视台办的外国人唱中国歌的比赛等等, 这些活动很受欢迎(3)。今后, 去中国学习的外国学生将会更多, 因为中国的经济发展得很快, 中国将会变得越来越吸引人。

(1) 唐朝 (Táng Cháo): Tang dynasty, 618–907　　(2) 国都 (guódū): capital

(3) 欢迎 (huānyíng): welcome

Questions:

1. 外國學生去中國主要學習什麼?

   外国学生去中国主要学习什么?

2. 今天的外國學生和唐朝的外國學生有什麼不同?

   今天的外国学生和唐朝的外国学生有什么不同?

3. 外國學生怎樣才能在中國上大學?

   外国学生怎样才能在中国上大学?

4. 除了學習以外, 外國學生在中國還做些什麼?

   除了学习以外, 外国学生在中国还做些什么?

C. Read the passage and answer the questions.

(Traditional Characters)

　　跟小王在一起壓力很大。他特別愛跟別人競爭。做數學題他要做得比別人快, 考試成績要比別人好, 辯論要比別人聲音大, 參加比賽一定要贏, 反正無論做什麼, 他都得比別人強。大家都有點兒受不了, 就開玩笑地對小王說, 不要那麼認真, 輕鬆一些, 否則他會比大家都容易得心臟病。

(Simplified Characters)

　　跟小王在一起压力很大。他特别爱跟别人竞争。做数学题他要做得比别人快, 考试成绩要比别人好, 辩论要比别人声音大, 参加比赛一定要赢, 反正无论做什么, 他都得比别人强。大家都有点儿受不了, 就开玩笑地对小王说, 不要那么认真, 轻松一些, 否则他会比大家都容易得心脏病。

▼ ▼

Questions (True/False):

( ) 1. 小王是一個很容易相處的人。

　　　　小王是一个很容易相处的人。

( ) 2. 朋友給小王的壓力很大。

　　　　朋友给小王的压力很大。

( ) 3. 小王喜歡大聲地開玩笑。

　　　　小王喜欢大声地开玩笑。

( ) 4. 小王不喜歡輸。

　　　　小王不喜欢输。

( ) 5. 小王有心臟病。

　　　　小王有心脏病。

D. In mainland China, Taiwan, and elsewhere in East Asia, parents often send their children to cram schools for additional instruction in various subjects. This phenomenon is now also catching on in the United States. Skim the ad found in a Chinese newspaper published in the United States and answer the questions.

(See the Appendix of Alternate Character Forms for simplified characters.)

Questions:

1. What subjects does the school teach in its after-school classes? List at least two.

2. What class size does the school offer for SAT classes?

E. It is estimated that there are more than 200,000 Chinese citizens studying abroad. These students represent tremendous human resources that the Chinese government wants to tap. To that end, it has been trying to lure more students back to China by offering various incentives and advertising in magazines that are targeted toward students overseas. Study the representation of such an advertisement, and answer the questions.

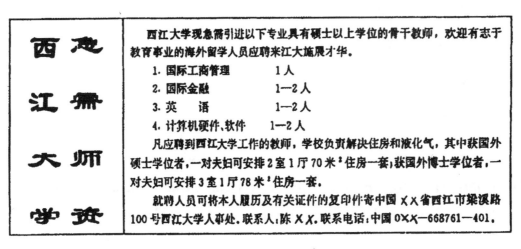

(See the Appendix of Alternate Character Versions for traditional characters.)

1. Circle the name of the institution.

2. How many positions is the institution trying to fill? Give the maximum number.

3. How many of these positions can you decipher? What are they?

4. What is the most important incentive that this institution is offering?

5. Circle the address of the institution.

F. Read the story and answer the questions.

(Traditional Characters)

畫蛇(1)添(2)足(3)

　　古時候有一個人，有一天他請朋友們喝酒，可是他的酒不夠多，所以對朋友們說：「我的酒你們幾個人喝，不夠，一個人又喝不完。請你們在地上畫一條蛇，

誰先畫完, 誰就先喝。" 有一個人先畫好了, 他拿起酒杯喝了一口, 看別人都沒畫完, 就說: "我還能給蛇畫上腳(4)呢!" 他還沒把腳畫好, 另一個人就把一條蛇畫完了, 把酒杯拿過去說: "蛇本來沒有腳, 你怎麼能給蛇加上腳呢? 這杯酒應該是我的。" 說完他就把酒都喝了。

(1)　蛇(shé): snake

(2)　添(tiān): to add

(3)　足(zú): (literary) foot

(4)　腳(jiǎo): foot

(Simplified Characters)

画蛇 (1)添(2)足(3)

　　古时候有一个人, 有一天他请朋友们喝酒, 可是他的酒不够多, 所以对朋友们说: "我的酒你们几个人喝, 不够, 一个人又喝不完。请你们在地上画一条蛇, 谁先画完, 谁就先喝。" 有一个人先画好了, 他拿起酒杯喝了一口, 看别人都没画完, 就说: "我还能给蛇画上脚(4)呢!" 他还没把脚画好, 另一个人就把一条蛇画完了, 把酒杯拿过去说: "蛇本来没有脚, 你怎么能给蛇加上脚呢? 这杯酒应该是我的。" 说完他就把酒都喝了。

(1) 蛇 (shé): snake   (2) 添 (tiān): to add

(3) 足 (zú): (literary) foot   (4) 脚 (jiǎo): foot

Questions:

1. Why did the host ask his guests to draw a snake on the ground?

2. Why did the first person to finish decide to add a few feet on the snake?

3. Why did the second person end up winning the contest?

4. What do you think is the moral of this parable?

IV. GRAMMAR & USAGE

A. Complete the sentences using 自然.

EXAMPLE: a: 聽説中國菜很難做。

　　　　　　　听说中国菜很难做。

　　　　　　b: 中國菜一點也不難做, <u>多做幾次自然就會了</u>。

　　　　　　　中国菜一点也不难做, <u>多做几次自然就会了</u>。

1. a: 我剛到, 對校園還不太熟悉。連圖書館在哪兒都不知道。

　　　我刚到, 对校园还不太熟悉。连图书馆在哪儿都不知道。

　 b: 別急, _____。

2. a: 這麼多漢字, 我記不住。

　　　这么多汉字, 我记不住。

　 b: 慢慢來, _____。

　　　慢慢来, _____。

3. a: 我太久沒運動了。跑了五分鐘就累得喘不過氣來。

　　　我太久没运动了。跑了五分钟就累得喘不过气来。

b: 沒關係, _____。

　　没关系, _____。

B. *Complete the sentences using* 害得.

EXAMPLE:　　我的同屋昨天晚上看球賽看到半夜, 害得我沒睡好覺。

　　　　　　　我的同屋昨天晚上看球赛看到半夜, 害得我没睡好觉。

1.　最近報上有文章说中國菜太油, 卡路里太多, _____。

　　最近报上有文章说中国菜太油, 卡路里太多, _____。

2.　我跟他説好七點在電影院門口見, 他差不多八點才來,

　　_____。

　　我跟他说好七点在电影院门口见, 他差不多八点才来,

　　_____。

3.　張先生和張太太常常吵架吵得很屬害。偶爾還當著孩子的面説些很難聽
　　的話, _____。

　　张先生和张太太常常吵架吵得很厉害。偶尔还当着孩子的面说些很难听
　　的话, _____。

C. *Fill in the blanks with the phrases provided.*

　　餓壞了, 氣壞了, 急壞了, 累壞了, 樂壞了
　　饿坏了, 气坏了, 急坏了, 累坏了, 乐坏了

1.　你去哪兒了? 你媽媽給你打了三天電話都沒找到你, 她_____, 你趕快
　　給她打個電話吧。

　　你去哪儿了? 你妈妈给你打了三天电话都没找到你, 她_____, 你赶快
　　给她打个电话吧。

2.　a: 今天我從早上一直忙到現在, 連吃飯的時間都沒有。

　　　今天我从早上一直忙到现在, 连吃饭的时间都没有。

　　b: 你一定_____。

3.　為了準備考試, 柯林三天沒睡覺, _____, 他決定考完試以後就回家
　　睡覺。

为了准备考试，柯林三天没睡觉，＿＿＿＿＿＿＿＿，他决定考完试以后就回家睡觉。

4. a: 柯林，這次比賽你贏了，高興吧？

    柯林，这次比赛你赢了，高兴吧？

    b: 是啊，總算得了第一，我 ＿＿＿＿＿＿＿＿。

    是啊，总算得了第一，我＿＿＿＿＿＿＿＿。

5. a: 哎，張天明想選《中國歷史》這門課，選上了嗎？

    哎，张天明想选《中国历史》这门课，选上了吗？

    b: 沒有。為了選這門課，他早上八點就去排隊，結果還是沒選上，把他＿＿＿＿＿＿＿＿。

    没有。为了选这门课，他早上八点就去排队，结果还是没选上，把他＿＿＿＿＿＿＿＿。

D. Based on your personal experience, answer the following questions using potential complements.

1. a: 今天的作業你做得完嗎？

    今天的作业你做得完吗？

    b: ＿＿＿＿＿＿＿＿＿＿＿＿＿＿＿＿＿＿＿＿＿＿＿＿＿＿＿＿。

2. a: 從你住的城市寄一封航空信到上海，兩天寄得到嗎？

    从你住的城市寄一封航空信到上海，两天寄得到吗？

    b: ＿＿＿＿＿＿＿＿＿＿＿＿＿＿＿＿＿＿＿＿＿＿＿＿＿＿＿＿。

3. a: 要是沒有醫療保險，你看得起病嗎？

    要是没有医疗保险，你看得起病吗？

    b: ＿＿＿＿＿＿＿＿＿＿＿＿＿＿＿＿＿＿＿＿＿＿＿＿＿＿＿＿。

4. a: 《中文聽說讀寫》在學校書店買得到買不到？

    《中文听说读写》在学校书店买得到买不到？

    b: ＿＿＿＿＿＿＿＿＿＿＿＿＿＿＿＿＿＿＿＿＿＿＿＿＿＿＿＿。

▼▼▼▼▼▼▼▼▼▼▼▼▼▼▼▼▼▼▼▼▼▼▼▼▼▼▼▼▼▼▼▼▼▼▼

E. Complete the sentences using 即使...也.

EXAMPLE: 我姑媽對人特別好, 即使不認識的人她也願意幫助。

我姑妈对人特别好, 即使不认识的人他也愿意帮助。

1. 這道數學習題難极了, _____。

   这道数学习题难极了, _____。

2. 王叔叔的病非常嚴重, _____。

   王叔叔的病非常严重, _____。

3. 這幾天這兒熱得像個大火爐, _____。

   这几天这儿热得像个大火炉, _____。

F. Fill in the blanks with vocabulary items from this lesson.

1. 這個學期張天明只選了兩門課, 所以很_____。

   这个学期张天明只选了三门课, 所以很_____。

2. 上個學期, 歷史課的教授讓學生整天背東西, 張天明覺得什麼也沒學到。
   張天明對這樣讓學生_____的教法很不以為然。

   上个学期, 历史课的教授让学生整天背东西, 张天明觉得什么也没学到。
   张天明对这样让学生_____的教法很不以为然。

3. 我的車的_____是跑得快、省油, 但_____是價錢稍微貴了一點。

   我的车的_____是跑得快、省油, 但_____是价钱稍微贵了一点。

4. 柯林的父母生了六個孩子, 所以經濟_____很重。

   柯林的父母生了六个孩子, 所以经济_____很重。

5. 老李後年的_____是考進法學院, 將來當律師。

   老李后年的_____是考进法学院, 将来当律师。

6. 張天華學習很自覺, 從來不需要別人_____。

   张天华学习很自觉, 从来不需要别人_____。

7. 學校籃球隊今年打得很糟, 第三場比賽就被＿＿＿＿＿＿＿＿了。

    学校篮球队今年打得很糟, 第三场比赛就被＿＿＿＿＿＿＿＿了。

G. *Do you approve or disapprove of the following scenarios? How about your parents? Write* 無所謂 /
无所谓 (wúsuǒwèi: *no big deal) or* 不以為然 / 不以为然 (*do not approve) next to each behavior.*

1. 沒有結婚, 和男朋友 / 女朋友住在一起。

    没有结婚, 和男朋友 / 女朋友住在一起。

    You: ＿＿＿＿＿＿＿＿   Your Parents: ＿＿＿＿＿＿＿＿

2. 沒有結婚就生孩子。

    没有结婚就生孩子。

    You: ＿＿＿＿＿＿＿＿   Your Parents: ＿＿＿＿＿＿＿＿

3. 結婚以後, 男的在家帶孩子, 女的在外面工作。

    结婚以后, 男的在家带孩子, 女的在外面工作。

    You: ＿＿＿＿＿＿＿＿   Your Parents:＿＿＿＿＿＿＿＿

V. TRANSLATION

A. *Translate the passage into English.*

(Traditional Characters)

    有一些國家重男輕女的現象十分嚴重。有時候婦女在社會上有沒有地位, 完全要看她能不能生男孩, 或者是她能生幾個男孩。男孩生得越多, 她的社會地位就越高。

(Simplified Characters)

    有一些国家, 重男轻女的现象十分严重。有时候妇女在社会上有没有地位, 完全要看她能不能生男孩, 或者是她能生几个男孩。男孩生得越多, 她的社会地位就越高。

▼▼▼▼▼▼▼▼▼▼▼▼▼▼▼▼▼▼▼▼▼▼▼▼▼▼▼▼▼▼

B. Translate the passage into English.

(Traditional Characters)

　　改革開放以來, 中國教育方面的情況變化很大, 政府特別強調減輕中小學學生的學習負擔, 要求老師少留功課, 讓孩子有更多的時間運動、休息, 有一個快樂的童年、和少年時代。但是望子成龍的父母為了讓孩子能考上好學校, 長大以後在社會上有競爭力, 週末總是找老師給孩子補習或者課後送孩子去學英文、電腦、或者彈鋼琴、畫畫等等。累得孩子喘不過氣來。

　　最近幾年, 因為大學收的學生比以前多了, 中學生上大學比較容易了。但是要考上好大學還是非常難。考不上好大學, 畢業以後就不容易找到好工作。所以中國的小學生、中學生的壓力還是很大。

(Simplified Characters)

　　改革开放以来, 中国教育方面的情况变化很大, 政府特别强调减轻中小学学生的学习负担, 要求老师少留功课, 让孩子有更多的时间运动、休息, 有一个快乐的童年、和少年时代。但是望子成龙的父母为了让孩子能考上好学校, 长大以后在社会上有竞争力, 周末总是找老师给孩子补习或者课后送孩子去学英文、电脑、或者弹钢琴、画画等等。累得孩子喘不过气来。

　　最近几年, 因为大学收的学生比以前多了, 中学生上大学比较容易了。但是要考上好大学还是非常难。考不上好大学, 毕业以后就不容易找到好工作。所以中国的小学生、中学生的压力还是很大。

高考壓力大　家長學生好辛苦

This is a headline from a Chinese newspaper. "高考" *refers to the college entrance examination in China. Can you understand what it says?*

(See the Appendix of Alternate Character Forms for simplified characters.)

C. Translate the sentences into Chinese. Remember one does not always need to use explicit passive markers in order to express passivity in Chinese.

1. Dinner is ready (cooked). Let's eat.

2. The report is done. We can relax now.

3. He was scolded by his piano teacher three times last week.

4. Last year she was elected "best student" by her classmates.

5. His foundation in math was established when he was in grade school.

D. Translate the passage into Chinese.

In many Asian countries the pressure on students is very great. Every day they have a lot of homework. They cannot even take a break on weekends: they have to attend cram schools. Teachers emphasize rote learning. In America teachers emphasize creativity and encourage students to think independently, but many people criticize the American educational system. They think that American teachers are not strict enough and fail to give students a solid foundation.

▼▼▼▼▼▼▼▼▼▼▼▼▼▼▼▼▼▼▼▼▼▼▼▼▼▼▼▼▼▼▼▼▼▼▼▼▼

E. Translate the passage into Chinese.

My older brother went to high school in China. His teachers were very strict. That's why he has a very good foundation in Chinese, English, and mathematics. My younger sister did not go to elementary school till after she came to America. She never had to memorize anything through mechanical repetition. Her teachers emphasized creativity. However, when she graduated, although her knowledge of English and history was very good, her math was rather shaky. Although the American educational method is good, my older brother feels that there are some problems with it, and that Chinese teaching methods are better.

VI. COMPOSITION

1. 談談你的中小學教育對你的學習態度和學習方法有什麼樣的影響。
   谈谈你的中小学教育对你的学习态度和学习方法有什么样的影响。

2. 要是你有孩子, 你希望他在什麼樣的教育制度下長大。為什麼?
   要是你有孩子, 你希望他在什么样的教育制度下长大。为什么?

I. LISTENING COMPREHENSION

A. Listen to the audio for the Textbook and answer the questions.

1. Why does Tianming have a gun in his room?

2. What do John and his family think of guns?

3. What is Zhang Tianming's view on owning a gun?

4. What is John's opinion on gun control?

B. Listen to the audio for the Workbook.

1. Listen to the passage and answer the multiple-choice questions.

   ( )   a. What were Lisa's parents worried about?

       1)   That it was not safe to travel to China.

       2)   That Lisa would not get used to Chinese customs.

       3)   That it was too hot to travel to China.

       4)   That Lisa and Tianming would exhaust themselves going to so many places.

   ( )   b. Lisa and Tianming did not want to join a tour group because

       1)   it would be more expensive.

       2)   none of the itineraries included Nanjing.

       3)   they wanted to stay put in Nanjing for several days.

       4)   they could not find a tour group.

   ( )   c. Lisa's parents called Tianming's father because

       1)   they wanted to invite him to have dinner before Lisa and Tianming left for China.

       2)   they wanted to know if it's safe to travel in China.

       3)   Lisa wanted them to call him.

       4)   they wanted to confirm the itinerary of the trip.

   ( )   d. Tianming's father told Lisa's parents that

       1)   Lisa and Tianming would be accompanied by Tianming's cousin.

       2)   there's virtually no crime in China.

3) he had seen no serious crime on his last trip.

4) he was going with them.

2. Listen to the passage and answer the multiple-choice questions.

( )   a. The thief hid

    1) under the bed.

    2) by the window.

    3) behind the door.

    4) in the attic.

( )   b. The two young people were

    1) insomniacs.

    2) newlyweds.

    3) starving.

    4) sick.

( )   c. The thief came out of hiding because he

    1) repented.

    2) was starving.

    3) became afraid.

    4) got sick.

( )   d. The thief claimed to be the young woman's

    1) doctor.

    2) tutor.

    3) student.

    4) cousin.

( )   e. The thief was exposed when

    1) people discovered on him the things that had been stolen.

    2) he failed to identify the woman.

    3) the woman denied that she knew him.

    4) he confessed.

II. SPEAKING EXERCISES

A. Practice asking and answering the questions with a partner before class.

1. 過生日的時候, 你希望你的好朋友送給你什麼生日禮物?

   过生日的时候, 你希望你的好朋友送给你什么生日礼物?

2. 什麼情況會讓你很緊張?

   什么情况会让你很紧张?

3. 美國哪些城市的犯罪率比較高?

   美国哪些城市的犯罪率比较高?

4. 美國憲法保障老百姓哪些權利?

   美国宪法保障老百姓哪些权利?

B. Practice speaking on the topics.

1. 美國政府應該通過什麼樣的手段來減少犯罪?

   美国政府应该通过什么样的手段来减少犯罪?

2. 辯論: 私人為什麼應該／不應該有槍?

   辩论: 私人为什么应该／不应该有枪?

III. READING COMPREHENSION

A. Read the passage and answer the questions.

(Traditional Characters)

　　這是美國南部的一個小城。一個秋天的夜晚, 約翰和他的太太從朋友家回來。約翰打開家門, 屋子裏黑黑的, 突然看見一個人向他跑來, 約翰以為是壞人來家裏搶劫, 就拿出手槍開了三槍, 那個人一下子倒在地上。約翰把燈打開, 發現躺在地上的不是別人, 而是他的兒子。原來, 他的兒子放假從學校回來, 想跟約翰開個玩笑, 就從衣櫃裏跳出來, 想嚇嚇(1)他們。那天晚上, 約翰的兒子在醫院裏死去。小城的人沒有怪約翰開槍。當地的人多半都有槍, 很多人說要是他們碰到這個情況, 也會開槍保護自己。他們認為錯並不在槍, 而是約翰的兒子不該開那樣的玩笑。

(1)　嚇 (xià): to frighten, startle

(Simplified Characters)

　　这是美国南部的一个小城。一个秋天的夜晚, 约翰和他的太太从朋友家回来。约翰打开家门, 屋子里黑黑的, 突然看见一个人向他跑来, 约翰以为是坏人来家里抢劫, 就拿出手枪开了三枪, 那个人一下子倒在地上。约翰把灯打开, 发现躺在地上的不是别人, 而是他的儿子。原来, 他的儿子放假从学校回来, 想跟约翰开个玩笑, 就从衣柜里跳出来, 想吓吓(1)他们。那天晚上, 约翰的儿子在医院里死去。小城的人没有怪约翰开枪。当地的人多半都有枪, 很多人说要是他们碰到这个情况, 也会开枪保护自己。他们认为错并不在枪, 而是约翰的儿子不该开那样的玩笑。

(1) 吓 (xià): to frighten, startle

(　) 1. When and where did the tragedy take place?
(　) 2. Where had John and his wife been?
(　) 3. Why did John fire three shots?
(　) 4. Whom had he shot?
(　) 5. How did local people react to the tragedy?
(　) 6. Who did they think was at fault?

B. Read the e-mail message that Tianming wrote to Tianhua and answer the questions. (Multiple Choice)

(Traditional Characters)

天華:

　　我的新同屋小李跟安德森不一樣, 很安靜, 什麼都怕。我今天買了一枝玩具(1)槍, 跟他開玩笑說是準備送給他的禮物, 他聽了緊張得不得了, 連碰都不敢碰一下, 老是怕槍會走火。我得馬上告訴他那不是真槍, 要不然他今天晚上一定睡不好覺。小李覺得讓私人買槍是很不理智的。但我認為買槍是憲法保障的權利。不過, 有時候我想, 要是全美國私人買的槍都像我的這枝玩具槍一樣, 都不是真的, 那該多好啊! 你説呢? 有空給我來電子郵件。

天明

(1) 玩具 (wánjù): toy

(Simplified Characters)

天华：

　　我的新同屋小李跟安德森不一样，很安静，什么都怕。我今天买了一枝玩具(1)枪，跟他开玩笑说是准备送给他的礼物，他听了紧张得不得了，连碰都不敢碰一下，老是怕枪会走火。我得马上告诉他那不是真枪，要不然他今天晚上一定睡不好觉。小李觉得让私人买枪是很不理智的。但我认为买枪是宪法保障的权利。不过，有时候我想，要是全美国私人买的枪像都我的这枝玩具枪一样，都不是真的，那该多好啊！你说呢？有空给我来电子邮件。

天明

(1)　玩具(wánjù): toy

（　）1. Zhang Tianming's new roommate is

　　　a.　as talkative as Anderson.

　　　b.　a hard-working student.

　　　c.　quiet and timid.

（　）2. What did Zhang Tianming buy?

　　　a.　A birthday gift for his sister.

　　　b.　A toy for himself.

　　　c.　A gun for Little Li.

（　）3. Little Li's reaction to the purchase

　　　a.　was fully justified because he knew the truth.

　　　b.　would be different if he knew the truth.

　　　c.　was not justified because he didn't know the truth.

（　）4. Zhang Tianming feels he needs to say something to Little Li in order to

　　　a.　soothe his nerves.

　　　b.　change his idea about the gift.

　　　c.　assure him of the good quality of the gift.

（　）5. Which of the following best characterizes Zhang Tianming's attitude toward gun control?

　　　a.　Decidedly for gun control.

　　　b.　Adamantly against gun control.

　　　c.　Ambivalent.

C. You may encounter written style Chinese while traveling in China. Skim the document and answer the questions.

旅客行李中严禁夹带的危险物品

为了保障飞行安全,旅客交运的行李和手提物品内不得夹带下列物品:

- 装有报警装置的手提箱和公文箱。
- 压缩气体(包括易燃气体、非易燃气体和毒气),如野炊用燃气。

- 带有传染病菌的物品。
- 炸药、弹药、烟花爆竹和照明弹(经承运人同意,限于体育运动用的小型枪械的弹药除外)。
- 腐蚀性物质(如酸、碱、汞和湿电池)。

- 易燃液体和固体(如打火机或加热用燃料、火柴和易燃品)。

- 氧化剂(如漂白粉和有机过氧化物)。
- 毒药。
- 放射性物质。
- 国际航空运输协会的《危险物品运输规定》中列出的其它限制性物品(如磁性物质或使旅客、机组人员讨厌或恼怒的物品)。

在自用合理数量内,旅客可以携带药品、医用器械、化妆用品、烟具(不包括汽油、打火机)、酒类。

(See the Appendix of Alternate Character Versions for traditional characters.)

1. What are the regulations about, based on the title of the document?

2. Where may you see such a document printed?

3. What is the document for?

4. What items cannot be brought? List one.

5. What items can be brought? List two.

D. Read the story and answer the questions.

(Traditional Characters)

樑(1)上君子(2)

　　你知道為什麼中國人把小偷(3)叫做 "樑上君子" 嗎? 原來, 中國漢朝(4)有一個姓陳的, 很會教育人。有一天晚上, 一個小偷在他家的屋樑上, 準備等沒有人的時候下來偷東西。姓陳的從外邊回來以後, 看見了小偷, 但是沒有馬上叫人來抓他, 而是把自己的孩子叫來, 很認真地對他們說: "一個人一定要經常提醒(5)自己不能做壞人。壞人不是生下來就是壞人, 而是因為經常做壞事, 慢慢才變成壞人, 就像樑上的那位君子一樣。" 小偷聽了嚇得從屋樑上掉(6)了下來。

(1) 樑(liáng): beam
(2) 君子(jūnzǐ): gentleman
(3) 小偷(xiǎotōu): thief
(4) 漢朝(Hàn Cháo): Han dynasty (206 BCE-220 CE)
(5) 提醒(tíxǐng): to remind
(6) 掉(diào): to fall; to drop

(Simplified Characters)

梁(1)上君子(2)

　　你知道为什么中国人把小偷(3)叫做 "梁上君子" 吗? 原来, 中国汉朝(4)有一个姓陈的, 很会教育人。有一天晚上, 一个小偷在他家的屋梁上, 准备等没有人的时候下来偷东西。姓陈的从外边回来以后, 看见了小偷, 但是没有马上叫人来抓他, 而是把自己的孩子叫来, 很认真地对他们说: "一个人一定要经常提醒(5)自己不能做坏人。坏人不是生下来就是坏人, 而是因为经常做坏事, 慢慢才变成坏人, 就像梁上的那位君子一样。" 小偷听了吓得从屋梁上掉(6)了下来。

(1) 梁(liáng): beam
(2) 君子(jūnzǐ): gentleman
(3) 小偷(xiǎotōu): thief
(4) 汉朝(Hàn Cháo): Han dynasty (206 BCE-220 CE)
(5) 提醒(tíxǐng): to remind
(6) 掉 (diào): to fall; to drop

1. What was Mr. Chen good at?

2. What was the thief doing on the beam?

3. What did Mr. Chen do when he spotted the thief?

4. What did Mr. Chen say to his children?

5. What was the thief's reaction?

6. What is "a gentleman on the beam"?

IV. GRAMMAR & USAGE

A. Complete the dialogues using 萬一 / 万一.

EXAMPLE:　　a: 現在交男女朋友真難! 我覺得由父母介紹也不錯。
　　　　　　　　現在交男女朋友真难! 我觉得由父母介绍也不错。

　　　　　　b: 我反對, <u>萬一碰上一個性格不開朗的</u>, 那怎麼辦?
　　　　　　　　我反对, <u>万一碰上一个性格不开朗的</u>, 那怎么办?

1.　a: 現在醫療保險那麼貴, 加上我的身體一向很健康, 等過兩年再保吧!
　　　　現在医疗保险那么贵, 加上我的身体一向很健康, 等过两年再保吧!

　　b: 那不行,＿＿＿＿＿＿＿＿＿＿＿＿＿＿＿＿＿, 到時候後悔就來不及了。
　　　　那不行,＿＿＿＿＿＿＿＿＿＿＿＿＿＿＿＿＿, 到时候后悔就来不及了。

2.　a: 我打算把我現在這份工作辭了。
　　　　我打算把我现在这分工作辞了。

　　b: 別辭, 你的工作是個鐵飯碗。而且現在沒有工作的人那麼多,
　　　　＿＿＿＿＿＿＿＿＿＿＿＿＿＿＿＿＿＿＿＿＿, 那你怎麼辦?

　　　　別辞, 你的工作是个铁饭碗。而且现在没有工作的人那么多,
　　　　＿＿＿＿＿＿＿＿＿＿＿＿＿＿＿＿＿＿＿＿＿, 那你怎么办?

3.　a: 他們兩個吵得那麼厲害, 好像還打架呢。你覺得我們應該不應該給
　　　　警察打電話?
　　　　他们两个吵得那么厉害, 好像还打架呢。你觉得我们应该不应该给
　　　　警察打电话?

▼▼▼▼▼▼▼▼▼▼▼▼▼▼▼▼▼▼▼▼▼▼▼▼▼▼▼▼▼▼▼▼▼▼▼

　　　b: 趕快找警察,＿＿＿＿＿＿＿＿＿＿＿＿＿＿, 那就來不及了。

　　　　 赶快找警察,＿＿＿＿＿＿＿＿＿＿＿＿＿＿, 那就来不及了。

B. Complete the dialogues using 簡直／简直.

EXAMPLE:　　a: 他说話那麼衝, 我簡直不能跟他討論事情。

　　　　　　　 他说话那么冲, 我简直不能跟他讨论事情。

　　　　　　b: 可不是嗎? 難怪沒有人願意跟他打交道。

　　　　　　　 可不是吗? 难怪没有人愿意跟他打交道。

1. a: 我隔壁同學放音樂, 聲音大極了, ＿＿＿＿＿＿＿＿＿＿＿＿＿＿。

　　 我隔壁同学放音乐, 声音大极了, ＿＿＿＿＿＿＿＿＿＿＿＿＿＿。

　 b: 我看你要麼到圖書館去學習, 要麼趕緊搬家吧!

　　 我看你要么到图书馆去学习, 要么赶紧搬家吧!

2. a: 那個紀錄片又長又沒意思, ＿＿＿＿＿＿＿＿＿＿＿＿＿。

　　 那个纪录片又长又没意思, ＿＿＿＿＿＿＿＿＿＿＿＿＿。

　 b: 這個紀錄片是沒有什麼意思, 但是沒辦法, 為了寫報告你最好看下去。

　　 这个纪录片是没有什么意思, 但是没办法, 为了写报告你最好看下去。

3. a: 昨天放假, 我帶朋友去夫子廟遊覽。那兒人山人海,

　　 ＿＿＿＿＿＿＿＿＿＿＿＿＿＿＿＿＿＿＿＿＿。

　　 昨天放假, 我带朋友去夫子庙游览。那儿人山人海,

　　 ＿＿＿＿＿＿＿＿＿＿＿＿＿＿＿＿＿＿＿＿＿。

　 b: 你怎麼選放假的時候去呢? 人擠人肯定沒意思。

　　 你怎么选放假的时候去呢? 人挤人肯定没意思。

C. Complete the dialogues using 只要.

EXAMPLE:　　a: 家裏有槍太危險了! 萬一走了火, 傷了人怎麼辦?

　　　　　　　 家里有枪太危险了! 万一走了火, 伤了人怎么办?

b: <u>只要你把槍放在安全的地方</u>, 不會有問題。

<u>只要你把枪放在安全的地方</u>, 不会有问题。

1. a: 我真怕考不上大學。

我真怕考不上大学。

b: 別怕, _____, 肯定考得上。

2. a: 他這一次病得這麼厲害, 真讓人著急。

他这一次病得这么厉害, 真让人着急。

b: 放心, _____, 他的病肯定會好。

放心, _____, 他的病肯定会好。

3. a: 漢字這麼多, 怎樣才記得住呢?

汉字这麼多, 怎样才记得住呢?

b: _____, 肯定記得住。 / 肯定记得住。

D. Complete the dialogues using 基本上.

EXAMPLE: a: 這個計劃只有一、兩點寫得不太清楚。(理想)

這個计划只有一、两点写得不太清楚。(理想)

b: 這個計劃<u>除了那一、兩點以外</u>, <u>基本上還是很理想的</u>。

这个计划<u>除了那一、两点以外</u>, <u>基本上还是很理想的</u>。

1. a: 她的丈夫不太喜歡陪她逛街。(體貼)

她的丈夫不太喜欢陪她逛街。(体贴)

b: 她的丈夫_____, _____。

2. a: 你的工作有時候得出差, 是不是很累啊? (輕鬆)

你的工作有时候得出差, 是不是很累啊? (轻松)

b: 我的工作_____, _____。

3. a: 這個孩子這麼愛看卡通片, 是不是不愛學習? (用功)

这个孩子这么爱看卡通片, 是不是不爱学习? (用功)

b: 這個孩子＿＿＿＿＿＿＿＿＿＿＿＿＿, ＿＿＿＿＿＿＿＿＿＿＿＿＿＿。

　　这个孩子＿＿＿＿＿＿＿＿＿＿＿＿＿, ＿＿＿＿＿＿＿＿＿＿＿＿＿＿。

E. Rewrite the sentences using 通過／通过.

EXAMPLE:　　警察調查了以後, 發現那些東西不是他偷的。

　　　　　　　警察调查了以后, 发现那些东西不是他偷的。

　　→ <u>警察通過調查</u>, 發現那些東西不是他偷的。

　　　　<u>警察通过调查</u>, 发现那些东西不是他偷的。

1. 醫生檢查了以後, 才知道老張有心臟病。

　　医生检查了以后, 才知道老张有心脏病。

　　→＿＿＿＿＿＿＿＿＿＿＿＿＿＿＿＿＿＿, 才知道老張有心臟病。

　　→＿＿＿＿＿＿＿＿＿＿＿＿＿＿＿＿＿＿, 才知道老张有心脏病。

2. 大家討論了以後, 決定選王先生為公司的新主管。

　　大家讨论了以后, 决定选王先生为公司的新主管。

　　→＿＿＿＿＿＿＿＿＿＿＿＿＿＿＿＿＿＿, 決定選王先生為公司的新主管。

　　→＿＿＿＿＿＿＿＿＿＿＿＿＿＿＿＿＿＿, 决定选王先生为公司的新主管。

3. 李教授介紹了以後, 大家才知道今天的客人是美國有名的詩人之一。

　　李教授介绍了以后, 大家才知道今天的客人是美国有名的诗人之一。

　　→＿＿＿＿＿＿＿＿＿＿＿＿＿＿＿＿＿＿, 大家才知道今天的客人是美國有
名的詩人之一。

　　→＿＿＿＿＿＿＿＿＿＿＿＿＿＿＿＿＿＿, 大家才知道今天的客人是美国有
名的诗人之一。

F. Fill in the blanks with vocabulary items from this lesson.

1. 毛毛, 你房間裏怎麼到處都是東西? 趕快收好, 別＿＿＿＿＿＿＿。

　　毛毛, 你房间里怎么到处都是东西? 赶快收好, 别＿＿＿＿＿＿＿。

2. 張天華想去紐約上醫學院, 可是她的父母怕一個女孩子住在紐約
太＿＿＿＿＿＿＿。

张天华想去纽约上医学院, 可是她的父母怕一个女孩子住在纽约太＿＿＿＿＿＿＿＿。

3. 張天華说她不怕, 紐約有很多＿＿＿＿＿＿＿保護老百姓的安全。

   張天华说她不怕, 纽约有很多＿＿＿＿＿＿＿保护老百姓的安全。

4. 美國的法律＿＿＿＿＿＿＿: 二十一歲以下不能喝酒。

   美国的法律＿＿＿＿＿＿＿: 二十一岁以下不能喝酒。

5. 許多外國人到美國來, 看到很多地方都＿＿＿＿＿＿＿吸煙, 感到有些不習慣。

   许多外国人到美国来, 看到很多地方都＿＿＿＿＿＿＿吸烟, 感到有些不习惯。

6. 美國憲法的第一條＿＿＿＿＿＿＿老百姓有言論自由。

   美国宪法的第一条＿＿＿＿＿＿＿老百姓有言论自由。

7. 這家商店販賣毒品, 被政府＿＿＿＿＿＿＿了。

   这家商店贩卖毒品, 被政府＿＿＿＿＿＿＿了。

8. 這個國家窮的很窮, 富的很富, 可以説是＿＿＿＿＿＿＿。

   这个国家穷的很穷, 富的很富, 可以说是＿＿＿＿＿＿＿。

V. TRANSLATION

A. Translate the sentences into Chinese. Take care to distinguish between 和 and 並/并.

1. Freedom of speech and assembly are rights guaranteed by the American Constitution.

2. At the meeting we discussed Ke Lin and Zhang Tianming's suggestion, and decided to adopt it. (採納 / 采纳: cǎinà)

3. The university passed the new regulation and decided to implement it immediately.

▼▼▼▼▼▼▼▼▼▼▼▼▼▼▼▼▼▼▼▼▼▼▼▼▼▼▼▼▼▼▼▼▼▼▼▼▼▼

4.　His cousin studied very hard. He passed (the examinations), got into a good college, and got a scholarship.

B. Fill in the blanks with the words provided and translate the passages into English.

並, 只要, 即使, 正, 害得, 通過, 看來, 萬一

并, 只要, 即使, 正, 害得, 通过, 看来, 万一

1.

(Traditional Characters)

　　很多人認為美國社會講究男女平等，＿＿＿＿＿＿有能力，願意做事，＿＿＿＿＿＿是女的也有機會做高職位主管。但有許多人不同意這個觀點。他們說政府＿＿＿＿＿＿各種不同手段來鼓勵婦女受教育、參加工作，＿＿＿＿＿＿有些男的沒有公平競爭的機會。這是一種新的男女不平等的現象。＿＿＿＿＿＿男女不平等的問題還沒有真正地解決。

(Simplified Characters)

　　很多人认为美国社会讲究男女平等，＿＿＿＿＿＿有能力，愿意做事，＿＿＿＿＿＿是女的也有机会做高职位主管。但有许多人不同意这个观点。他们说政府＿＿＿＿＿＿各种不同手段来鼓励妇女受教育、参加工作，＿＿＿＿＿＿有些男的没有公平竞争的机会。这是一种新的男女不平等的现象。＿＿＿＿＿＿男女平等的问题还没有真正地解决。

2.

(Traditional Characters)

非法移民在社會上不但沒有什麼地位，_____常受各方的批評。
_____因為他們是非法(fēifǎ)進的美國，所以_____出了什麼事，有時候連警察也幫不了他們的忙。

(Simplified Characters)

非法移民在社会上不但没有什么地位，_____常受各方的批评。
_____因为他们是非法(fēifǎ)进的美国，所以_____出了什么事，有时候连警察也帮不了他们的忙。

C. Translate the passage into Chinese:

Many Americans think that having a gun to protect oneself is an important right guaranteed by the Constitution. In their view, this right is as important as freedom of speech. Others disagree. They believe that too many Americans have guns, that it is too easy to buy guns, and that the government should ban gun commercials on TV.

D. Translate into Chinese a journal entry from Ke Lin's mother.

America is a free country. The Constitution ensures people have freedom of speech, freedom of assembly, and freedom to bear arms. In school, teachers encourage students to develop their imagination and seldom require students to do mechanical memorizing. Some students do not respect their teachers. They verbally abuse their teachers, and even bring drugs and guns into classrooms. The crime rate has gone up. The government tries to fight crime by hiring more cops and building (蓋/盖: gài) more jails. However, some policemen don't treat their jobs seriously and some even become criminals themselves. What has happened to this society?

VI. COMPOSITION

你認為每個人都應該有權利買槍嗎? 為什麼?

你认为每个人都应该有权利买枪吗? 为什么?

第十九課 ▲ 動物與人
第十九课 ▲ 动物与人

I. LISTENING COMPREHENSION

A. Listen to the audio for the Textbook and answer the questions.

1. How many protests has Ke Lin participated in over the past few days?

2. Why is Zhang Tianming looking for Ke Lin?

3. Is Ke Lin going to see the game with Zhang Tianming? Why or why not?

4. What's Zhang Tianming's view on animal experiments?

5. Does Ke Lin think it is right to sacrifice animals to save people's lives?

B. Listen to the audio for the Workbook.

1. Listen to the passage and answer the questions.

   New Vocabulary:

   存活 (cúnhuó): to survive; to remain alive   竹子 (zhúzi): bamboo

   a. Why do the Chinese call the panda *xióngmāo*?

   b. What did the Chinese government do in the 1970s?

   c. What could foreign zoos do to exhibit pandas?

   d. What two factors made the number of pandas decrease?

2. Listen to the passage and answer the questions.

New Vocabulary:

代表(dàibiǎo): to represent   兔(子)(tùzi): rabbit   尾巴(wěiba): tail

Questions:

(   ) a. 1974 was the year of the
    1) rabbit.
    2) sheep.
    3) horse.
    4) tiger.

(   ) b. 1976 was the year of the
    1) dragon.
    2) sheep.
    3) rabbit.
    4) horse.

(   ) c. 1978 was the year of the
    1) sheep.
    2) horse.
    3) tiger.
    4) rabbit.

(   ) d. People were reluctant to have children in the year of the sheep because they believed that
    1) their children would have unhappy lives.
    2) it was usually a time of famine.
    3) their children would die young.
    4) their children would be less intelligent.

(   ) e. People were reluctant to get married in the year of the rabbit because they feared that
    1) their marriage would not last.
    2) their marriage would be an unhappy one.
    3) they would have too many children.
    4) their spouse would commit adultery.

(   ) f. The year of the rabbit comes after the year of the
    1) sheep.
    2) horse.
    3) tiger.
    4) dragon.

(   ) g. The year of the rabbit comes before the year of the
    1) sheep.
    2) horse.

▼▼▼

    3) tiger.

    4) dragon.

h. What is *shēngxiào*?

    For more information on *shēngxiào*, see Lesson 15 of *Integrated Chinese*, Level 1.

II. SPEAKING EXERCISES

A. Practice asking and answering the questions with a partner before class.

1. 你會為了什麼事情上街抗議?

    你会为了什么事情上街抗议?

2. 你覺得什麼樣的抗議行為有點兒太過份?

    你觉得什么样的抗议行为有点儿太过分?

3. 要是你看到有人虐待孩子, 你會怎麼辦?

    要是你看到有人虐待孩子, 你会怎么办?

4. 美國或中國政府現在在動物保護方面面臨的最大難題是什麼?

    美国或中国政府现在在动物保护方面面临的最大难题是什么?

B. Practice speaking on the following topics.

1. 你反對通過動物實驗來研究藥物嗎? 為什麼?

    你反对通过动物实验来研究药物吗? 为什么?

2. 請談談生態不平衡會帶來什麼樣的問題。

    请谈谈生态不平衡会带来什么样的问题。

III. READING COMPREHENSION

A. Read the passage and answer the questions. (True/False)

(Traditional)

    高先生是一位有名的動物保護主義(zhǔyì)者。他一向反對用動物做藥物試驗, 他家的人也從來不穿用動物皮毛做的衣服。高先生養了一隻很可愛的小狗, 他對小狗就像對自己五歲的兒子小寶一樣好。有一天, 幾個朋友來看高先

▼▼▼▼▼▼▼▼▼▼▼▼▼▼▼▼▼▼▼▼▼▼▼▼▼▼▼

生, 高先生又談起動物保護的重要: "你們憑什麼説人比動物更重要? 正是因為很多人有這種想法, 他們才去破壞自然, 讓那些又可愛又可憐的動物一天比一天減少。如果不改變(gǎibiàn)這種觀念, 總有一天我們會自食其果的!" 正在這時, 一位朋友在外邊叫起來: "不好了, 小寶和小狗都掉(diào)到河裏了!" 高先生一聽就跑了出去, 一邊跑一邊喊: "快救我的兒子!"

(Simplified)

高先生是一位有名的动物保护主义(zhǔyì)者。他一向反对用动物做药物实验, 他家的人也从来不穿用动物皮毛做的衣服。高先生养了一只很可爱的小狗, 他对小狗就像对自己五岁的儿子小宝一样好。有一天, 几个朋友来看高先生, 高先生又谈起动物保护的重要: "你们凭什么说人比动物更重要? 正是因为很多人有这种想法, 他们才去破坏自然, 让那些又可爱又可怜的动物一天比一天减少。如果不改变(gǎibiàn)这种观念, 总有一天我们会自食其果的!" 正在这时, 一位朋友在外边叫起来: "不好了, 小宝和小狗都掉(diào)到河里了!" 高先生一听就跑了出去, 一边跑一边喊: "快救我的儿子!"

Questions: (True/ False):

(　) 1. Mr. Gao thinks that it's important to protect animals.

(　) 2. Mr. Gao worries that there will be fewer and fewer animals available for experiments in the future.

(　) 3. Mr. Gao's family agrees with his view on animal protection.

(　) 4. Mr. Gao's friends agree with him completely.

(　) 5. Mr. Gao tells his friends that people are not any more important than animals.

(　) 6. Mr. Gao loves his dog as much as he loves his son.

B. *Answer the questions after reading the passage.*

舞獅／舞狮

舞龍／舞龙

(Traditional Characters)

　　動物在世界各國風俗中都佔 (zhàn) 有很重要的地位，中國也一樣。比如，以前在中國，小男孩常常戴虎頭帽(1)，穿虎頭鞋。端午節的時候，中國人要賽龍舟。過新年的時候，中國人要放鞭炮、舞獅(2)、舞龍。現在在國外，每當中國新年的時候，中國城的舞獅、舞龍表演往往吸引很多人去觀看。在中國，不僅 (bùjǐn) 漢族 (Hànzú) 舞獅，有的少數民族 (shǎoshùmínzú) 也有舞獅的習慣，比如中國南方的壯族(3)。壯族的舞獅很特別，他們把很多凳子(4) 摞 (5) 起來，前邊的一個人拿著球引 (yǐn) 獅子爬 (6) 到凳子頂上。獅子是由兩個人扮演 (bànyǎn) 的，所以要爬到最上邊的凳子上，非常困難。大家敲鑼打鼓(7)，又喊又叫，十分熱鬧。雖然已經二十一世紀了，大家對這些民間風俗還是很喜歡的。

(1)　…帽(mào): hat; 帽子
(2)　…獅(shī): lion; 獅子
(3)　壯族(Zhuàng zú): Zhuang nationality
(4)　凳子(dèngzi): bench
(5)　摞(luò): to pile up
(6)　爬(pá): to climb
(7)　敲鑼打鼓(qiāo luó dǎ gǔ): to beat gongs and drums

(Simplified Characters)

　　动物在世界各国风俗中都占(zhàn)有很重要的地位，中国也一样。比如，以前在中国，小男孩常常戴虎头帽(1)，穿虎头鞋。端午节的时候，中国人要赛龙舟。过新年的时候，中国人要放鞭炮、舞狮(2)、舞龙。现在在国外，每当中国新年的时候，中国城的舞狮、舞龙表演往往吸引很多人去观看。在中国，不仅(bùjǐn)汉族(Hànzú)舞狮，有的少数民族(shǎoshùmínzú)也有舞狮的习惯，比如中国南方的壮族(3)。壮族的舞狮很特别，他们把很多凳子(4)摞(5)起来，前边的一个人拿着球引(yǐn)狮子爬(6)到凳子顶上。狮子是由两个人扮演(bànyǎn)的，所以要爬到最上边的凳子上，非常困难。大家敲锣打鼓(7)，又喊又叫，十分热闹。虽然已经二十一世纪了，大家对这些民间风俗还是很喜欢的。

(1)　…帽(mào): hat; 帽子
(2)　…狮(shī): lion; 狮子
(3)　壮族(Zhuàng zú): Zhuang nationality
(4)　凳子(dèngzi): bench
(5)　摞(luò): to pile up
(6)　爬(pá): to climb
(7)　敲鑼打鼓 qiāo luó dǎ gǔ): to beat gongs and drums

虎頭鞋 / 虎头鞋

Questions:

1. Give an example of the popularity of the tiger in Chinese folk costumes.

2. Is the lion dance confined to the Han people?

3. Describe the Zhuang lion dance.

4. In Chinese communities the dragon boat race is often associated with a particular festival. What is that festival?

5. What do all the events mentioned in the passage have in common?

C. Answer the questions after reading the story.

(Traditional Characters)

朝(1)三暮(2)四

　　從前有個養猴子的人, 大家都叫他狙公(3), 意思是猴子先生。狙公養了很多猴子, 他知道猴子的脾氣。他說的話猴子們也聽得懂。

　　狙公的猴子都很喜歡吃一種果子, 每天都要吃很多, 狙公沒有錢給猴子買那麼多的果子了, 只好少給猴子吃點果子, 可是怕猴子不高興, 於是就想了個辦法。

▼▼▼▼▼▼▼▼▼▼▼▼▼▼▼▼▼▼▼▼▼▼▼▼▼▼▼▼▼▼▼▼▼▼▼▼▼

有一天早上, 狙公對猴子們說: "從現在起, 我每天早上給你們三個果子, 晚上四個, 你們說好不好? " 猴子們聽了都說不好, 覺得給得太少。狙公於是笑著說: "那麼, 早上四個, 晚上三個, 好不好? " 猴子們聽了, 個個都很高興, 都不說什麼了。

"朝三暮四" 這句話就是從這個故事來的。但是這個成語有特別的意思: 一個人一下兒這樣, 一下兒那樣, 變來變去。

(1) 朝(zhāo): (literary) morning　　　(2) 暮(mù): (literary) dusk

(3) 狙公(Jūgōng): a person's name

(Simplified Characters)

朝(1)三暮(2)四

　　从前有个养猴子的人, 大家都叫他狙公(3), 意思是猴子先生。狙公养了很多猴子, 他知道猴子的脾气。他说的话猴子们也听得懂。

　　狙公的猴子都很喜欢吃一种果子, 每天都要吃很多, 狙公没有钱给猴子买那么多的果子了, 只好少给猴子吃点果子, 可是怕猴子不高兴, 于是就想了个办法。

▼▼

有一天早上, 狙公对猴子们说: "从现在起, 我每天早上给你们三个果子, 晚上四个, 你们说好不好?" 猴子们听了都说不好, 觉得给得太少。狙公於是笑着说: "那么, 早上四个, 晚上三个, 好不好?" 猴子们听了, 个个都很高兴, 都不说什么了。

"朝三暮四" 这句话就是从这个故事来的。但是这个成语有特别的意思: 一个人一下儿这样, 一下儿那样, 变来变去。

(1) 朝 (zhāo): (literary) morning   (2) 暮 (mù): (literary) dusk

(3) 狙公 (Jūgōng): a person's name

Questions:

1. Why was the man called Jugong?

2. Why did Jugong want to stop feeding so many nuts to the monkeys?

3. Why did the monkeys prefer the second plan?

4. How did the second feeding plan differ from the first one?

5. What does the idiom 朝三暮四 mean?

IV. GRAMMAR & USAGE

A. Complete the dialogues using 憑什麼 / 凭什么.

EXAMPLE: a: 小李又加薪了。

         小李又加薪了。

       b: 我們工作得那麼努力都沒有加薪, <u>小李憑什麼加薪</u>?

         我们工作得那么努力都没有加薪, <u>小李凭什么加薪</u>?

1. a: 請你不要吸煙, 我受不了煙味。

     请你不要吸烟, 我受不了烟味。

   b: 這兒不是你的家, _____?

     这儿不是你的家, _____?

2. a: 我不懂老師為什麼生物成績只給我一個B, 沒給我A。

   我不懂老师为什么生物成绩只给我一个B, 没给我A。

   b: 你做實驗常常做不出結果, _____?

   你做实验常常做不出结果, _____?

3. a: 請你不要說這些亂七八糟難聽的話。

   请你不要说这些乱七八糟难听的话。

   b: 憲法保障我有言論自由, _____?

   宪法保障我有言论自由, _____?

B. Complete the dialogues using 儘量 / 尽量.

EXAMPLE: a: 醫生, 我父親出院以後, 應該注意些什麼?

             医生, 我父亲出院以后, 应该注意些什么?

            b: 他應該每天吃藥, <u>儘量多休息</u>。

              他应该每天吃药, <u>尽量多休息</u>。

1. a: 她懷孕以後, 先生對她特別體貼。

   她怀孕以后, 先生对她特别体贴。

   b: 可不是嗎? 家務事都是他做, _____。

   可不是吗? 家务事都是他做, _____。

2. a: 這兩天放假, 你為什麼不出去走走?

   这两天放假, 你为什么不出去走走?

   b: 過年過節到處都是人, 我_____。

   过年过节到处都是人, 我_____。

3. a: 最近的電視節目越做越糟。孩子看了很容易學壞。

   最近的电视节目越做越糟。孩子看了很容易学坏。

   b: 可不是嗎? 因為我怕我的孩子受不好的影響, _____。

   可不是吗? 因为我怕我的孩子受不好的影响, _____。

C. Fill in the blanks using 因為 / 因为 *or* 為了 / 为了.

1. _____省錢, 我決定畢業後搬回家住。

   _____省钱, 我决定毕业后搬回家住。

2. _____我沒有工作、沒有錢, 畢業後我只好搬回家住。

   _____我没有工作、没有钱, 毕业后我只好搬回家住。

3. 爸爸說: "我這樣做是_____你好。"

   爸爸说: "我这样做是_____你好。"

4. 許多人認為_____減少犯罪, 政府應該立法禁止槍枝買賣。

   许多人认为_____减少犯罪, 政府应该立法禁止枪枝买卖。

5. _____很多中國人重男輕女, 所以很多女孩生下來沒人要, 真可憐。

   _____很多中国人重男轻女, 所以很多女孩生下来没人要, 真可怜。

6. _____保護動物, 政府設立了許多動物保護區。

   _____保护动物, 政府设立了许多动物保护区。

D. Complete the sentences using 而.

EXAMPLE: 表哥為了學習美國文化<u>而到美國留學</u>。

             表哥为了学习美国文化<u>而到美国留学</u>。

1. 小高為了提高中文聽力水平_____。

   小高为了提高中文听力水平_____。

2. 為了保護動物_____是沒有道理的。

   为了保护动物_____是没有道理的。

3. 因為輸了球_____是很不應該的。

   因为输了球_____是很不应该的。

E. Complete the dialogues using 其中.

EXAMPLE: a: 那個人為什麼被警察帶走了?

             那个人为什么被警察带走了?

b: 他犯了很多罪, <u>其中有非法賭博、吸毒、偷竊、和搶劫</u>。

他犯了很多罪, <u>其中有非法赌博、吸毒、偷窃、和抢劫</u>。

1. a: 你昨天去動物園看到什麼動物了?

你昨天去动物园看到什么动物了?

b: 我看到的動物很多, ＿＿＿＿＿＿＿＿＿＿＿＿＿＿＿＿＿。

我看到的动物很多, ＿＿＿＿＿＿＿＿＿＿＿＿＿＿＿＿＿。

2. a: 昨天報上有一條新聞, 談到中國現在面臨的難題。

昨天报上有一条新闻, 谈到中国现在面临的难题。

b: 對, 我也看到了。文章中提到了好幾個方面的問題, ＿＿＿＿＿＿＿。

对, 我也看到了。文章中提到了好几个方面的问题, ＿＿＿＿＿＿＿。

3. a: 你去年暑假去什麼地方旅行了?

你去年暑假去什么地方旅行了?

b: 我遊覽了南京的許多名勝古蹟, ＿＿＿＿＿＿＿＿＿＿＿＿＿。

我游览了南京的许多名胜古迹, ＿＿＿＿＿＿＿＿＿＿＿＿＿。

警察的好朋友／警察的好朋友

▼▼▼▼▼▼▼▼▼▼▼▼▼▼▼▼▼▼▼▼▼▼▼▼▼▼▼▼▼▼▼▼▼▼▼▼▼▼

F. Rewrite the sentences using 由於 / 由于.

EXAMPLE: 中國南方地少人多, 許多人移民他處, 往外發展。

中國南方地少人多, 許多人移民他处, 往外发展。

→ 由於中國南方地少人多, 所以許多人搬到別的地方, 往外發展。

由于中国南方地少人多, 所以许多人搬到别的地方, 往外发展。

1. 中西部在鬧水災, 我們不能坐火車, 得坐飛機。

中西部在闹水灾, 我们不能坐火车, 得坐飞机。

→ _____。

2. 前幾年美國經濟情況不好, 很多人找不到工作。

前几年美国经济情况不好, 很多人找不到工作。

→ _____。

3. 我們學校的教練很努力, 學校的運動員在比賽中拿到了好幾面金牌和銀牌。

我们学校的教练很努力, 学校的运动员在比赛中拿到了好几面金牌和银牌。

→ _____。

G. Match the verbs in the left column with the nouns and phrases in the right column to form verb-object phrases. Some verbs may be used more than once.

1. 研究 / 研究	a. 措施 / 措施
2. 抗議 / 抗议	b. 抗議 / 抗议
3. 保護 / 保护	c. 環境 / 环境
4. 組織 / 组织	d. 動物 / 动物
5. 虐待 / 虐待	e. 虐待動物 / 虐待动物
6. 犧牲 / 牺牲	f. 老年癡呆症 / 老年痴呆症
7. 採取 / 采取	

▼▼▼▼▼▼▼▼▼▼▼▼▼▼▼▼▼▼▼▼▼▼▼▼▼▼▼▼▼▼▼▼▼▼▼

H. Fill in the blanks with the words provided.

(Traditional Characters)

禁止, 手段, 採取, 通過, 犯罪, 保障, 提高

　　最近十幾年來, 中國政府為了降低(jiàngdī: to lower)人口出生率, ＿＿＿＿＿＿了各種 ＿＿＿＿＿＿。但是社會學家認為, 解決人口問題最根本的方法是 ＿＿＿＿＿＿婦女的社會地位, 從法律上 ＿＿＿＿＿＿ 婦女的權利。為此, 中國人大 ＿＿＿＿＿＿了婦女和兒童權利保護法, ＿＿＿＿＿＿ 販賣婦女等各種 ＿＿＿＿＿＿行為。

(Simplified Characters)

禁止, 手段, 采取, 通过, 犯罪, 保障, 提高

　　最近十几年来, 中国政府为了降低(jiàngdī: to lower)人口出生率, ＿＿＿＿＿＿了各种 ＿＿＿＿＿＿。但是社会学家认为, 解决人口问题最根本的方法是 ＿＿＿＿＿＿妇女的社会地位, 从法律上 ＿＿＿＿＿＿妇女的权利。为此, 中国人大 ＿＿＿＿＿＿ 了妇女和儿童权利保护法, ＿＿＿＿＿＿ 贩卖妇女等各种 ＿＿＿＿＿＿行为。

V. TRANSLATION

A. Translate the passage into Chinese.

There is an elementary school near our home. Yesterday I saw many parents arrive at the school. I heard that a teacher had hit a boy. The principal said that the reason that the teacher had hit the student was that he was making fun of the teacher. The parents thought even if the student had done something wrong, the teacher should only have educated him. In order to avoid parents' protesting, the school asked the teacher to resign. Some teachers thought that was unfair. However, the parents thought the teacher had brought the consequence on himself.

B. Translate the passage into Chinese.

I think animal abuse is barbaric behavior. Neither do I approve of animal dissection for research for new medicines. We should protect animals and maintain the ecological balance as much as we can, and make our world better and better.

VI. COMPOSITION

What do you think of animal protection groups such as PETA? Do you agree with their message and their tactics?

注意動物保護 / 注意动物保护

第二十課 ▲ 環境保護
第二十课 ▲ 环境保护

I. LISTENING COMPREHENSION

A. Listen to the audio for the Textbook and answer the questions.

1. Why couldn't Zhang Tianming find Li Zhe?

2. Who was responsible for the pollution?

3. Why did the government rather than the chemical plant sponsor the research?

4. Why did the chemical plant claim that it couldn't afford to clean up the mess?

5. What kind of environmental damage had the chemical plant caused? Give two examples.

B. Listen to the audio for the Workbook.

1. Listen to the passage and answer the multiple-choice questions.

New Vocabulary: 蘋果 / 苹果 (píngguǒ): apple

( ) a. Anna used to be a
   1) college professor.
   2) reporter.
   3) news junkie.
   4) movie star.

( ) b. Anna has not read a newspaper or watched TV for a year and a half because
   1) she is too busy raising her three children.
   2) she can no longer afford newspapers or cable TV.
   3) the media coverage makes her anxious.
   4) she has never been interested in any form of journalism.

( ) c. According to the media a few months ago, apples
   1) were a good source of nutrition.
   2) were unsafe.
   3) had been endorsed by a well-known film star as a health food.
   4) were in short supply.

2. Listen to the passage and answer the following questions.

   a. When did the incident happen?

   b. Where did it happen?

   c. When the residents of the town woke up, in what condition was the river?

   d. What had happened to the river?

   e. What was the factory director's excuse?

   f. What were the consequences for the residents?

   g. What changes had the factory brought to the town?

   h. What question did the residents begin to ponder?

II. SPEAKING EXERCISES

A. Practice asking and answering the questions with a partner before class.

1. 這幾天你都在忙些什麼?
   这几天你都在忙些什么?

2. 什麼樣的地方是大學城?
   什么样的地方是大学城?

3. 怎麼樣可以減少對空氣的污染?
   怎么样可以减少对空气的污染?

4. 哪幾種污染會對人體健康造成很大的危害?
   哪几种污染会对人体健康造成很大的危害?

B. Practice speaking on the following topics.

1. 請談談政府應該採取什麼措施來鼓勵私人工廠治理三廢問題。
   请谈谈政府应该采取什么措施来鼓励私人工厂治理三废问题。

2. 請談談核能發電的優缺點。

請談談核能发电的优缺点。

III. READING COMPREHENSION

A. Read the passage and answer the questions. (True/False)

(Traditional Characters)

　　對許多發展中國家來說, 在發展經濟的同時如何保護環境是一個大難題。很多第三世界國家認為, 對他們來說發展經濟比環境保護更重要, 等經濟發展了以後再來考慮環境保護也不晚。在他們看來, 保護熱帶雨林雖然重要, 但是他們首先要解決的是老百姓的生存問題。他們也認為許多西方國家對環境造成的污染比發展中國家嚴重得多, 所以西方國家應該負更大的責任。

(Simplified Characters)

　　对许多发展中国家来说, 发展经济的同时如何保护环境是一个大难题。很多第三世界国家认为, 对他们来说发展经济比环境保护更重要, 等经济发展了以后再来考虑环境保护也不晚。在他们看来, 护热带雨林虽然重要, 但是他们首先要解决的是老百姓的生存问题。他们也认为许多西方国家对环境造成的污染比发展中国家严重得多, 所以西方国家应该负更大的责任。

(　) 1. The views and sentiments expressed in the passage represent those of developed countries.

(　) 2. In the view of many developing countries, environmental protection can be addressed after they have accumulated sufficient economic resources.

(　) 3. Developing countries concede that they are major polluters.

(　) 4. Many countries see economic development and environmental protection as incompatible.

B. Read the passage and answer the questions. (True/False)

(Traditional)

　　張天明的表哥在一家化工廠工作。他和太太女兒住的地方離化工廠很近。他的工作不錯, 薪水也很高。可是最近化工廠排出的廢氣給附近的居民帶來了嚴重的污染。因為解決污染問題會增加產品成本, 所以化工廠說他們沒有能力解決。附近的許多居民都給政府寫信, 要求化工廠關門。表哥知道空氣污染會影響他和家人的身體健康, 可是化工廠一關門他就失業了。他想來想去, 不知道怎麼辦才好。

(Simplified)

　　张天明的表哥在一家化工厂工作。他和太太女儿住的地方离化工厂很近。他的工作不错, 薪水也很高。可是最近化工厂排出的废气给附近的居民带来了严重的污染。因为解决污染问题会增加产品成本, 所以化工厂说他们没有能力解决。附近的许多居民都给政府写信, 要求化工厂关门。表哥知道空气污染会影响他和家人的身体健康, 可是化工厂一关门他就失业了。他想来想去, 不知道怎麼办才好。

Questions (True/False):

(　) 1. Zhang Tianming's cousin doesn't have to worry about long commutes to work.

(　) 2. His job is dirty, and his wages are low.

(　) 3. The chemical plant denies that it releases anything harmful into the air.

(　) 4. To protect themselves, the residents near the plant keep their windows closed at all times.

(　) 5. Because the residents complained to the government, the plant was closed and the workers are now unemployed.

(　) 6. Zhang Tianming's cousin is ambivalent about how to address his plant's pollution problem.

C. Look at the card and answer the questions.

(See the Appendix of Alternate Character Versions for traditional characters.)

1. Where could one find such a card displayed?

2. What does the card suggest its readers do?

3. Would you follow its suggestion? Why or why not?

▼▼▼▼▼▼▼▼▼▼▼▼▼▼▼▼▼▼▼▼▼▼▼▼▼▼▼▼▼▼▼▼

D. Answer the questions after reading the story.

(Traditional Characters)

竭澤而漁(1)

　　春秋時期(770–476 BCE)楚國攻打晉國(2)。當時楚國是大國，晉國是小國。晉文公(3)問他的大官狐偃(4)怎樣才能打贏楚國。狐偃說：“如果是送禮物，越精美(5)越好，如果是打仗(6)，越奸詐(7)越好。所以打楚國得用計策(8)。”晉文公把狐偃的建議告訴他的另一個大官雍季(9)。雍季不同意狐偃的看法，他說：“千萬不要‘竭澤而漁’。把池塘(10)的水都抽乾了(11)，當然能捉到魚，可是第二年就沒有魚了。把樹林說的樹都燒光了，當然獵得到動物，但是第二年就沒有動物了。奸詐也一樣，可能偶爾用一次行，但是下一次就不能再用了，所以這不是長遠的辦法。”可是雍季沒有更好的建議，晉文公只能用狐偃的辦法。晉文公用狐偃的辦法打贏了楚國，但是他卻重賞(12)雍季。大家都覺得奇怪。晉文公說：“狐偃的話只能幫我解決這一次的問題，可是雍季的話卻對我更有用。”

　　現在大家用“竭澤而漁”來比喻(13)人沒有限制地、不顧後果地索取(14)。

(1)　竭澤而漁(jié zé ér yú)
(2)　晉(Jìn)國: State of Jin
(3)　晉文公: Duke Wen of Jin
(4)　狐偃(Húyàn): a person's name
(5)　精美(jīngměi): exquisite
(6)　打仗(dǎ zhàng): to go to war
(7)　奸詐(jiānzhà): deception; treachery
(8)　計策(jìcè): scheme
(9)　雍季(Yōngjì): a person's name
(10)　池塘(chítáng): pond

(11) 抽乾 (chōu gān): to drain completely (12) 重赏 (zhòng shǎng): to reward lavishly

(13) 比喻 (bǐyù): to describe; metaphor (14) 索取 (suǒqǔ): to take; to ask for; to demand

(Simplified Characters)

竭泽而渔(1)

　　春秋时期(770-476 BCE)楚国攻打晋国(2)。当时楚国是大国, 晋国是小国。晋文公(3)问他的大官狐偃(4)怎样才能打赢楚国。狐偃说: "如果是送礼物, 越精美(5)越好, 如果是打仗(6), 越奸诈(7)越好。所以打楚国得用计策(8)。" 晋文公把狐偃的建议告诉他的另一个大官雍季(9)。雍季不同意狐偃的看法, 他说: "千万不要'竭泽而渔'。把池塘(10)的水都抽乾了(11), 当然能捉到鱼, 可是第二年就没有鱼了。把树林里的树都烧光了, 当然猎得到动物, 但是第二年就没有动物了。奸诈也一样, 可能偶尔用一次行, 但是下一次就不能再用了, 所以这不是长远的办法。" 可是雍季没有更好的建议, 晋文公只能用狐偃的办法。晋文公用狐偃的办法打赢了楚国, 但是他却重赏(12)雍季, 大家都觉得奇怪。晋文公说: "狐偃的话只能帮我解决这一次的问题, 可是雍季的话对我更有用。"

　　现在大家用 "竭泽而渔" 来比喻(13)人没有限制地、不顾後果地索取(14)。

(1) 竭泽而渔 (jié zé ér yú) (2) 晋 (Jìn)国: State of Jin

(3) 晋文公: Duke Wen of Jin (4) 狐偃 (Húyàn): a person's name

(5) 精美 (jīngměi): exquisite (6) 打仗 (dǎ zhàng): to go to war

(7) 奸诈 (jiānzhà): deception; treachery (8) 计策 (jìcè): scheme

(9) 雍季 (Yōngjì): a person's name (10) 池塘 (chítáng): pond

(11) 抽干 (chōu gān): to drain completely (12) 重赏 (zhòng shǎng): to reward lavishly

(13) 比喻 (bǐyù): to describe; metaphor (14) 索取 (suǒqǔ): to take; to ask for; to demand

Questions:

1. Why couldn't Jin have defeated Chu without resorting to a scheme?

2. What was Huyan's suggestion to Duke Wen?

3. Why did Yongji disapprove of Huyan's suggestion?

4. Why did Duke Wen lavishly reward Yongji instead of Huyan?

IV. GRAMMAR & USAGE

A. Fill in the blanks using 為什麼 ／ 为什么 *or* 怎麼 ／ 怎么.

1. 他＿＿＿＿＿＿＿＿還沒有來? 平時他八點就到學校了, 現在都十點半了。

   他＿＿＿＿＿＿＿＿还没有来? 平时他八点就到学校了, 现在都十点半了。

2. 你＿＿＿＿＿＿＿上這所大學? 這所大學很有名吧?

   你＿＿＿＿＿＿＿上这所大学? 这所大学很有名吧?

3. 平平, 你已經十歲了, ＿＿＿＿＿＿＿還要媽媽幫你穿衣服?

   平平, 你已经十岁了,＿＿＿＿＿＿＿还要妈妈帮你穿衣服?

B. Fill in the blanks using 往往 *or* 常常.

1. 你十年沒來看我了, 以後你要＿＿＿＿＿來。

   你十年没来看我了, 以后你要＿＿＿＿＿来。

2. 我＿＿＿＿＿想去南京遊覽, 可是一直沒有機會。

   我＿＿＿＿＿想去南京游览, 可是一直没有机会。

3. 研究新藥＿＿＿＿＿得用動物做實驗。

   研究新药＿＿＿＿＿得用动物做实验。

4. 大學一年級的新生＿＿＿＿＿不知道選什麼專業。

   大学一年级的新生＿＿＿＿＿不知道选什么专业。

C. Fill in the blanks with the appropriate phrases.

1. 改革開放以後的犯罪率比改革開放以前的犯罪率＿＿＿＿＿。(很高 ／ 高多了)

   改革开放以后的犯罪率比改革开放以前的犯罪率＿＿＿＿＿。(很高 ／ 高多了)

2. 你母親現在的身體怎麼樣?_____。(好多了 / 好得多)

   你母亲现在的身体怎么样?_____。(好多了 / 好得多)

3. 發展中國家的環保意識比發達國家_____。(薄弱得多 / 有一點薄弱)

   发展中国家的环保意识比发达国家_____。(薄弱得多 / 有一点薄弱)

D. Complete the sentences.

1. 我以前的女朋友結婚, 請我去參加她的婚禮, 我實在不知道應該怎麼辦。
   去吧, _____, 不去吧, _____。

   我以前的女朋友结婚, 请我去参加她的婚礼, 我实在不知道应该怎么办。
   去吧, _____, 不去吧, _____。

2. 她找男朋友很挑剔, _____吧, 她不喜歡, _____吧,
   她也不喜歡。

   她找男朋友很挑剔,_____吧, 她不喜欢, _____吧,
   她也不喜欢。

3. 用動物做實驗研究新藥常常引起爭論, 用吧, _____,
   不用吧, _____。

   用动物做实验研究新药常常引起争论。用吧, _____,
   不用吧, _____。

E. Complete the dialogues using 以為 / 以为.

EXAMPLE: a: 你怎麼現在才來? 我等你已經等了一個多鐘頭了。
       你怎么现在才来? 我等你已经等了一个多钟头了。

       b: <u>我以為現在才八點</u>。非常對不起。
       <u>我以为现在才八点</u>。非常对不起。

1. a: 那門統計學的課你怎麼上了一半就不上了?
      那门统计学的课你怎么上了一半就不上了?

   b: 我_____, 沒想到那麼難, 所以就不上了。
      我_____, 没想到那么难, 所以就不上了。

2. a: 你態度認真, 做事負責, 為什麼不申請那個工作?

　　你态度认真, 做事负责, 为什么不申请那个工作?

　b: 我＿＿＿＿＿＿＿＿＿＿＿＿＿＿＿＿＿＿＿, 所以沒申請。

　　我＿＿＿＿＿＿＿＿＿＿＿＿＿＿＿＿＿＿＿, 所以没申请。

3. a: 哎, 你怎麼病得這麼厲害? 難道你沒去看病?

　　哎, 你怎么病得这么厉害? 难道你没去看病?

　b: 沒去。我＿＿＿＿＿＿＿＿＿＿＿＿＿＿＿, 沒想到病得越來越厲害。

　　没去。我＿＿＿＿＿＿＿＿＿＿＿＿＿＿＿, 没想到病得越来越厉害。

F. Complete the dialogues using 造成.

1. a: 在附近建化學工廠, 工作機會就多了, 有什麼不好? (污染)

　　在附近建化学工厂, 工作机会就多了, 有什么不好? (污染)

　b: 當然不好, ＿＿＿＿＿＿＿＿＿＿＿＿＿＿。

　　当然不好, ＿＿＿＿＿＿＿＿＿＿＿＿＿＿。

2. a: 他們整天不是吵架就是打架, 是不是要離婚了? (影響)

　　他们整天不是吵架就是打架, 是不是要离婚了? (影响)

　b: 他們想離婚, 可是孩子那麼小, 怕＿＿＿＿＿＿＿＿, 所以不離了。

　　他们想离婚, 可是孩子那么小, 怕＿＿＿＿＿＿＿＿, 所以不离了。

3. a: 現在的電腦真厲害, 什麼事都能做。(失業)

　　现在的电脑真厉害, 什么事都能做。(失业)

　b: 就是因為電腦什麼都能做, ＿＿＿＿＿＿＿＿＿＿＿＿＿。

　　就是因为电脑什么都能做, ＿＿＿＿＿＿＿＿＿＿＿＿＿。

G. Fill in the blanks with vocabulary items from this lesson.

1. 這個工廠每年＿＿＿＿＿＿大量的三廢, 對當地的環境造成很大的污染。

　这个工厂每年＿＿＿＿＿＿大量的三废, 对当地的环境造成很大的污染。

2. 這種藥很_____, 我吃了兩片, 病就好了。

    这种药很_____, 我吃了两片, 病就好了。

3. 張教授今天不能來, 所以_____我來參加這個討論會。

    张教授今天不能来, 所以_____我来参加这个讨论会。

4. 這件事很_____, 我得好好考慮考慮。

    这件事很_____, 我得好好考虑考虑。

5. 化工廠關門, 造成很多工人_____。

    化工厂关门, 造成很多工人_____。

6. 你這個決定是錯誤的, 將來後果_____。

    你这个决定是错误的, 将来后果_____。

7. 小林整天在實驗室裏做化學_____, 寫報告。

    小林整天在实验室里做化学_____, 写报告。

8. 這個地方的經濟最近這幾年發展得太慢, 得_____發展。

    这个地方的经济最近这几年发展得太慢, 得_____发展。

汽車排放的廢氣／汽车排放的废气

▼▼▼▼▼▼▼▼▼▼▼▼▼▼▼▼▼▼▼▼▼▼▼▼▼▼▼▼▼▼▼▼▼▼▼▼▼▼▼

V. TRANSLATION

A. Translate the passages into Chinese.

1. America is one of the world's big energy [producing and consuming] nations. But America is unlike China. In America most power plants use oil to generate electricity. In addition, there are many nuclear power plants in America. Although nuclear energy causes little pollution to the environment, many people oppose nuclear energy because they are concerned that nuclear power plants are not safe enough.

2. My family lives in a small town in the southern part of America. The natural environment there is very good. The sky is blue, the mountains are green, and the water is very clean. Because there are no factories there, there is no pollution. Recently, the state government proposed to build (建: jiàn) an incinerator (焚化爐 ／ 焚化炉: fénhuàlú) near our home, which drew the opposition of all of the residents of the town. They all went to the local government to protest. They believe that if this kind of incinerator were built, it would cause environmental pollution, and the consequences would be unthinkable. Eventually, the municipal government decided to build the incinerator elsewhere.

B. Translate an entry from Xiao Zhang's diary into Chinese.

Because of the need to develop the economy, many countries underestimate the importance of protecting the environment. As a result, the decrease of rain forests has led to ecological imbalance. Many animals are on the verge of extinction. In addition, the global climate has become abnormal. More and more people have incurable diseases. In order to find the medicine for these diseases, scientists have to use animals for medical experiments. However, there are organizations protesting this and claiming that animal experiments are barbaric. On the other hand, is it humane to see people die from diseases?

VI. COMPOSITION

請你談談發展中國家的經濟和環境哪個更重要。
请你谈谈发展中国家的经济和环境哪个更重要。

VOCABULARY INDEX (CHINESE-ENGLISH)

Traditional	Simplified	Pinyin	Part of Speech	English	Lesson
奔		bēn	v	run; fly to	12
笨		bèn	adj	stupid	1
比喻		bǐyù	v	describe; metaphor	20
變化	变化	biànhuà	n	change	14
鱉	鳖	biē	n	soft-shell turtle	9
採納	采纳	cǎinà	v	adopt; accept	18
草		cǎo	n	grass	2
朝代		cháodài	n	dynasty	11
成為	成为	chéngwéi	v	become	7
池塘		chítáng	n	pond	20
重		chóng	adv	renew; repeat; again	14
抽乾	抽干	chōu gān	vc	drain completely	20
抽煙	抽烟	chōu yān	vo	smoke (a cigarette)	2
抽煙斗	抽烟斗	chōu yāndǒu	vo	smoke a pipe	2
雌		cí	adj	(of animals) female	15
刺穿		cì chuān	vc	pierce through	8
存活		cúnhuó	v	survive; remain alive	19
打官司		dǎ guānsī	vo	sue	15
打仗		dǎ zhàng	vo	go to war	20
代表		dàibiǎo	v	represent	19
戴眼鏡	戴眼镜	dài yǎnjìng	vo	wear glasses	2
當兵	当兵	dāng bīng	vo	serve in the army	15
凳子		dèngzi	n	bench	19
電扇	电扇	diànshàn	n	electric fan	3
電梯	电梯	diàntī	n	elevator	6
掉		diào	v	fall; drop	18
電子郵件	电子邮件	diànzǐ yóujiàn	n	e-mail	10
對方	对方	duìfāng	n	each other	14
對上	对上	duì shang	vc	match	14
盾		dùn	n	shield	8
發榜	发榜	fā bǎng	vo	publish a list of successful candidates or applicants	5
飯碗	饭碗	fànwǎn	n	rice bowl	3
防病		fáng bìng	vo	prevent illness	16
放火		fàng huǒ	vo	set fire; commit arson	12
焚化爐	焚化炉	fénhuàlú	n	incinerator	20
駙馬	驸马	fùmǎ	n	emperor's son-in-law	14
蓋	盖	gài	v	build	18
趕走	赶走	gǎn zǒu	vc	drive away	12
幹活	干活	gàn huó	vo	work	12
告示		gàoshì	v	announcement	12

Traditional	Simplified	Pinyin	Part of Speech	English	Lesson
根據	根据	gēnjù	v	on the basis of	3
公元		gōngyuán	n	"common era," i.e., CE	16
貢獻	贡献	gòngxiàn	n	contribution	16
掛	挂	guà	v	hang	2
怪物		guàiwù	n	monster	12
官		guān	n	official	7
歸	归	guī	v	return; 回來	1
國都	国都	guódū	n	capital of the country	11, 17
汗		hàn	n	sweat	9
盒子		hézi	n	box	12
互聯網	互联网	hùliánwǎng	n	Internet	10
畫	画	huà	n	picture; painting	2
歡迎	欢迎	huānyíng	v	welcome	17
皇帝		huángdì	n	emperor	11
火柴		huǒchái	n	matches	2
計策	计策	jìcè	n	scheme	20
記賬	记账	jì zhàng	vo	keep accounts; do bookkeeping	1
嫁		jià	v	marry	7
奸詐	奸诈	jiānzhà	adj	deception; treachery	20
建		jiàn	v	build	20
降低		jiàngdī	v	lower	19
郊區	郊区	jiāoqū	v	outskirts; suburbs	11
腳	脚	jiǎo	n	foot	17
竭澤而漁	竭泽而渔	jié zé ér yú		drain the pond to get all the fish; kill the goose that lays the golden eggs	20
經濟頭腦	经济头脑	jīngjì tóunǎo	n	smarts for finance	1
精美		jīngměi	adj	exquisite	20
驚訝	惊讶	jīngyà	adj	surprised; astonished	15
井		jǐng	n	well	9
決定	决定	juédìng	v	decide	3
君子		jūnzǐ	n	gentleman	18
口		kǒu	m	measure word for a well	9
樑	梁	liáng	n	beam	18
獵人	猎人	lièrén	n	hunter	12
摞		luò	v	pile up	19
旅遊城市	旅游城市	lǚyóu chéngshì	n	tourist city	12
麻醉		mázuì	v	anaesthetize	16
馬球	马球	mǎqiú	n	polo	13
矛		máo	n	spear	8
...帽		mào	n	hat; 帽子	19
眉頭	眉头	méitóu	n	eyebrows	11
滅亡	灭亡	mièwáng	v	perish; die out	14

▼▼▼▼▼▼▼▼▼▼▼▼▼▼▼▼▼▼▼▼▼▼▼▼▼▼▼▼▼▼▼▼▼▼▼▼

Traditional	Simplified	Pinyin	Part of Speech	English	Lesson
暮		mù		(literary) dusk	19
墓地		mùdì	n	graveyard; cemetery	6
泥人		nírén	n	terracotta figures	11
農人	农人	nóngrén	n	farmer	12
女籃	女篮	nǔlán	n	women's basketball; 女子籃球 / 女子篮球	15
男籃	男篮	nánlán	n	men's basketball; 男子籃球 / 男子篮球	15
爬		pá	v	climb	19
盤子	盘子	pánzi	n	plate	3
顰	颦	pín	v	knit one's eyebrows; (literary) 皺眉	11
蘋果	苹果	píngguǒ	n	apple	20
遷	迁	qiān	v	move (to another place)	6
敲鑼打鼓	敲锣打鼓	qiāo luó dǎ gǔ		beat gongs and drums	19
(青)蛙		(qīng)wā	n	frog	9
情況	情况	qíngkuàng	n	situation	3
請柬	请柬	qǐngjiǎn	n	invitation letter	1
裙子		qúnzi	n	skirt	15
思想家		sīxiǎngjiā	n	philosopher; 哲學家	6
蛇		shé	n	snake	17
神仙		shénxian	n	god; deity	12
聲音	声音	shēngyīn	n	sound	12
…獅	…狮	shī	n	lion; 獅子 / 狮子	19
手錶	手表	shǒubiǎo	n	watch	2
手提箱		shǒutíxiāng	n	briefcase	2
書法家	书法家	shūfǎjiā	n	calligrapher	7
索取		suǒqǔ	v	take; ask for; demand	20
太傅		tàifù	n	Grand Master; tutor to the crown prince	7
太陽	太阳	tàiyáng	n	sun	12, 17
逃跑		táopǎo	v	run and escape	12
踢		tī	v	kick	13
提醒		tíxǐng	v	remind	18
添		tiān	v	add	17
頭髮	头发	tóufa	n	hair (on the human head)	15
兔子		tùzi	n	rabbit	12, 15, 19
退回		tuì huí	vc	return (something to a person/shop)	6
挖墓		wā mù	vo	dig graves	6
外地		wàidì	n	places other than where one is	12
玩具		wánjù	n	toy	18
圍著	围着	wéi zhe		around	17
尾巴		wěiba	n	tail	19
無所謂	无所谓	wúsuǒwèi	adv	no big deal	17

Traditional	Simplified	Pinyin	Part of Speech	English	Lesson
嚇	吓	xià	v	frighten; startle	18
嚇跑	吓跑	xià pǎo	vc	frighten into running away	12
仙丹		xiāndān	n	elixir	12
羨慕	羡慕	xiànmù	v/adj	envy; envious	11
小偷		xiǎotōu	n	thief	18
效		xiào	v	imitate; (literary) 模仿, 仿效	11
雄		xióng	adj	(of animal) male	15
(女)婿		(nǚ)xù		(literary) son-in-law	7
藥物學	药物学	yàowùxué	n	materia medica	16
俑		yǒng	n	figurines buried with the dead in ancient times	13
宰相		zǎixiàng	n	prime minister	7
丈夫		zhàngfu	n	husband	12
朝		zhāo	n	(literary) morning	19
治病		zhì bìng	vo	treat an illness	16
重賞	重赏	zhòng shǎng		reward lavishly	20
皺	皱	zhòu	v	wrinkle; furrow	11
竹子		zhúzi	n	bamboo	19
專業	专业	zhuānyè	n	major	2
轉	转	zhuàn	v	turn; revolve	17
撞		zhuàng	v	run into	12
自私		zìsī	adj	selfish	17
足		zú	n	foot (literary)	17
尊敬		zūnjìng	adj/v	respectful; respect	12

PROPER NOUNS

Traditional	Simplified	Pinyin	English	Lesson
本草綱目	本草纲目	Běncǎo Gāngmù	*Materia Medica*	16
查爾斯敦	查尔斯敦	Chá'ěrsīdūn	Charleston	12
嫦娥		Cháng'é	name of a goddess	12
陳朝	陈朝	Chén Cháo	Chén Dynasty	14
東施		Dōngshī	a person's name	11
感恩節	感恩节	Gǎn'ēnjié	Thanksgiving	12
漢朝	汉朝	Hàn Cháo	the Han Dynasty	18
漢代	汉代	Hàn Dài	the Han Dynasty	13
華陀	华陀	Huà Tuó	a person's name	16
狐偃		Húyàn	a person's name	20
晉國	晋国	Jìnguó	State of Jin	20
晉文公		Jìnwéngōng	Duke Wen of Jin	20
狙公		Jūgōng	a person's name	19
李時珍	李时珍	Lǐ Shízhēn	a person's name	16
孟子		Mèngzǐ	Mencius	6
南卡		Nánkǎ	South Carolina	12
南美洲		Nánměizhōu	South America	13
歐洲	欧洲	Ōuzhōu	Europe	13
傷寒論	伤寒论	Shānghán Lùn	*On Febrile Diseases*	16
聖誕節	圣诞节	Shèngdàn Jié	Christmas	12
孫山	孙山	Sūn Shān	a person's name	5
唐朝		Táng Cháo	Tang dynasty	17
田登		Tián Dēng	a person's name	12
王羲之		Wáng Xīzhī	a person's name	7
郗		Xī	a Chinese surname	7
西施		Xīshī	a person's name	11
雍季		Yōngjì	a person's name	20
張仲景	张仲景	Zhāng Zhòngjǐng	a person's name	16
莊子	庄子	Zhuāngzǐ	Zhuangzi	9
壯族	壮族	Zhuàng zú	the Zhuang nationality	19

VOCABULARY INDEX (ENGLISH-CHINESE)

English	Traditional	Simplified	Pinyin	Part of Speech	Lesson
▲A▲					
add	添		tiān	v	17
adopt; accept	採納	采纳	cǎinà	v	18
anaesthetize	麻醉		mázuì	v	16
announcement	告示		gàoshì	v	12
apple	蘋果	苹果	píngguǒ	n	20
around	圍著	围着	wéi zhe		17
▲B▲					
bamboo	竹子		zhúzi	n	19
beam	樑	梁	liáng	n	18
beat gongs and drums	敲鑼打鼓	敲锣打鼓	qiāo luó dǎ gǔ		19
become	成為	成为	chéngwéi		7
bench	凳子		dèngzi	n	19
box	盒子		hézi	n	12
briefcase	手提箱		shǒutíxiāng	n	2
build	蓋	盖	gài	v	18
build	建		jiàn	v	20
▲C▲					
calligrapher	書法家	书法家	shūfǎjiā	n	7
capital of the country	國都	国都	guódū	n	11, 17
change	變化	变化	biànhuà	n	14
climb	爬		pá	v	19
"common era," i.e., CE	公元		gōngyuán	n	16
contribution	貢獻	贡献	gòngxiàn	n	16
▲D▲					
deception; treachery	奸詐	奸诈	jiānzhà	adj	20
decide	決定	决定	juédìng	v	3
describe; metaphor	比喻		bǐyù	v	20
dig graves	挖墓		wā mù	vo	6
drain completely	抽乾	抽干	chōu gān	vc	20
drain the pond to get all the fish; kill the goose that lays the golden eggs	竭澤而漁	竭泽而渔	jié zé ér yú		20
drive away	趕走	赶走	gǎn zǒu	vc	12
(literary) dusk	暮		mù		19
dynasty	朝代		cháodài	n	11
▲E▲					
each other	對方	对方	duìfāng	n	14
electric fan	電扇	电扇	diànshàn	n	3
elevator	電梯	电梯	diàntī	n	6
elixir	仙丹		xiāndān	n	12

▼▼▼▼▼▼▼▼▼▼▼▼▼▼▼▼▼▼▼▼▼▼▼▼▼▼▼▼▼▼▼▼▼▼▼▼

English	Traditional	Simplified	Pinyin	Part of Speech	Lesson
e-mail	電子郵件	电子邮件	diànzǐ yóujiàn	n	10
emperor	皇帝		huángdì	n	11
emperor's son-in-law	駙馬	驸马	fùmǎ	n	14
envy; envious	羨慕	羡慕	xiànmù	v/adj	11
exquisite	精美		jīngměi	adj	20
eyebrows	眉頭	眉头	méitóu	n	11
▲F▲					
fall; drop	掉		diào	v	18
farmer	農人	农人	nóngrén	n	12
(of animal) female	雌		cí	adj	15
figurines buried with the dead in ancient times	俑		yǒng	n	13
foot	腳	脚	jiǎo	n	17
foot (literary)	足		zú	n	17
frighten; startle	嚇	吓	xià	v	18
frighten into running away	嚇跑	吓跑	xià pǎo	vc	12
frog	(青)蛙		(qīng)wā	n	9
▲G▲					
gentleman	君子		jūnzǐ	n	18
go to war	打仗		dǎ zhàng	vo	20
god; deity	神仙		shénxian	n	12
Grand Master; tutor to the crown prince	太傅		tàifù	n	7
grass	草		cǎo	n	2
graveyard; cemetery	墓地		mùdì	n	6
▲H▲					
hair (on the human head)	頭髮	头发	tóufa	n	15
hang	掛	挂	guà	v	2
hat	...帽		mào	n	19
hunter	獵人	猎人	lièrén	n	12
husband	丈夫		zhàngfu	n	12
▲I▲					
imitate	效		xiào	v	11
incinerator	焚化爐	焚化炉	fénhuàlú	n	20
Internet	互聯網	互联网	hùliánwǎng	n	10
invitation letter	請柬	请柬	qǐngjiǎn	n	1
▲K▲					
keep accounts; do bookkeeping	記賬	记账	jì zhàng	vo	1
kick	踢		tī	v	13
knit one's eyebrows	顰	颦	pín	v	11
▲L▲					
lion	...獅	...狮	shī	n	19
lower	降低		jiàngdī	v	19

▼▼▼▼▼▼▼▼▼▼▼▼▼▼▼▼▼▼▼▼▼▼▼▼▼▼▼▼▼▼▼▼▼▼▼▼▼▼

English	Traditional	Simplified	Pinyin	Part of Speech	Lesson
▲M▲					
major	專業	专业	zhuānyè	n	2
(of animal) male	雄		xióng	adj	15
marry	嫁		jià	v	7
match	對上	对上	duì shang	vc	14
matches	火柴		huǒchái	n	2
materia medica	藥物學	药物学	yàowùxué	n	16
measure word for a well	口		kǒu	m	9
men's basketball	男籃	男篮	nánlán	n	15
monster	怪物		guàiwù	n	12
morning	朝		zhāo	n	19
move (to another place)	遷	迁	qiān	v	6
▲N▲					
no big deal	無所謂	无所谓	wúsuǒwèi	adv	17
▲O▲					
official	官		guān	n	7
on the basis of	根據	根据	gēnjù	v	3
outskirts; suburbs	郊區	郊区	jiāoqū	v	11
▲P▲					
perish; die out	滅亡	灭亡	mièwáng	v	14
philosopher	思想家		sīxiǎngjiā	n	6
picture; painting	畫	画	huà	n	2
pierce through	刺穿		cì chuān	vc	8
pile up	摞		luò	v	19
places other than where one is	外地		wàidì	n	12
plate	盤子	盘子	pánzi	n	3
polo	馬球	马球	mǎqiú	n	13
pond	池塘		chítáng	n	20
prevent illness	防病		fáng bìng	vo	16
prime minister	宰相		zǎixiàng	n	7
publish a list of successful candidates or applicants	發榜	发榜	fā bǎng	vo	5
▲R▲					
rabbit	兔子		tùzi	n	12, 15, 19
remind	提醒		tíxǐng	v	18
renew; repeat; again	重		chóng	adv	14
represent	代表		dàibiǎo	v	19
respectful; respect	尊敬		zūnjìng	adj/v	12
return	歸	归	guī	v	1
return (something to a person/shop)	退回		tuì huí	vc	6
reward lavishly	重賞	重赏	zhòng shǎng		20

English	Traditional	Simplified	Pinyin	Part of Speech	Lesson
rice bowl	飯碗	饭碗	fànwǎn	n	3
run; fly to	奔		bēn	v	12
run and escape	逃跑		táopǎo	v	12
run into	撞		zhuàng	v	12
▲S▲					
scheme	計策	计策	jìcè	n	20
selfish	自私		zìsī	adj	17
serve in the army	當兵	当兵	dāng bīng	vo	15
set fire; commit arson	放火		fàng huǒ	vo	12
shield	盾		dùn	n	8
situation	情況	情况	qíngkuàng	n	3
skirt	裙子		qúnzi	n	15
smarts for finance	經濟頭腦	经济头脑	jīngjì tóunǎo	n	1
smoke (a cigarette)	抽煙	抽烟	chōu yān	vo	2
smoke a pipe	抽煙斗	抽烟斗	chōu yāndǒu	vo	2
snake	蛇		shé	n	17
soft-shell turtle	鱉	鳖	biē	n	9
son-in-law	(女)婿		(nǚ)xù		7
sound	聲音	声音	shēngyīn	n	12
spear	矛		máo	n	8
stupid	笨		bèn	adj	1
sue	打官司		dǎ guānsī	vo	15
sun	太陽	太阳	tàiyáng	n	12, 17
surprised; astonished	驚訝	惊讶	jīngyà	adj	15
survive; remain alive	存活		cúnhuó	v	19
sweat	汗		hàn	n	9
▲T▲					
tail	尾巴		wěiba	n	19
take; ask for; demand	索取		suǒqǔ	v	20
terracotta figures	泥人		nírén	n	11
thief	小偷		xiǎotōu	n	18
tourist city	旅遊城市	旅游城市	lǚyóu chéngshì	n	12
toy	玩具		wánjù	n	18
treat an illness	治病		zhì bìng	vo	16
turn; revolve	轉	转	zhuàn	v	17
▲W▲					
watch	手錶	手表	shǒubiǎo	n	2
wear glasses	戴眼鏡	戴眼镜	dài yǎnjìng	vo	2
welcome	歡迎	欢迎	huānyíng	v	17
well	井		jǐng	n	9
women's basketball	女籃	女篮	nǚlán	n	15
work	幹活	干活	gàn huó	vo	12
wrinkle; furrow	皺	皱	zhòu	v	11

PROPER NOUNS

English	Traditional	Simplified	Pinyin	Lesson
a Chinese surname	郗		Xī	7
a person's name	東施		Dōngshī	11
a person's name	華陀	华陀	Huà Tuó	16
a person's name	狐偃		Húyàn	20
a person's name	狙公		Jūgōng	19
a person's name	李時珍	李时珍	Lǐ Shízhēn	16
a person's name	孫山	孙山	Sūn Shān	5
a person's name	田登		Tián Dēng	12
a person's name	王羲之		Wáng Xīzhī	7
a person's name	西施		Xīshī	11
a person's name	雍季		Yōngjì	20
a person's name	張仲景	张仲景	Zhāng Zhòngjǐng	16
Charleston	查爾斯敦	查尔斯敦	Chá'ěrsīdūn	12
Chén Dynasty	陳朝	陈朝	Chén Cháo	14
Christmas	聖誕節	圣诞节	Shèngdàn Jié	12
Duke Wen of Jin	晉文公		Jìnwéngōng	20
Europe	歐洲	欧洲	Ōuzhōu	13
Han Dynasty	漢朝	汉朝	Hàn Cháo	18
Han Dynasty	漢代	汉代	Hàn Dài	13
Materia Medica	本草綱目	本草纲目	Běncǎo Gāngmù	16
Mencius	孟子		Mèngzǐ	6
name of a goddess	嫦娥		Cháng'é	12
On Febrile Diseases	傷寒論	伤寒论	Shānghán Lùn	16
South America	南美洲		Nánměizhōu	13
South Carolina	南卡		Nánkǎ	12
State of Jin	晉國	晋国	Jìnguó	20
Tang dynasty	唐朝		Táng Cháo	17
Thanksgiving	感恩節	感恩节	Gǎn'ēnjié	12
Zhuangzi	莊子	庄子	Zhuāngzǐ	9
Zhuang nationality	壯族	壮族	Zhuàng zú	19

Page 34

汤　类

海鲜酸辣汤 (2–4人)	7.95	大肠猪血汤 (2–4人)	6.95
海鲜豆腐羹 (2–4人)	7.95	沙茶猪血汤 (2–4人)	6.95
西湖牛肉羹 (2–4人)	7.95	姜丝腰花汤 (2–4人)	7.25
香菇肉羹 (2–4人)	7.95	姜丝鱼干空心菜汤 (2–4人)	6.95
花枝羹 (2–4人)	7.95	姜丝蛤蜊汤 (2–4人)	7.95
鱿鱼汤 (2–4人)	7.95	蚵仔汤 (2–4人)	7.95
酸菜鱿鱼汤 (2–4人)	7.95	酸菜豆腐汤 (2–4人)	6.25
酸菜肚丝汤 (2–4人)	6.95	菠菜豆腐汤 (2–4人)	6.25
麻辣肚丝汤 (2–4人)	6.95	榨菜肉丝汤 (2–4人)	6.25
		鸡茸玉米汤 (2–4人)	6.50

Page 43

Page 57

學生　李大成　系　　　　授予　文　學學士學位。

江蘇武進　人，一九八二年

十一月生。在上海外國語學院

校（院）　英語　系

　　　　英語　專業　　　　校（院）長　　學位評定委員會主席

修業四年，成績及格，準予

畢業。經審核符合《中華人

民共和國學位條例》規定，

2003 年 7 月 10 日

證書編號：

Page 71

房屋出租

近 Northgate mall

三房兩厅

兩個厕所

有冰箱，洗衣机

月租：$1375

有意请电：425 ****

房屋出租

$180-$350

有共用电话

及电视CABLE，近公车站

有意者请电：

682 ****

Page 98

姓名	王小梅	星座	雙子座
性別		出生年月	1976 年 6 月 14 日
身高	165 cm	體重	48 kg
所在城市	北京	老家	海澱
國籍	中國	血型	O 型
婚姻狀況	未婚	體型	保密
休息日	雙休六七	月收入	保密
學歷	大學專科	畢業學校	北京醫科大學
兄妹情況	兄妹兩人以上	專業	眼科
工作情況	在職	從事職業	醫生
吸烟	不吸		
喝酒	偶爾		
住房	與父母同住	汽車	有買車計劃
擅長（愛好）	聽音樂、跑步		
性格自介	活潑開朗,外向,溫柔體貼,不拘小節,害羞,老實,敏感,快言快語		

Page 103

安琪小姐 大專學歷， 24歲，未婚，出身於北京一高知家庭，身高 1.67 米，知書達理，端莊美麗，溫柔善良，聰慧能幹，身材健美。愛好體育，擅長烹調及室內設計。能說一口流利地道的英語（托福成績 617 分）， 現在國內一家外商獨資公司工作。 欲尋一位有事業心，眞誠善良，品德高尚，具有碩士以上學歷的海外男士爲侶（以在美加爲宜）。有意者請寄簡歷、全身近照、電話號碼及婚姻狀況證明。來信請寄： 100083　　中國北京市海澱區暫安處一號魏淑珍轉安琪小姐收。

Page 104

留學人員徵婚需填表格							
姓　名		性　別		出生日期		民　族	
籍　貫		身　高		相　貌		學　歷	
愛　好		職　業		護照號		所在國	
居留身份				婚姻狀況			
有無子女				身體狀況			
通訊地址						電　話	
其它情況							
要求對方							

Page 105

立體電影　獨家放映
燎原電影院小廳
《馴獅三郎》
放映時間：1：30　3：00
4：30　6：00　7：30
長壽路600號　電話：2539254

Page 118

今 明 電 視

4月11日　星期一
中央電視臺　五頻道
23:35　4集連續劇:特區警察
③④
上海電視臺　八頻道
10:17　包青天:眞假狀元(1)
23:01　故事片:風雨相思雁
上海電視臺　十四頻道
0:20　楊貴妃(28)
東方電視臺　廿頻道
21:54　臺灣電視連續劇:末
代皇孫(54)
上海敎育電視臺(26頻道)
19:59　音樂專題:軍歌聲聲
4月12日　星期二
中央電視臺　五頻道
20:05　14集連續劇:還是那
條街⑤
上海電視臺　八頻道
20:10　包青天:眞假狀元(2)
上海電視臺　十四頻道
23:38　楊貴妃(29)
東方電視臺　廿頻道
21:53　末代皇孫(55)
上海敎育電視臺(26頻道)
20:13　七彩講壇　話劇《冰山
情》

Page 119

中 視

08000122 xx
05:30　我们两家都是人
06:00　新天地无用之
银河战警
06:30　早安！您的气象新闻
08:30　快乐生活王　（普）
09:00　文茜小妹大　（普）
10:00　戏说乾隆　（普）
11:00　亲亲你是我的宝贝
12:00　中视午间新闻
13:00　神医侠侣　（普）
14:30　奈何花　（普）
15:30　黄色手帕　（普）
16:30　机兽新世纪　│
17:00　七龙珠　（普）
17:00　网球王子　（普）
17:57　大小同心ABC　（普）
18:00　大家来说笑　（普）
19:00　中视新闻全球报导
20:00　神医侠侣　（普）
21:30　我们两家都是人
22:00　世界非常奇妙　（普）
22:30　文茜小际大　（普）
23:30　黄色手帕　（普）
00:30　中视夜线新闻
01:30　我的秘密花园　（普）
02:30　午夜我们两家都是人
03:00　午夜文茜小妹大
04:00　午夜MIT台湾志

Page 127

▼▼

明 日
中央電視臺

●中央電視臺—1
6:00 走近科學
9:24 連續劇：西游記（縮編版）
（22-24）
12:38 今日說法
●中央電視臺—新聞頻道
6:30 媒體廣場
11:00 整點新聞
12:00 新聞 30 分
●中央電視臺—2
9:00 中國證券
9:48 健康之路
10:43 廣告經濟信息中心特別節目
12:00 全球資訊榜
●中央電視臺—3
7:45 文化訪談錄
8:20 中國音樂電視
9:05 劇場：東北一家人（38-40）
11:55 曲苑雜壇
12:30 快樂驛站
12:45 曲苑雜壇
●中央電視臺—4
7:10 探索·發現
8:00 新聞 60 分
9:00 連續劇：表演系的故事（8）
10:15 動畫城
11:10 走遍中國
●中央電視臺—5
6:00 健身房
9:00 早安中國
10:00 實況錄像：2005 年焦作 U17 乒乓球挑戰賽
●中央電視臺—6
6:51 故事片：東歸英雄傳
8:36 故事片：神女峰的迷霧
12:59 紀錄片長廊：飲食文化：世界蛋糕縱覽：澳門
●中央電視臺—7
7:30 科技博覽
8:30 動畫城
9:19 智慧樹
11:30 人與自然
12:30 致富經

●中央電視臺—8
6:00 每日佳藝（佳藝劇場）：隱秘的激情（第二部）（20）（哥倫比亞）
7:46 連續劇：再見阿郎（55-58）
11:38 連續劇：閑人馬大姐（133、134）
12:51 魅力 100 分：武裝特警（5、6）
●中央電視臺—10
7:55 教科文行動之科學發現篇
9:35 走近科學
10:05 教科文行動
11:05 科技之光
12:05 地圖上的故事
12:15 希望·英語雜志
●中央電視臺—11
6:00 九州大戲臺
7:35 名段欣賞
8:45 九州大戲臺（地方版）:越劇:灰闌記（周燕萍、鄭曼麗、李寶嬴主演）
12:05 跟我學
12:40 名段欣賞
●中央電視臺 –12
8:15 大家看法
8:35 道德觀察
9:00 第一綫
10:25 法治視界
12:00 中國法治報道
12:30 大家看法
●中央電視臺 –少兒頻道
6:00 中國動畫
8:00 中國動畫
9:20 （首播）中國動畫
10:00 動漫世界
10:30 快樂體驗
11:00 中國動畫
12:00 中國動畫
12:30 新聞袋袋褲
●中央電視臺 –（音樂頻道）
10:21 CCTV·音樂廳（214）
12:40 影視留聲機（214）

Page 131

波士顿 **环 球 旅 行 社**

L. B. N. INTERNATIONAL TRAVEL

经验丰富・服务周到
电脑订位・包君满意

● 代理国内外廉价机票
● 代办国际旅游与签证

‖‖‖‖‖‖‖每周营业七天 9：30AM～6：30PM‖‖‖‖‖‖‖

地址：665 PASQUINELLI DRIVE, SUITE 103

TEL：五五五－八八八

Page 137

京倫飯店位于北京市中心，

無論是商務旅行還是旅游觀光均十分便利。

乘車前往北京國際機場祇需三十分鐘，

乘車前往天安門廣場僅十分鐘，

毗鄰中國國際貿易中心、商務區及大使區。

Page 138

房 价 表	
	NT$
单人房	7,600
双人房（一大床）	7,900
双人房（二单床）	7,900
精致套房	13,000
景隅套房	17,000
行政套房	18,000
豪华套房	30,000
＊＊＊＊总统套房	40,000
加床	800

■ 住宿迁出时间：中午 12 点

● 上列价格自 2004 年 1 月 1 日起生效，金额以新台币
计费并已包含 5% 加值营业税。

● 10% 服务费另计。

● 价格有所异动时，不再另行通知。

● 提供宾士轿车往返机场的接送服务。

● 可接受的信用卡：
美国运通卡（AE）、大来卡（Diners）、万事达卡（Mater）
威士卡（Visa）、JCB 卡、联合信用卡。

Page 139

郵 2102

中國郵政
LA POSTE CHINOISE
國際、港、澳函件收據
Récépissé de dépôt d'un envoi
☐ 挂號　Recommandé
☐ 保價　Avec valeur déclarée

函件號碼　　（貼挂號條碼標籤下聯）
No. _____

函件種類（挂號函件填）
Catégorie d'envoi (A n'utiliser que pour
les envois recommandes)
☐ 信函　☐ 印刷品　☐ 小包
　Lettre　　Imprimé　　　Petit paquet
☐ 盲人讀物　☐ 印刷品專袋
　Cécogramme　　Sac M
保價金額 Valeur déclarée
元　　　　　　特別提款權
Yuan _____　　**DTS** _____
特別標記 Mention Spécial
☐ 航空　　　☐ 快遞
　Avion　　　　Exprés
資費數額
Taxe percue _____
收寄人員簽名和收寄局日戳
Signateur de
bureau d'origine

Page 157

▼▼▼▼▼▼▼▼▼▼▼▼▼▼▼▼▼▼▼▼▼▼▼▼▼▼▼▼▼▼▼▼▼▼▼▼

說明：

Indications:

1. 憑此據可在一年以內辦理查詢。

   La réclamation sera admise à la présentation de ce réecépissé dans le délai d'un an à compter du lendemain du jour de dépôt de l'envio.

2. 請將收件人名址填入下列格內以備查詢。

   Veuillez inscrire, ci‑après, le nom et l'adresse du desti‑nataire pour la réclamation

Page 158

中 华 邮 政
挂 号 邮 件 收 件 回 执

邮件种类	号码	（由邮局收寄人员填写）
投 递 记 要		收件人姓名地址（请寄件人填写）

（供查询时填写）　　（请收件人填写）　　□□□－□□

附上原挂号收据影印本一件　请查收　　　年　月　日　　邮局　　□
该机构收发单位代收讫　　君收讫
经查上述邮件已于　年　月　日妥投

挂号邮件壹件　盖章　收件人　　年　月　日收到第　　投递士戳　□　号

先生
小姐

投 递 后 邮 戳　　　收 寄 局 邮 戳

Page 159

南京中山陵

句容茅山

南京中華門

南京鄭和墓

南京朝天宮

南京秦淮風光帶

南京中山植物園

南京紫霞湖

南京紫金山天文臺

南京栖霞山

南京玄武湖

南京桂子山石柱林

南京湯山風景區

南京長江大橋

南京明孝陵

南京總統府

南京莫愁湖

南京雨花臺

南京固城湖

南京長江二橋

Page 176

邊防
檢查　入境登記卡　　　中國公民 (含港澳臺) 填寫
　　　　　　　　　　　　請使用中文填寫，　　內請劃 ✓

　　　　　　　　　　　　　　　　　　　　　　男　　　官方使用
姓　名　　　　　　　　　　　　　　　　　　女

證件號碼　　　　　　　　　出生　　　年　　月　　日　　證件種類
　　　　　　　　　　　　　日期
簽注號碼　　　　　　　　　國籍 (地區)
簽注簽發地　　　　　　　　中國　(香港　澳門　臺灣　)
船名/車次　　　　　　　　入境事由 (祇能填寫一項)
/航班號
　　　　　　　　　　　　　會議/商務　　訪問　　觀光/休閑
來自何地　　　　　　　　　探親訪友　　就業　　學習
　　　　　　　　　　　　　返回常住地　定居　　其他
國內住址

以上申明眞實完整。如有不　簽名　　　入境日期　　　出入境管理局
實填報，願承擔由此引起的　　　　　　年　　月　　日　　公安部監制
一切法律責任。　　　　　　　　　　　　　　　　　　J(03.12)

Page 184

邊防
檢查　出境登記卡　　　中國公民 (含港澳臺) 填寫
　　　　　　　　　　　　請使用中文填寫，　　內請劃 ✓

　　　　　　　　　　　　　　　　　　　　　　男　　　官方使用
姓　名　　　　　　　　　　　　　　　　　　女

證件號碼　　　　　　　　　出生　　　年　　月　　日　　證件種類
　　　　　　　　　　　　　日期
國籍 (地區) 中國　(香港　澳門　臺灣　)　出境事由 (祇能填寫一項)
航班號
車次　　　　　　　　　　　會議/商務　　訪問　　觀光/休閑
船名
　　　　　　　　　　　　　探親訪友　　就業　　學習
來自何地　　　　　　　　　返回常住地　定居　　其他
　　　　　　　　　　　　　　　　　　　　　　　　　出入境管理局
國內住址

以上申明眞實完整。如有不　簽名　　　出境日期　　　公安部監制
實填報，願承擔由此引起的　　　　　　年　　月　　日
一切法律責任。　　　　　　　　　　　　　　　　　　J(03.12)

Page 184

中国国际航空公司
AIR CHINA

尊敬的國航旅客，如果您沒有需要托運的行李，請到"無托運行李值機專用櫃臺"辦理乘機手續。

Page 186

世界青棒賽
昨天战绩

义大利胜南 非		6:0
日 本胜荷 兰		4:2
巴拿马胜澳 洲		12:2
美 国胜德 国		10:4
古 巴胜南 韩		3:2

Page 209

中國足球隊勝澳門藍白隊

據新華社澳門二月二十七日電應澳門藍白體育會的邀請，中國國家足球隊今天下午在這裏同藍白隊進行了一場友誼賽，以三比零獲勝。

中國隊在上半時進行到第二十六分鐘時攻進第一個球，又分別在下半時第八十四分和第八十九分時又下兩城。

Page 214

专教美术

画家授课，耐心有序
儿童至成人
卡通，素描，水彩，油画
国画，电脑设计，摄影

Page 229

国贸人员

· 女,38岁以下

· 大学或大学以上毕

· 三年以上国贸经验

· 英语说写流利或具第二外

国语者佳

· 具独立作业能力

Page 247

中國平安保險公司

西湖游船游客人身安全保險證

貳   角

Page 265

门诊时间：

上午 8:00~12:00
下午 14:00~17:50
晚上 18:30~21:30
※ 国定假日 · 照常门诊
※ 周日仅上午看诊

Page 266

一 般 外 科
神 经 外 科

Page 271

M 补习班

英文·数学·物理·化学·生物

课业辅导班（G6-G12）

培养孩子良好的读书及思考习惯

归纳思考 (Inductive Thinking) 法教学，让孩子轻松学习

让您的孩子在升学竞争中一路领先，挺进名校热门科系

定期追踪，您能随时掌握孩子的学习状况

SAT 先修班，让孩子预习考试内容，习惯考试方式

SAT I & II 高分班

地毯式复习考试范围，增加考试信心

一对一特别班，针对学生弱点加强，保证满意

一对二家教班，经济实惠，效果显著

Page 279

西急 西江大學現急需引進以下專業具有碩士以上學位的骨幹教師，歡迎有志於
江需 教育事業的海外留學人員應聘來江大施展才華。
大師
學資 1. 國際工商管理　　　　1人
2. 國際金融　　　　　　1-2人
3. 英　　語　　　　　　1-2人
4. 計算機硬件、軟件　　1-2人

凡應聘到西江大學工作的教師，學校負責解決住房和液化氣，其中獲國外
碩士學位者，一對夫婦可安排 2室 1廳 70米² 住房一套；獲國外博士學位者，一
對夫婦可安排 3室 1廳 78米² 住房一套。

就聘人員可將本人履歷及有關證件的復印伯寄中國 ×× 省西江市梁溪路
100號西江大學人事處。聯系人：陳 ××。聯系電話：中國 0××-668761-401。

Page 280

高考压力大　家长学生好辛苦

Page 288

旅客行李中嚴禁夾帶的危險物品

爲了保障飛行安全，旅游交運的行李和手提物品内不得夾帶下列物品：

· 裝有報警裝置的手提箱和公文箱。
· 壓縮氣體（包括易燃氣體、非易燃氣體和毒氣），如野炊用燃氣。

· 帶有傳染病菌的物品。
· 炸藥、彈藥、烟花爆竹和照明彈（經承運人同意，限于體育運動用的小型
　槍械的彈藥除外）。
· 腐蝕性物質（如酸、碱、汞和濕電池）。

· 易燃液體和固體（如打火機或加熱用燃料、火柴和易燃品）。

· 氧化劑（如漂白粉和有機過氧化物）。
· 毒藥。
· 放射性物質。
· 國際航空運輸協會的《危險物品運輸規定》中列出的其它限制性物品
　（如磁性物質或使旅客、機組人員討厭或惱怒的物品）。

在自用合理數量内，旅客可以携帶藥品、醫用器械、化妝用品、烟具（不包
括汽油、打火機）、酒類。

Page 296

感謝您爲環保所作的貢獻

通過我們共同的努力

我們節約了無比珍貴的水資源

您的選擇

就是對環境最大的幫助

如果您使用過的毛巾不用更換，請挂在架子上，

其它位置的毛巾我們將爲您更換

Page 324